Sovereign Wealth Funds

Sovereign Wealth Funds

States Buying the World

Lixia Loh PhD

GLOBAL
professional
publishing

© Global Professional Publishing Ltd 2010

Apart from any fair dealing for the purpose of research or private study, or criticism or review, as permitted under the Copyright, Designs and Patents Act 1988, this publication may only be reproduced, stored or transmitted, in any form or by any means, with the prior permission in writing of the publisher, or in the case of reprographic reproduction in accordance with the terms and licences issued by the Copyright Licensing Agency. Enquiries concerning reproduction outside those terms should be addressed to the publisher. The address is below:

Global Professional Publishing Ltd
Random Acres
Slip Mill Lane
Hawkhurst
Cranbrook
Kent TN18 5AD
Email: publishing@gppbooks.com

Global Professional Publishing believes that the sources of information upon which the book is based are reliable, and has made every effort to ensure the complete accuracy of the text. However, neither Global Professional Publishing, the authors nor any contributors can accept any legal responsibility whatsoever for consequences that may arise from errors or omissions or any opinion or advice given.

ISBN 978-1-906403-51-5

Printed by Good News Digital Books

For full details of Global Professional Publishing titles in Finance and Banking see our website at:
www.gppbooks.com

CHAPTER 1

Origins, Sources, Size, Objectives and Reasons: Why Some Commentators are Concerned at the Rise of SWFs

1.1 What are SWFs?

SWFs are not a new phenomenon. They were introduced in the 1950s but little research has been done on them. In addition, there was little media interest on their investments prior to 2007. Basically SWFs were the brainchild of the British colonial government and were set up by commodity-rich countries which had abundant foreign reserves from commodity exports to help them accumulate savings funds. Information about these funds is always kept at a low profile and their investment activities are a mystery.

Despite their long history SWFs it is only during the last few years that they have been of interest to investors, policymakers and academics. The Kuwait Investment Fund was the first SWF set up in 1953 to invest the revenue from its oil industry. Following this, Kiribati established the Revenue Equalisation Reserve Fund in 1956 and the Singaporean government set up Temasek Holdings in 1974 to invest the country's budget surplus. Papua New Guinea set up the Mineral Resources Stabilisation Fund in 1974 and the Abu

Dhabi Investment Authority (ADIA) was launched by the UAE in 1976. Most of these funds, with the exception of Temasek Holdings, were set up to invest revenues from commodity exports. Due to the success of ADIA, Norway's Government Pension Fund, – Global and the Government of Singapore Investment Corporation (GIC), countries with excess foreign reserves from either sale of commodities or exports have set up similar funds, thus resulting in the unprecedented growth in the assets under the SWF management. Table 1.1 shows that most of these funds were set up after 2000.

The first wave of SWFs was initiated by the British colonial administration. The Kuwait Investment Board (now the Kuwait Investment Authority) was set up in 1953. In 1956, the British colonial administration of the Gilbert Islands in the Pacific Ocean set up the Kiribati Revenue Equalisation Reserve Fund to manage revenues from phosphate deposits. The objective was to generate long-term income for future generation. The rationale for these early funds was to establish a source for long-term, continuing income because the resources of these countries would eventually be depleted. The second wave of SWFs came during the oil boom when oil-producing countries established stabilisation funds to accumulate the revenue from oil exports. These funds provided budgetary support and were, and are, used to stabilise the national economy from volatility in international commodity prices. Examples of such funds include the ADIA (Abu Dhabi Investment Authority) formed in 1976, the Brunei Investment Fund formed in 1983 and the Norway's Government Pension Fund – Global – founded in 1990. Other oil-rich countries such as Russia and Venezuela have also since set up SWFs to invest revenues from their oil production after the huge surge in oil prices between 2000 and 2008.

Non-commodity SWFs are largely funded by excess foreign reserves and budget surpluses. Singapore was the first country to set up a SWF using its fiscal surplus, with Temasek established in 1974. GIC followed in 1981. After the Asian Crisis, many East Asian countries (in particular China and South Korea) accumulated huge foreign reserves. The Korea Investment Corporation was set up in 2005 and the China Investment Corporation (CIC) in 2007. However, there are some new SWFs which are neither commodity-based nor set up to soak up excess liquidity in their country. They are merely imitating the success of the longer-established SWFs.

Does a SWF represent a government or does it operate separately from that government? The term "Sovereign Wealth Fund" was coined by Andrew

Rozanov of State Street Global Advisors[1] in 2005 to describe the investment funds created by nations. The US Treasury defines SWF as a government investment vehicle funded by foreign exchange assets and managed separately from official reserves.[2] As has been pointed out by the IMF, special purpose government funds, which are usually called sovereign wealth funds, are classified as "captive financial institutions rather than investment funds given the nature of their liabilities. They would not be classified as a financial corporation" because SWFs normally receive funds from the state and not from issuing shares and units to the public.[3] Due to the various definitions of SWFs, the number cited in different reports varies. For example, the Monitor Group Report in 2008 identified 36 SWFs[4] while the Deutsche Bank 2007 Report states that there are more than 40.[5] As far as China is concerned, the China Investment Corporation is regarded as the SWF of the country but not for the State Administration of Foreign Exchange. It is difficult to define a SWF based on the legal nature of such funds because governments could change the legal framework that governs the fund. Thus it will be more sensible to identify whether a government investment vehicle is a SWF by judging the characteristics of the fund. However, despite the many definitions of SWFs, they generally share the following characteristics:

- they are owned by a sovereign government.
- they are managed separately from the sovereign central bank, ministry of finance and treasuries.
- they invest in a portfolio of assets of different risk profiles.
- they have a long-term investment horizon.
- unlike pension funds, they have no explicit individual liabilities.
- they can either operate as a separate legal entity from the government or they can legally be part of the government or central banks.

---

1 State Street Global Advisors is the fund management arm of the US custody bank, State Street Corporation.
2 Robert Kimmitt "Public footprints in private markets-sovereign wealth and the world economy," Foreign Affairs, January/ February 2008.
3 *International Monetary Fund (IMF) 6th Balance of Payment Manual, par. 4.75. December 2008.* https://www.imf.org/external/pubs/ft/bop/2007/pdf/BPM6.pdf
4 William Miracky, Davis Dyer, Drosten Fisher, Tony Goldner, Loic Lagarde and Vicente Piedrahita "Assessing the risks, The behaviors of sovereign wealth funds in the global economy," Monitor Group, June 2008.
5 Steffen Kern, "Sovereign wealth funds- State investments on the Rise. Deutsche Bank Research," September 2007. http://www.dbresearch.com/PROD/CIB_INTERNET_EN-PROD/PROD0000000000215270.pdf

SWFs can be managed by any of three entities – national government, central banks/statutory boards and private fund managers. (However, the distinction between private- and state-owned fund is not clear for some of the Middle East SWFs as they are either owned by the ruler or the ruling family of their respective countries, and hence there is confusion with regard to the ownership of the SWFs.) At the heart of rise of SWFs is the desire of these governments to get a higher risk-return trade-off for the country's national wealth. In this way SWFs serve as a vehicle for governments to participate in financial investment in the global markets. This could also be seen as their attempt to build a "piggy bank" for rainy days. The Norwegian government has recently dipped into its "piggy bank" to cushion the effects of recession.[6]

SWFs are different from state-owned enterprises (SOEs) and state pension funds. SOEs can be defined as companies in which the state has significant control through full, majority or significant ownership. Usually they have core businesses such as those providing essential services to the domestic market. Although SOEs sometimes invest overseas, they do not usually do so substantially and they mainly hold major stakes in domestic companies. In addition, the assets held by SOEs are not as diversified as those of SWFs. They normally invest in companies which are related to their core businesses and do not actively invest in financial assets. Pension funds differ from SWFs in that they have explicit individual liabilities and there is a continuous stream of fixed payments. Pension funds are mostly denominated in local currency and usually have no or low exposure to foreign investments. Norway's Government Pension Fund – Global and the Australian Government Future Fund are different from normal pension funds, and are classified as SWFs because they mainly act as fund saving organisations, and their pension payment obligations are some way in the future. According to this investment pattern, SWFs have a higher risk appetite than SOEs and pension funds. Another distinct feature is that SWFs are established to manage wealth while SOEs and pension funds are established to save funds. There can be a fine line between a SWF and a SOE but in general a fund is classified as a SWF if the source comes from the proceeds of commodities or foreign reserves and if it mainly serves as a financial investor.

The Asian and Middle Eastern SWFs, because of their high profile investments in western financial institutions and their lack of disclosure, have generated a lot of speculation in the media. Nine out of the ten biggest funds

---

6 David Ibison, "Norway dips into oil fund for NKr20bn stimulus," *Financial Times*, 26 January 2009. http://www.ft.com/cms/s/0/5cd3812a-ebbd-11dd-8838-0000779fd2ac.html?nclick_check=1

are from Asia and the Middle East and recent activities of these funds in the global markets suggest that they are more aggressive in their investment approach and are prepared to take significant stakes in foreign companies. They are also actively seeking high-risk high-return investments in emerging markets. On the other hand, Norway's Government Pension Fund - Global and the Australian Government Future Fund, which are saving funds for future pension obligations, do not hold large stakes in the companies they invest in and are passive investors with a lower risk appetite.

1.2   Sources of SWFs

Initially, most of these funds were set up using revenues from commodities, particularly oil. But over the years more funds were set up using a country's fiscal surplus and foreign reserves. As shown in Table 1.1, most of the SWFs are still funded from commodity revenues, predominantly oil and gas exports. These revenues are generated from taxes, export duties and profits from state-owned enterprises. In these resource-rich countries, the SWFs serve two purposes. Firstly, they help to stabilise government expenditure and export revenue in times of volatile commodity prices. Secondly, they act as a means of accumulating savings for future generations as their natural resources are non-renewable. Both ADIA, Norway's Government Pension Fund – Global and Russia's Oil Stabilisation Fund share these objectives.

Another source is fiscal surplus and foreign reserves. This source mainly comes from the accumulation of reserves used for the management of inflexible exchange rate systems. After the Asian crisis, many East Asian countries have been aggressively building up their foreign reserves to defend their currencies in the event of future currency speculation. In addition, most of these countries are major net exporters and have accumulated vast current account surpluses during the global economic boom. Traditionally, foreign reserves were invested in government bonds from developed countries, particularly the US. However, as the level of foreign reserves grew bigger than that required to defend their currencies, the Asian central banks began to shift some of their reserves to investment agencies such as SWFs to reap a higher rate of return. For example, the GIC was set up in 1981 and funded by the Monetary Authority of Singapore (MAS) using its foreign reserves.[7] Having

---

7   There were wide speculations that GIC has used the saving fund, Central Provident Fund (CPF) for investment. At the press conference to mark GIC's 20th anniversary, Singapore's Senior Minister Lee Kuan Yew had stressed that GIC does not dip into the CPF fund. Reported by Ignatius Low, Singapore

accumulated a vast amount of foreign reserves from its export and direct foreign investment, China's CIC was launched in 2007. The rise of these non-commodity SWFs is the result of global imbalances – high balance of payment deficits in developed countries and high balance of payments surpluses in Asia, and an undervaluation of currencies in Asia. Despite the continued rise of Asian SWFs, the size of non-commodity SWFs is still smaller than the commodity-based SWFs.

1.3   Size of the SWFs

Estimates of the size of SWFs are fairly arbitrary. They are hindered by the fact that most of these funds do not publish the value of the assets they have under management. A report by the Monitor Group[8] in 2008 stated that the value of SWFs is estimated to be between US$1.9 trillion and US$ 2.9 trillion. On the other hand research conducted by Deutsche Bank in 2007 estimated SWFs to be worth over US$3.1 trillion.[9] The IMF report in 2008 estimated the value of SWFs to be between US$2 and 3 trillion.[10] The largest SWFs, Abu Dhabi Investment Authority, Government Investment Corporation of Singapore, Norway's Government Pension Fund – Global, Kuwait Investment Authority, China Investment Corporation (Central Huijin Investment Corporation is China Investment Corporation, see Chapter 4 for detail), Stabilisation Fund of the Russian Federation and Singapore's Temasek Holdings, are from oil-rich countries and East Asian countries with high foreign reserves. These individual SWFs manage assets that are worth more than US$100 billion. The ten biggest SWFs hold more than 80% of the total holdings. ADIA is estimated to be the biggest SWF with assets of $875 billion. The top five SWFs, with the exception of the GIC, were established by commodity-exporting countries. Smaller funds which manage less than US$1 billion include Venezuela's Investment Fund for Macroeconomic Stabilisation, Kiribati's Revenue Equalisation Reserve Fund, Chile's Pension Reserve Fund, Uganda's Poverty Action Fund, and Papua New Guinea's Mineral Resources Stabilisation Fund. (See Table 1.1 for a list of the SWFs and the value of assets under management).

Strait Times, 23 May 2001.
8   See Note 4.
9   See Note 5.
10 "International Monetary Fund (2008) Sovereign Wealth Funds – A Work Agenda" Prepared by the Monetary and Capital Markets and Policy Development and Review Departments, IMF. In collaboration with other Departments. Approved by Mark Allen and Jamie Caruana. February 2008.

Table 1.1: An Overview of Sovereign Wealth Funds 2008-2009

COUNTRY	NAME OF FUND	ASSETS UNDER MANAGEMENT USD BN	YEAR FOUNDED	SOURCE
United Arab Emirates	Abu Dhabi Investment Authority (ADIA)	875	1976	Oil
Saudi Arabia	SAMA Foreign Holdings	433	NA	Oil
Singapore	Government of Singapore Investment Corporation (GIC)	330	1981	Non-commodity
Norway	Government Pension Fund - Global (GPFG)	301	1990	Oil
Kuwait	Kuwait Investment Authority (KIA)	265	1953	Oil
China	China Investment Company Ltd.	200	2007	Non-commodity
Hong Kong	Hong Kong Monetary Authority Investment Portfolio	173	1998	Non-commodity
Russia	Stabilization Fund of the Russian Federation (SFRF)	157	2003	Oil
Singapore	Temasek Holdings	134	1974	Non-commodity
China	Central Hujin Investment Corp.	100	2003	Non-commodity
Qatar	Qatar Investment Authority (QIA)	60	2000	Oil
Libya	Reserve Fund	50	NA	Oil
Algeria	Revenue Regulation Fund	47	NA	Oil
Australia	Australian Government Future Fund (AGFF)	44	2004	Non-commodity
Kazakhstan	Kazakhstan National Fund (KNF)	38	2000	Oil, gas metal
Ireland	National Pensions Reserve Fund (NPRF)	31	2001	Non-commodity
Brunei	Brunei Investment Agency (BIA)	30	1983	Oil
South Korea	Korea Investment Corporation (KIC)	30	2006	Non-commodity
United States of America	Alaska Permanent Reserve Fund Corporation (APRF)	29	1976	Oil
Malaysia	Khazanah Nasional BHD (KNB)	26	1993	Non-commodity
Canada	Alberta Heritage Fund (AHF)	16	1976	Oil

COUNTRY	NAME OF FUND	ASSETS UNDER MANAGEMENT USD BN	YEAR FOUNDED	SOURCE
Taiwan	Taiwan National Stabilisation Fund (TNSF)	15	2000	Non-commodity
United States of America	New Mexico State Investment Office Trust Funds	15	1958	Non-commodity
Iran	Foreign Exchange Reserve Fund	15	1999	Oil
Nigeria	Excess Crude Account	11	2004	Oil
New Zealand	New Zealand Superannuation Fund	10	2003	Non-commodity
Oman	State General Stabilisation Fund (SGSF)	8.2	1980	Oil, gas
Chile	Economic and Social Stabilisation Fund (ESSF)	6	2007	Copper
Botswana	Pula Fund	4.7	1993	Diamonds, copper
United States of America	Permanent Wyoming Mineral Trust Fund (PWMTF)	3.2	1974	Minerals
Norway	Government Petroleum Insurance Fund (GPIF)	2.6	1986	Oil
Azerbaijan	State Oil Fund	1.5	1999	Oil
East Timor	Timor-Leste Petroleum Fund	1.2	2005	Oil, gas
Venezuela	Investment Fund for Macroeconomic Stabilisation (FIEM)	0.8	1998	Oil
Kiribati	Revenue Equalisation Reserve Fund (RERF)	0.6	1956	Phosphates
Chile	Chile Pension Reserves Fund	0.6	2007	Copper
Uganda	Poverty Action Fund	0.4	1998	Aid
Papua New Guinea	Mineral Resources Stabilisation Fund (MRSF)	0.2	1974	Minerals
Mauritania	National Fund for Hydrocarbon Reserves	0	2006	Oil, gas
United Arab Emirates	Dubai Intern Financial Centre Investments (DIFC)	NA	2002	Oil
Angola	Reserve Fund for Oil	NA	2007	Oil

Sources: Deutsche Bank Research 2007, IFSL Research 2008 and SWF Institute

Though the size of SWFs is relatively small at the moment as compared to other financial vehicles, their growth undoubtedly warrants attention from policymakers and international investors (see Figure 1.1 on the size of assets under management in 2008). SWFs managed 6% of the total assets under management by the end of 2008. This amount is small when compared to mutual funds, pension funds and insurance funds though it is bigger than hedge funds and private equity funds. However, if SWFs were to grow to $12 trillion by 2015 (4 times the size of its current value, this industry will play a major role in the fund management industry and could significantly alter the role of government in the private sector.

Figure 1.1: Size of Assets under Management at the end of 2008

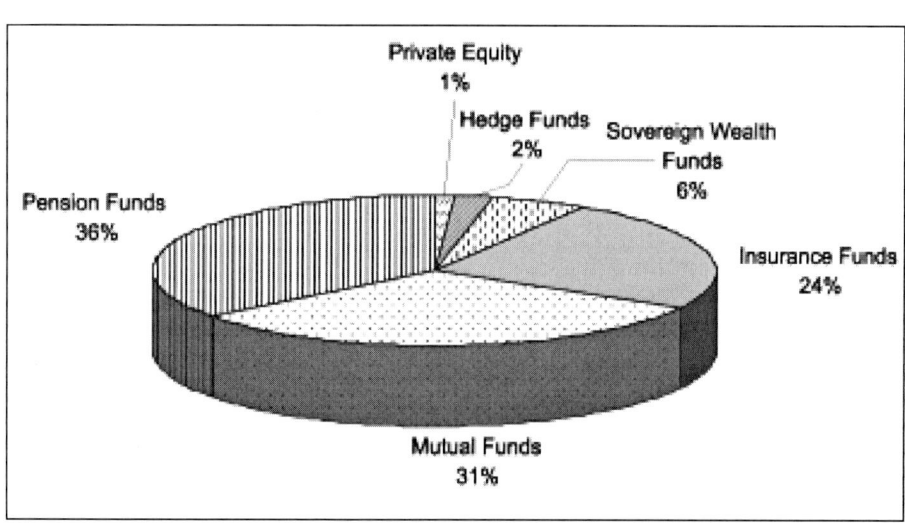

Source: Data from Maslakovic (2009) Sovereign Wealth Funds 2009, IFSL Report.

1.4 Objectives of SWFs

In general, most SWFs share similar characteristics but they are a heterogeneous group with different policy objectives. The IMF has identified five types of SWFs based on their main objectives:[11]

a) Stabilisation funds – established by government to insulate the budget and the economy against commodity (usually oil) price fluctuations, e.g. Stabilisation Fund of the Russian Federation.

---
11 See Note 10.

b) Saving funds – to invest proceeds from non-renewable assets into financial assets to fund long-term objectives for future generations. This type of fund also mitigates the effects of Dutch disease,[12] e.g. Kuwait Investment Authority.
c) Reserve investment corporations – formed to increase returns on reserves, e.g. Korea Investment Corporation.
d) Development funds - typically help to finance socio-economic projects or promote industrial policy for economic development, e.g. Singapore's Temasek Holdings.
d) Pension reserve funds – different from individual pension contributions. They are owned by governments and set up to finance future public pensions, e.g. Australian Government Future Fund.

This said, the objectives of some funds may change over time. For example, Temasek initially focused on Singapore's logistics industry. Over the years, it has become more diversified and now its assets extend to various industries and the fund is looking for higher returns from its investments. For other SWFs such as ADIA, the initial objective was to use the fund to cushion the effects of volatile oil prices. As the fund grew bigger, it had sufficient reserves to meet its stabilisation objectives and it is now looking for substantial returns on its assets. Similarly, CIC was set up to increase returns on China's foreign reserves but the fund has increasingly been used to accumulate commodities for the country's consumption in anticipation of higher commodity prices. As a result of the specific situation when it was established, CIC also assumes the role of investing in domestic banks (see Chapter 4 on CIC domestic investments). Clearly most SWFs carry multiple objectives which then change over time and the recent recession has seen some governments planning to use SWFs to cushion the effects of recession and indeed some have already done so.

Applying Hotelling's Rule for efficient resource depletion, an oil-exporting countries should be indifferent as between keeping its oil resources underground on the one hand and receiving a market rate of return on the sale of oil on the other. If the returns on oil sales are low, they will reduce the supply thus resulting in higher oil prices. In fact, however, oil-exporting countries are able to achieve a higher return on oil sales using SWFs as an investment vehicle. Their incentive for maintaining a consistent supply of oil

---

12 Dutch disease refers to the deindustrialisation of a nation's economy that occurs when the discovery of natural resources raise the value of that nation's currency. This makes manufactured goods less competitive with other nations and leads to higher import and lower export.

is mainly due to the higher rate of return they can earn on equity rather than on oil. In contrast to using SWFs for stabilising commodity prices, extracting and selling oil results in running down capital resources and such countries need to smooth their consumption levels for future generations when resources will have been exhausted. Thus revenues can be fully reinvested in financial, physical or human capital (Hartwick's Rule for Intergenerational Equity). Laura Tyson from Haas School of Business comments that the Gulf States have been behaving responsibly by trying to generate a higher living standard for their citizens over the next 100 years, and not squandering their petrodollars on the high life as they did in the 1970s.[13] The oil exporters now have to invest most of their oil proceeds overseas because of the diminishing returns in their domestic markets and the huge flow of oil proceeds in their small domestic market that would result in Dutch disease. A SWF helps to transform the oil proceeds into other forms of wealth so as to accumulate capital for future generations. While providing governments with liquidity in times of low asset prices or shortages of reserves, SWFs are also set up by commodity exporting countries to shield their economies against volatility in the commodity markets.

Non-commodity SWFs provide governments with alternatives for investing their foreign reserves. Central banks that invest large amount of foreign reserves in government bonds are highly exposed to interest rate risk, inflation risk and currency risk. This lack of diversification by central banks would mean that the value of foreign reserves would be adversely affected should the prices of debt securities fall. Traditionally most of the surplus was invested in US treasuries and other developed country government debts. However, the decline of the US dollar and the low returns on US treasuries may be the reasons for the Asian central banks to supplement this passive approach with a proactive approach to maximise returns using SWFs. Returns of government bonds from the UK and other EU countries have also been falling due to the poor economic climates in these countries (see Chapter 3 on the returns of government bonds from developed countries). Using a SWF to broaden their asset classes, governments can achieve a higher return without significantly increasing the risk and sometimes a similar return can be achieved with a lower risk.

Thus Asian governments, particularly the Chinese government, regard the creation of a SWF as a solution to hedging the risk of US dollar depreciation and to meeting the needs of their monetary policies. China is, in fact, the

---

13 "The rise of state capitalism," *The Economist*, Special Reports, 18 September 2008.

largest holder of US treasuries and had accumulated $9 trillion by September 2007.[14] The Chinese government is concerned about their vulnerability in holding such a high volume of foreign reserve in US treasuries. The possibility of a big devaluation of the US dollar, given the state of its economy and the size of its trade deficit and budget deficit, is a clear possibility. And China is not the only country which is diversifying its foreign reserves into SWFs. South Korea launched its first SWF in 2005 using its foreign reserves. While still holding a huge proportion of the country's foreign reserves in US treasuries, Japan also plans to set up the country's first SWF to diversify some of its investments. In these cases, SWFs serve as an investment vehicle for governments to diversify out of specifically US assets and provide an avenue for investing in high-return, high-risk assets. In addition, SWFs also offer an alternative to investing foreign reserves in liquid financial markets that allow assets to be converted to cash readily to meet balance of payment needs. Thus governments can both meet the need to hold liquid assets and obtain a return higher than government debts. Countries such as India and Sri Lanka, for example, which do not have SWFs have limited possibilities for diverting their foreign reserves out of US dollars. The Indian Central Bank sold dollars to buy 200 tonnes of gold in an attempt to avoid losses due to possible US dollar depreciation in November 2009[15] and the move was followed by the Sri Lankan Central Bank.[16] In general, the move by numerous central banks to swap dollar reserves for other alternative liquid assets at the same time would result in an excessive demand for a single asset such as gold. This attempt to diversify foreign reserves would not be a good alternative because it would cause a large upward swing in asset prices. Diversifying foreign reserves with a wider range of assets avoids the volatility resulting from such large fluctuations in financial markets and gives governments more flexibility in managing their national wealth. Such diversifications also enables governments to invest in assets denominated in the currencies of their major trading partners to minimise exchange rate risks. In the past, most Asian central banks held their foreign reserves in US dollars and Euros but given the economic climates in these countries coupled with the higher growth expected in emerging

---

14 Wayne, M. Morrison and Marc Labonte, "China's holdings of US securities: Implications for the US economy", Congressional Research Service Report for Congress, May 19, 2008.
15 James Kamont and Javier Blas, "India sells dollars for 200 tonnes gold and lift bullions at all-time high," Financial Times, 4 November 2009. http://www.ft.com/cms/s/0/2b5e1908-c8e3-11de-8f9d-00144feabdc0.html
16 Joe Leahy, "Sri Lanka follows India move to buy gold," Financial Times, 5 November 2009. http://www.ft.com/cms/s/0/8fd6288a-ca23-11de-a5b5-00144feabdc0.html

markets, holding reserves in multiple currencies would reduce the exchange rate risk (see Chapter 5 on IMF's prediction on US dollar).

Central banks issue bonds in the domestic market to absorb excess liquidity – the sterilisation and cost of these domestic bonds has to be funded. A higher rate of return on the sterilisation bond is needed to attract a demand for the bonds in order for the sterilisation policy to successfully absorb the excess liquidity. The high returns from SWFs can meet this high funding cost. The Chinese government has been issuing sterilisation bonds to absorb the excess liquidity in its domestic market and prior to setting up CIC, the People Bank of China established the State Administration of Foreign Exchange (SAFE) in 1997 to manage its foreign reserves. Coincidently, SAFE started when the Chinese government began to increase its bond issues. Following this, the SAFE Investment Company was established in Hong Kong to invest in foreign equity.

Recently, France has set up its first SWF to protect domestic companies. However, it fails to meet any of the objectives identified by the IMF. This appears to be a political rather than a commercial move. Basically, SWFs are established on the basis of strong commodity exports and high foreign reserves and the high balance of payment surplus explains why most SWFs invest globally but not domestically. SWFs are used by these countries to insulate against volatile commodities prices and obtain a high return on their foreign reserves. While France has set up a SWF to protect its domestic companies, it is difficult to say if other European countries, despite not having exportable commodities and running balance of payment deficits, will follow such a move.

From the above objectives, we can see that SWFs are used by governments as an insurance against potential future problems. This appears to be more important for both developing and less developed nations. In analysing Singapore's GIC, Clarke and Monk (forthcoming) have argued that Singapore's SWFs reflect the government's commitment to self-insurance due to the size of the country, its geographical setting and its lack of resources. The GIC is an insurance to underwrite the country's autonomy, long-term welfare and the stability of its financial systems.

1.6 Why are some Commentators Concerned by the Growth of SWFs?

The recent aggressive investment approach of SWFs and their growing size have generated a huge interest in these funds, especially in their operations, structures and investment strategies. Ten of the biggest funds are from Asia and the Middle East. With the increasing oil prices and the high foreign reserves of these countries, the value of assets under SWF management is set to grow further to an estimated $12 trillion by 2015.[17] This indicates a shift of financial power from the West to the East and a rise in state capitalism. SWFs represent a challenge to free markets and reverse the effort of capitalists over the past decade to minimise the role of the state and to promote the free market. During his presidential election, President Barack Obama made the following comment on SWFs: "I am obviously concerned if these… sovereign wealth funds are motivated by more than just market considerations, and that's obviously a possibility."[18] The fear of deploying economic resources for security purposes generates the strongest opposition to the creation and growth of SWFs.

The number of media reports on SWFs were second only to the subprime crisis since the financial crisis in 2007. Most of the arguments and debates against SWFs point to the potentially negative impacts on the security of the recipient countries and on the financial markets. A lack of understanding of these funds and the numerous media reports have created more doubt and fear on SWFs' activities among the general public. The continous growth of SWFs and their lack of transparency instill more fear among policymakers and the general public that SWFs will be utilised by economic powers to achieve their political agendas. There have been cases where investments by SWFs were blocked by recipient countries because of political lobbying and public opposition. For example, Dubai Port's investment in US ports was eventually sold to a US company. In response to the rise of SWFs and their investment activities in the global market, countries such as the US and Germany have tightened the regulations on foreign direct investments in their countries. There is fear that with the continuous growth of SWFs, the West will further

---
17 Steven Jen, "How big could sovereign wealth funds be by 2015?" Morgan Stanley Perspectives, 4 May 2007.
18 "Obama says concerned about sovereign wealth funds," Reuters, 7 February 2008. Reported by Jeff Mason, edited by Stuart Grudgings.
http://www.reuters.com/article/politicsNews/idUSN0742347120080208

increase its level of protectionism, thus resulting in a reversal of globalisation. The subprime crisis and the credit crunch have led to the nationalisation of financial institutions. The budget deficit in the West provides an opportunity for SWFs to invest in failing western companies. This rise of nationalisation is different from what has happened in the past because it is no longer the local government that bails out the ailing companies but foreign governments who provide the necessary liquidity. The bailout activities of SWFs act like cross-border nationalisations which worries developed countries.

SWFs were particularly thrust into the limelight in the recent financial crisis when they bought stakes in western financial institutions to provide the then much needed liquidity in the banking sector. For example, the ADIA bought a 4.9% stake in Citigroup and the GIC bought a 7.9% stake in Union Bank of Switzerland (UBS) during the subprime crisis. What makes SWFs different from other types of institutional investors? Why do these funds cause uneasiness among policymakers? Are the size, the speed of growth and the secrecy associated with SWFs the main causes of worry or is it the shift from market capitalism to state capitalism that causes the uneasiness? Lawrence Summers, the former US Secretary of the Treasury, raised the alarm about SWF investments in the OECD countries:

> *The government of Qatar is seeking to gain control of J. Sainsbury, one of the Britain's largest supermarket chains. Gazprom, a Russian conglomerate, in effect controlled by the Kremlin, has strategic interests in the energy sectors of a number of countries and even a stake in Airbus. Entities controlled by the government of China and Singapore are offering to take a substantial stake in Barclays, giving it more heft in its effort to pull off the world's largest banking merger, with ABN Amro. (Summers 2007).*[19]

The growing size and power of SWFs have raised a number of issues. The main concern is whether countries holding these funds will use them to advance their political ambitions rather than for commercial purposes. SWFs from Asia and the Middle East operate in a secret manner and have limited disclosure on their investment strategies and asset allocation. Furthermore, most top SWFs are from countries without full democratic rights and they are taking

---

19 Lawrence Summers, "Funds that stake capitalist logic," *Financial Times*, 29 July 2007. http://www.ft.com/cms/s/2/bb8f50b8-3dcc-11dc-8f6a-0000779fd2ac.html

substantial stakes in private companies. Will they be politically aggressive as Russia's Gazprom has shown? Secondly, with regard to the impact of SWFs on financial stability in markets, there is fear that SWFs could destabilise these markets. In addition, most countries have traditionally invested their reserves in US treasuries and diversifying out of US treasuries may result in a plunge in the value of US treasuries and the government debt of other developed countries. Thirdly, a conflict of interest may arise between SWFs and the recipient countries where these funds are invested. The SWFs investments would have macroeconomic implications for the local governments, particularly on investment in strategic industries. Fourthly, unregulated SWFs may encourage the rise of protectionism in recipients' countries. The fear that governments of SWFs will use cross-border investment as a political tool would block globalisation which will reverse the decade's effort on globalisation and international trade. The US government has blocked several SWFs' and SOEs' investments citing security and China's CIC has threatened to boycott countries which use 'national security' as an excuse for protectionism.[20] Finally, is the increasing size of SWFs a return of state capitalism? Is the formation of SWFs an undesirable policy which will eventually lead to the demise of the free market? These concerns have arisen mainly due to the lack of information and understanding about SWFs. A broader understanding of the history, size, organisational structure, activities and implications of SWFs is needed.

---

20 Martin Arnold, "China funds warns against protectionism," Financial Times, 11 December 2007. http://www.ft.com/cms/s/0/c3096c9a-a77e-11dc-a25a-0000779fd2ac.html

CHAPTER 2
Structure, Governance and Proposed International Guidelines

This chapter examines the structure and corporate governance of SWFs, most of which are operated in secrecy and have brought concern to policymakers, recipient countries and investors. There is limited information on how these funds are operated and how their assets are allocated. What public information is available only comes in the form of occasional press releases and media reports. This lack of regular public information is very similar to the situation for hedge funds and private equity firms but, unlike SWFs, the strong criticism of hedge funds and private equity firms is usually not related to national security and economic dominance. In particular, the corporate governance of SWFs face harsh criticism because the shareholders of these funds are governments. When the shareholders are governments, there is a risk that the investment vehicle will be used to achieve political agendas hence there is a need for an emphasis on proper corporate governance and disclosure in SWFs' operations.

The lack of transparency and international rules to regulate the SWFs has raised concerns regarding their activities and motives (see Chapter 1).

This Chapter aims to provide some clarity on the funds' operations focussing on the role of government. The corporate structure of SWFs and the organisational structure of five of the largest – ADIA, GIC, Temasek, CIC and GPFG will be discussed. Next, the current governance and transparency of SWFs will be examined with reference to Truman's (2008) Scoreboard and Linaburg-Maduell Transparency Index. The current and proposed international guidelines with regard to the funds' operations and the resulting compliance after the proposed guidelines will also be discussed.

2.1 Corporate Structure

SWFs can exist as separate legal entities from the state or the central bank, or they can fall within a pool of assets managed by the central bank, statutory agencies or the Ministry of Finance. They can be established under specific constitutional laws, general fiscal (budget or fiscal responsibility) laws, or under the central bank law. Some SWFs, for instance the China Investment Corporation, Temasek and the Government Investment Corporation of Singapore, are established as separate legal entities which have a governance structure that clearly differentiates an owner, a governing body and a board of management. For SWFs which are established as a pool of assets without a separate legal entity (e.g. GPFG, Russia's National Wealth Fund, Reserve Fund and Timor-Leste's Petroleum Fund), the owners may exercise the authority of governing bodies through organisational units such as the ministry of finance or a parliamentary committee.

In a survey conducted by the International Working Group of Sovereign Wealth Funds[1] (IWG) in 2008, respondents from 20 SWF countries claimed that while their institutional framework which aims to provide the SWFs with operational independence is still accountable to the government, independent operation is ensured by establishing a separate legal entity or by delegating the management to the central bank or a ministry. Though government officials are frequently appointed to the SWF governing bodies, these appointments are for a long duration and there is often a limit on the number of seats for government officials. But there are also a number of SWFs which do not set a limit on the number of government officials appointed to the governing bodies. The appointment and removal of members are legislated for to ensure operational independence. Like most private corporations, those SWFs with a separate legal entity are managed by a board of directors. The board is headed by the Chief Executive Officer (CEO) who is either chosen by government

---

[1] *International Working Group of Sovereign Wealth Funds (IWG) was established in 2008 which comprises 26 IMF member countries which has SWFs.*

officials or elected by the Board of Directors itself. To ensure accountability, the SWFs are required to disclose their audited financial accounts and submit regular reports to the shareholders (which can be the Ministry of Finance, central bank and/or the parliament).

If SWFs are not a separate legal entity, they may be directly governed by government officials. The central bank, ministries or statutory agencies will delegate responsibility to the SWF's operational management. To ensure accountability, the ministry of finance will report the activities of a SWF to the parliament. The audited financial accounts will be presented annually.

2.2 Examples of Five Large SWFs

To gain a better understanding of the structure of SWFs, five large SWFs, namely the UAE's Abu Dhabi Investment Authority (ADIA), the Singapore Government's Investment Corporation (GIC) and Temasek Holdings, the China Investment Corporation (CIC) and Norway's Government Pension Fund – Global (GPFG) are examined. Since GIC and Temasek were established with different sources of funds and operate in a different manner, a detailed examination will provide insights into the different operations by the same government. The operational secrecy of some of these SWFs and their large amounts of transactions have generated a lot of media attention.

2.2.1   Abu Dhabi Investment Authority (ADIA)

According to information from their official website, ADIA is a premier global institutional investor which focuses on the investment of equities, bonds, treasuries and real estate. The fund's mission is to secure and maintain the current and future prosperity of the Emirates of Abu Dhabi through the prudent management of their investment assets.

ADIA was established by the founder of the UAE in 1976 to invest the surpluses of the Abu Dhabi government. According to an interview with the managing Director in 2008,[2] the fund grows at an annual rate of 10%. Its Board of Directors is chaired by the President of the UAE and consists of various government officials. The organisational structure of ADIA has a very clear operational structure (Figure 2.1). The Investment Department, which deals

---
2   Emily Thornton and Stanley Reed , "Inside the Abu Dhabi Investment Authority," Business Week, 6 June 2008.

Figure 2.1: The Organisational Structure of Abu Dhabi Investment Authority

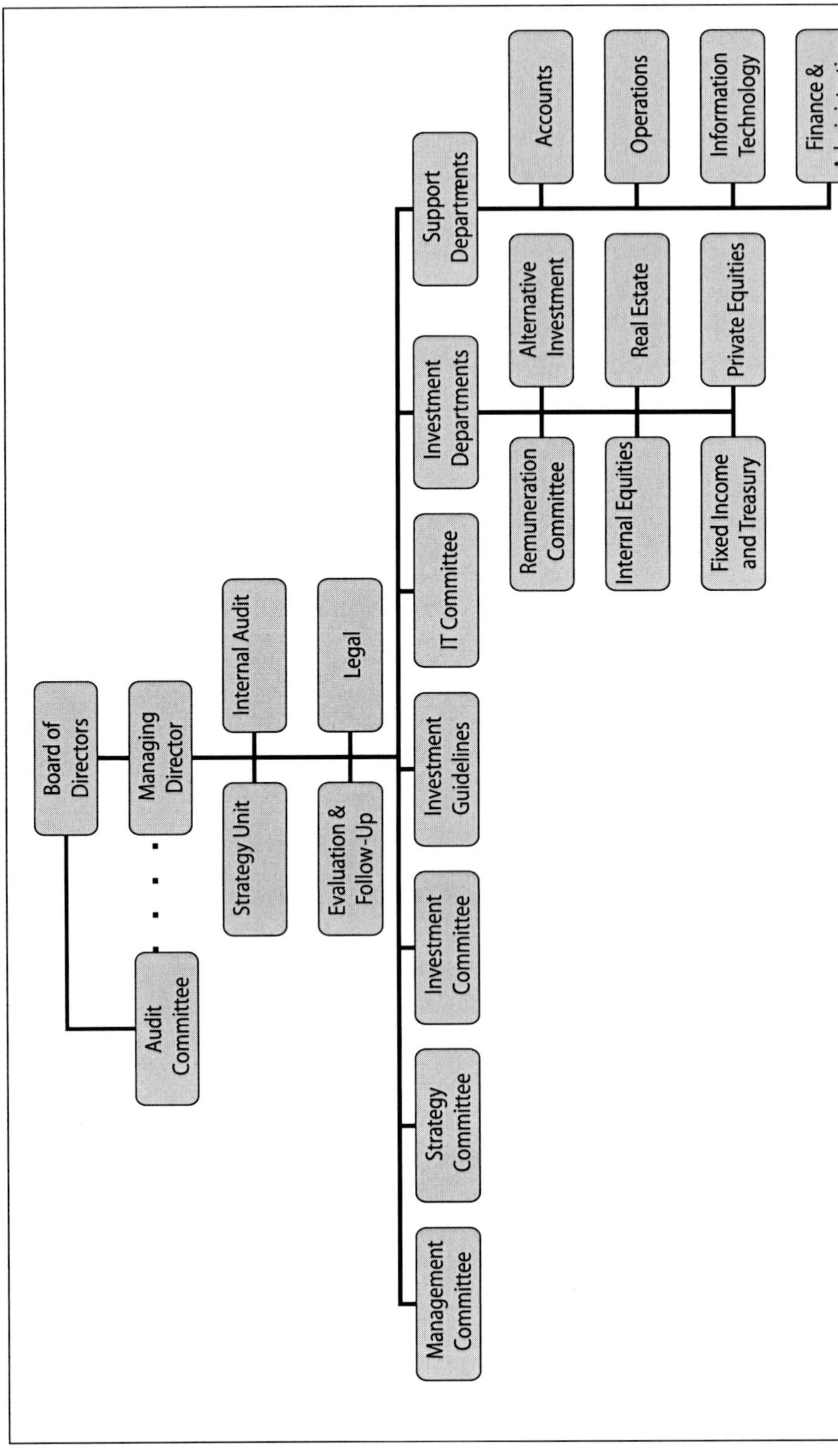

Source: http://www.adia.ae/ADIA_AE_structure.asp?navLoc=structure

with different aspects of its investment activities, consists of six investment functions: external equities, internal equities, fixed income and treasury, alternative investment, real estate and private equities. These investment departments report directly to the Managing Director who is accountable to the Board of Directors (refer to Appendix 1 for the Board of Directors).

Besides the two major departments – the Investment Departments and the Support Departments, ADIA has five committees to deal with important decisions. They are the Investment Committee, Strategy Committee, Guidelines Committee, Management Committee, I.T. Committee, Compensation Committee and the Audit Committee. Although the Board of Directors consists only of local government officials, about 70% of the 1,100 professionals working at ADIA are foreigners due to the small pool of talent available in the UAE. Many of the foreign and local staff members were educated in the West. The fund Managing Director, Sheikh Khalifa, has delegated a significant role to Jean-Paul Villain who first joined the Fund in 1982. He is currently heading the Investment Strategy and Asset Allocation of the Fund and is also a Board Member of the Abu Dhabi Commercial Bank.[3] Prior to joining ADIA, Jean-Paul Villain was with Bank Paribas. Al-Hajeri, the Executive Director, personally invited Chris Koski to head the ADIA Infrastructure Investment Unit. He was appointed the Global Head of Infrastructure in 2007 and was promised a free rein to run the Unit. In January 2009, ADIA appointed another expatriate, Bill Schwab, as the Global Head of Real Estate.[4] He will be responsible for leading a team of professionals in managing and implementing ADIA's global investment strategy in the real estate sector. Besides having its own in-house investment professionals, ADIA uses external asset managers, fund managers and other advisors to manage its diversified portfolio.

2.2.2 Government of Singapore Investment Corporation (GIC)

GIC was established in Singapore in 1981 using the country's foreign reserves. It manages the nation's foreign reserve fund on behalf of the government and the Monetary Authority of Singapore. It was established as a private company but is wholly owned by the government. Operating with a network

---
3 The Expat 50, The region's most influential expatriates. Profile of Jean-Paul Villain, Arabian Business.com. http://www.arbianbusiness.com/expat-powerlist/profile/1189
4 Abu Dhabi, UAE, "Abu Dhabi Investment Authority appoints Bill Schwab as Global Head of Real Estate," Abu Dhabi Investment Authority Press release, 8 January 2009. http://www.adia.ae/PDFs/Bill_Schwab_8_Jan.pdf

SOVEREIGN WEALTH FUNDS

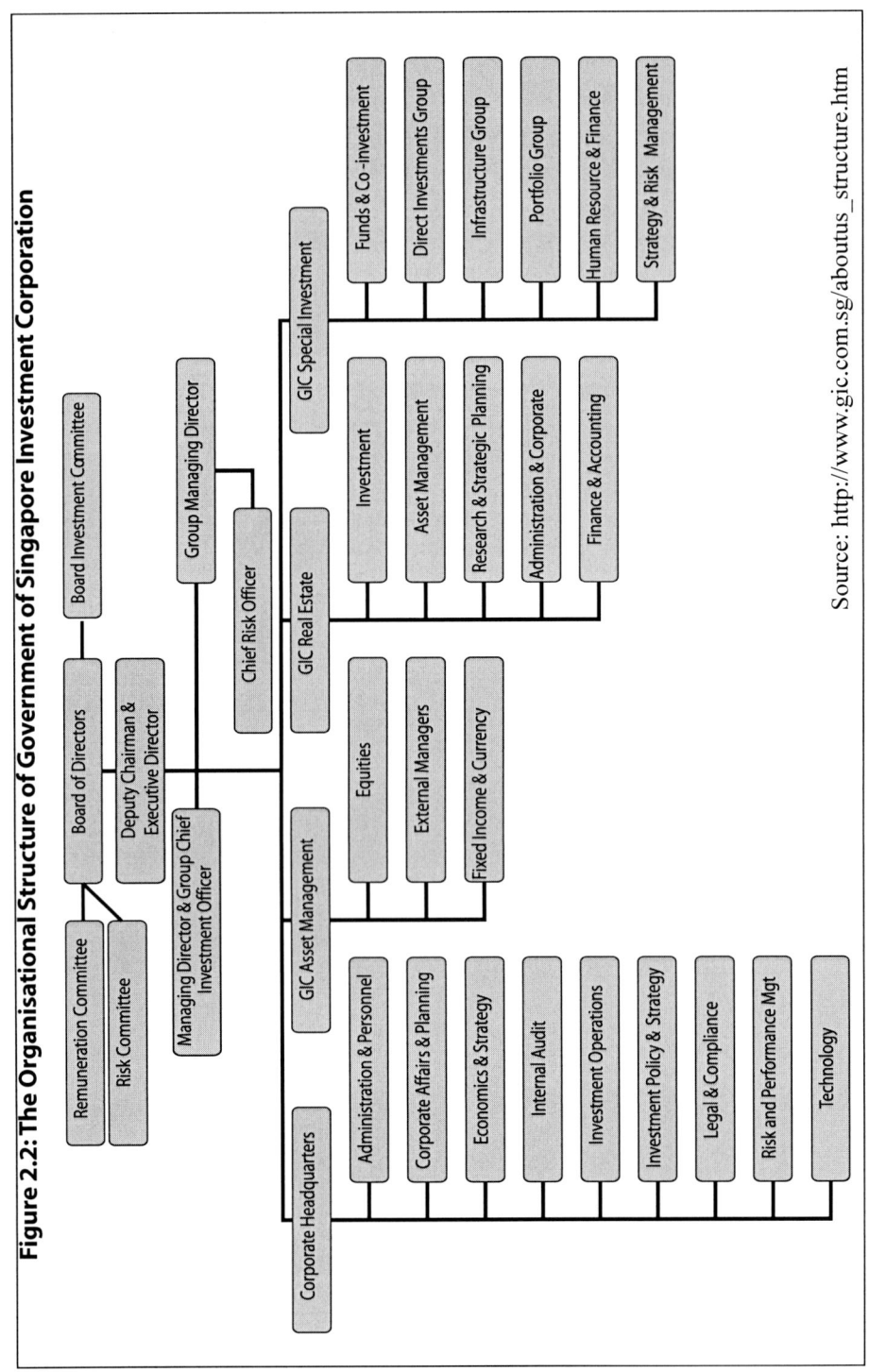

Figure 2.2: The Organisational Structure of Government of Singapore Investment Corporation

Source: http://www.gic.com.sg/aboutus_structure.htm

of eight worldwide offices, GIC is a global investment management company which invests internationally in equities, fixed income, foreign exchange, commodities, money markets, alternative investments, real estate and private equity. The objective of the Fund is to achieve good long-term returns on Singapore's national wealth while seeking to outperform some of the market indices in the medium term.

The Board of Directors is chaired by the country's founding father, Lee Kuan Yew. There are two Deputy Chairman, Prime Minister Lee Hsein Loong and Former Deputy Prime Minister Dr Tan Keng Yam. The Board of Directors consists of government officials from various ministries and government agencies, members from the Government-Linked Corporations[5] (GLC) and personnel from the senior management of GIC (see Appendix 2 for the list of Directors and various positions held outside GIC). The Deputy Chairman (cum Executive Director) reports to the Board of Directors and is in charge of GIC's operation, assisted by the Managing Director and the Group Managing Director. There are four divisions, one taking charge of corporate issues and three dealing with investments in different areas. GIC's Asset Management Division is responsible for managing GIC's external managers. The Real Estate Division is responsible for GIC's direct and indirect real estate investments and the division has also formed a number of subsidiaries (e.g. Reco Shahzan (M) Sdn Bhd and Reco Pearl Pte Ltd) to handle its overseas real estate investments. GIC Special Investment Division works as a private equity unit and deals with investments involving venture capital, leverage buyout, infrastructure, distress situations and other special situation investments. GIC employs both local and overseas professionals in its management team, with staff from 25 nationalities working in its worldwide offices.

The Ministry of Finance represents the Singaporean government in dealing with GIC, hence it is accountable to the Ministry of Finance and the Monetary Authority of Singapore (MAS). GIC is given the autonomy to invest but works within the risk tolerance levels and investment objectives set by the government and MAS. GIC is designated as the "Fifth Schedule" company under the Constitution of the Republic of Singapore and to a certain extent its operation comes under the President of Singapore who has the right to any information concerning GIC. The appointment and removal of directors requires the assent of the President. In addition, GIC financial statements and

---

5 Government-linked Corporation (GLC) is commercial company run as a private enterprise but with the Singaporean government as the only shareholder or the major shareholder. GLCs are owned by the government and invested through Temasek Holdings Ltd. Example of GLCs are the Singapore Airlines Ltd and the Singapore Technologies Engineering Ltd.

proposed budgets are submitted to the President for approval. The accounts of GIC are subject to regular audits by the Auditor General.

To ensure that GIC's operations are ethically and fiscally sound, three separate committees with independent advisors were set up. The Investment Committee evaluates and makes appropriate recommendations to the Board on matters relating to investment policy. The Risk Committee evaluates the risks undertaken by GIC and examines its risk management process and system. The Remuneration Committee oversees GIC's remuneration policies and its executive compensation. The members of these committees are basically made up of Directors, with the exception of Ho Tian Yee from the Risk Committee. He is one of the external fund managers who invest for GIC as the Managing Director and Chief Investment Officer of Pacific Asia Asset Management. In the Investment Committee, there are four external advisors, two of whom are professionals in the finance industry while two are academics from the UK and the US. For the Risk Committee, there is one external advisor, the Managing Director of Goldman Sachs Asset Management in the US (see Appendix 2 for the list of Members of the Committees).

Within GIC internal management, there is an additional unit called the Corporate Affairs and Planning Department (CADP) that deals with corporate policies and governance, relationship management with its clients (Singapore Ministry of Finance and MAS), accounting and budgeting. CADP also reports GIC's statutory accounts to the Council of Presidential Advisors.

2.2.3 Temasek Holdings

Singapore Temasek Holdings was established in 1974 by the Singapore Ministry of Finance as an exempt private company. According to its official website, Temasek Holdings is an Asian investment house with its main investment focus on Asia. It has achieved more than 18% compound annual return since its inception. Under the Singapore Companies Act (Chapter 50), an exempt private company should have less than 20 shareholders and no corporate shareholder and can be exempted from filing its audited financial statements with the public registry. In 1991, Temasek was designated a Fifth Schedule Company,[6] with the primary objective of developing industries for economic development. In the early days, Temasek invested in several key industries such as logistics and technology which formed part of Singapore's industrial policies. Unlike GIC, Temasek is an active shareholder which is

---
6 See GIC above on the requirement on the right of President over a Fifth Schedule Company.

involved in the operation of these companies through voting rights. As Temasek expands, it invests not only in the regional market but also in the global market. Unlike other SWFs which set their investment objective as obtaining high returns for their assets, Temasek investments have primarily focused on building key industries in Singapore and making use of Singapore's comparative advantages to invest in the region. Its mission is to create and maximise long-term shareholder value as an active investor and shareholder of successful enterprises.

Unlike other SWFs, some of Temasek's investments are funded through bond issuance, commercial borrowings, divestment proceeds and occasional asset injections from the Ministry of Finance. Another difference between Temasek and other SWFs is that the former issued a Yankee bond in 2005 and has a credit rating of AAA from Standard and Poor's. Unlike GIC, it holds direct investments in companies and the Fund takes an active role in the operation of those investments.

The Board of Directors is chaired by S Dhanabalan who held several cabinet posts until his retirement from politics. Within its Board of Directors, there are three expatriate directors. Simon Israel was appointed in 2005 and others are from the private sector except for Teo Ming Kian who also holds a position in the Prime Minister's Office. Temasek generated a lot of media attention when Ho Ching, the wife of the Prime Minister, was appointed to head Temasek's operations in 2004. In a surprising move, Ho Ching resigned as CEO after Temasek made huge losses overseas.[7] Charles Goodyear, who was appointed the Director in February 2009, was to take over the reins of Temasek in October 2009 and become the first expatriate to run Temasek. According to the official statement, seven out of nine Directors in its Board are independent Directors. In a press interview, S Dhanabalan stressed the importance of having different people holding the posts of Chairman and CEO. Temasek wants to make the Board feels at ease in questioning and examining the management proposals (refer to Appendix 3 for the list of Directors).[8]

Three months before Goodyear was to become CEO, Temasek announced that due to differences in strategic issues Goodyear has resigned and Ho Ching was to remain as CEO. These announcements have left many locals and foreigners questioning Temasek's moves. When it was announced that

---

[7] Kevin Lim and Saeed Azhar, "Temasek CEO Ho Ching to quit after rocky ride," Reuters, 6 February 2009. http://www.reuters.com/articles/asiaDealsNews/idUSTRES5152CA2009/0206

[8] Conrad Raj and Patrick Daniel, "Firms in its stable will have chairman, chief executive functions separated," Singapore Business Times, 25 June 1999.

SOVEREIGN WEALTH FUNDS

Figure 2.3: The Organisational Structure of Temasek Holdings

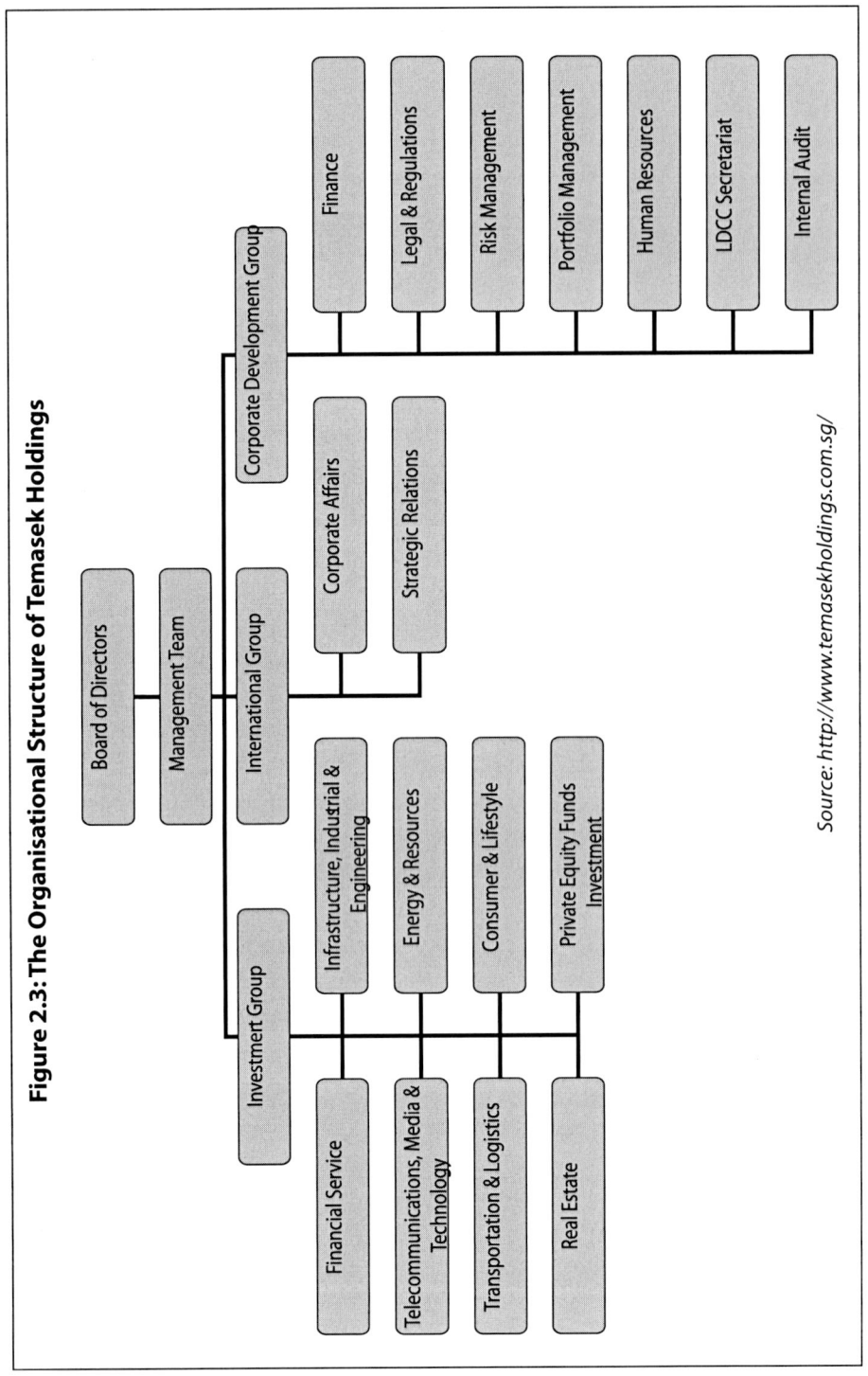

Source: http://www.temasekholdings.com.sg/

Ho Ching would step down as CEO, many had speculated that she was under pressure to resign due to Temasek's huge losses in overseas investments. However, Temasek defended the move and claimed that the replacement was not due to performance.[9] It was widely speculated that Goodyear was squeezed out by Ho Ching.[10] Shortly after the announcement of Goodyear's resignation, Temask announced that it had recouped most of its losses from the subprime crisis and its portfolio was valued at just 7% below its peak of S$185 billion in March 2008.[11] Singapore's Minister of Finance, Tharman Shanmugaratnam raised the point, in a parliamentary speech, that the Temasek CEO should ideally be a Singaporean.[12] Despite the unclear signals Temasek gave on its boardroom shuffles, Temasek is still seen as the model for other Asian SWFs. Even though the corporate governance and disclosure policy of Norway's Government Pension Fund- Global is considered the "golden standard" in the SWF industry, Temasek's model is being viewed as "acceptable" because it publishes its annual account to give an overview of its policies and operations. These, though not as detailed as Norway's Government Pension Fund- Global, are more open than those of ADIA and the Brunei Investment Agency, for example.

The Management Team is divided into three core groups: the Investment Group, the International Group and the Corporate Development Group. It is headed by the CEO and reports to the Board of Directors. Within the Investment Group there are eight divisions which handle investments including those in the financial services, telecommunications, media and technology, transport and logistics, real estate, infrastructure, industrial and engineering, energy and resources, consumer and lifestyle and private equity funds investment. Temasek has offices in Asia and Mexico (refer to the organisational chart of Temasek in Figure 2.3).

Previously, Temasek did not have to disclose its financial statements and investment portfolios despite pressure from the general public. However, its level of transparency has increased tremendously following its plan to issue bonds in 2005. To issue corporate bonds Temasek had to reveal its operations

---

[9] John Burton, "Temasek said Goodyear will not be chief," *Financial Times*, 21 July 2009. http://www.ft.com/cms/s/0/6fc55des-75db-11de-84c7-00144feadbc0.html

[10] Richard Wachman, "Temasek abandons plan to install Chip Goodyear as Chief Executive," *Guardian UK*, 21 July 2009. http://www.guardian.co.uk/business/2009/jul9/21/temasek-chip-goodyear-resignation

[11] Kevin Brown, "Temasek gain $30bn from market rally," *Financial Times*, 17 September 2009. http://www.ft.com/cms/s/0/16bb3f42-a32e-11de-ba74-00144feabdc0.html

[12] Joy Fang, "Temasek CEO ideally Singaporean," *Asiaone.com*, 19 August 2009. http://business.asiaone.com/Business/News/Story/A1Story20090819-161923.html

and accounts to two credit rating agencies, Standard and Poor's and Moody. Currently, Temasek has published detailed financial statements (including their asset portfolio), as well as information on the Directors and their positions outside Temasek in their official website.

In moving from a secretive operation to a policy of complete disclosure a year before its public offer of Yankee Bonds in 2005, Temasek is attempting to distance itself from being labelled as a SWF. It claims that because it needs to raise funds in the same way as any other company in the private sector through various sources, it does not qualify as a SWF.[13] So Temasek is unlike other SWFs where the government is the only source of funding in also raising funds in the capital markets.

2.2.4 China Investment Corporation (CIC)

CIC, one of the latest players in the SWF industry, generated a lot of publicity even before its launch in 2007. This was due to China's huge amount of foreign reserves and the government's lack of transparency in most activities. The West is sceptical about CIC's commitment to investment for higher returns on its foreign reserves. In particular, policymakers are worried that the Chinese government is using the CIC as a veil to mask its political ambitions and as an investment vehicle to control key foreign infrastructure and industries. However, until now there has been no evidence to show that the Chinese government has used the CIC to advance its political purposes.

The CIC is established as a wholly state-owned company under the Company Law of the People's Republic of China. It is funded through the issuance of special bonds worth RMB1.55 trillion by the Ministry of Finance and the funds raised are used to purchase foreign reserves to be used as capital by the CIC. The net effect of this is that $200 billion in The People's Bank of China was replaced with bonds which the Ministry of Finance will pay off from interest payments from the CIC.[14] When CIC was established in 2007, it bought out Huijin Investment Ltd which was set up in 2003 to recapitalise and stabilise China's major state-owned commercial banks. According to the official statement, the CIC's investment is not restricted to any particular class of assets or region of investment. In fact, the CIC is modelled after Singapore's

---

13 "Guidelines to avoid investment friction restriction reached," Ministry of Foreign Affair Press Release, March 22 2008. http://app.mfa.gov.sg/pr/read_content.asp?View,9632
14 Ziemba, Rachel, "How is China Funding the Chinese Investment Corporation (CIC)?" RGE Analysts' EconoMonitor web log, 7 December 2007. http//www.rgemonitor.com/blog/economonitor/230764/

Temasek Holding which invests in both domestic and international markets and is accountable to the Ministry of Finance. CIC differed from other SWFs in terms of its capital structure. "Capital" was treated as a loan from the Ministry of Finance and the CIC was required to pay back interest to the Ministry. However, this capital structure was changed in September 2009 and the CIC is now only required to pay a regular dividend instead.

The Board of Directors oversees the operations and performance of the Fund. It is headed by Lou Jiwei who is the Chairman and CEO. Of the eleven members of the Board of Directors, five are non-executive directors, two are independent directors and one is an employed director, while the rest are executive directors. The executive directors are all former state employees while the non-executive and independent directors are from various state agencies (see Appendix 4 for a list of Directors and Committee Members). In his analysis of CIC, Cognato (2008) commented that the Vice Chairman and Chief Investment Officer, Gao Xiping, is more likely to have a direct say in investment decisions despite Lou Jiwei having been been the most visible representative of the Fund.

In addition, the Board of Supervisors of CIC oversees the company's corporate governance and accounting and financial activities. It ensures that there is an appropriate level of supervision and accountability within CIC's operations. Most of these members hold position in other regulatory agencies. The Executive Committee is responsible for the daily operation and reports to the Board of Directors and State Council. All the seven members of the Executive Committee served in state agencies prior to joining CIC (see Appendix 4 for information about the executive committee cited from the CIC website). According to the CIC official statement, there are three committees: the International Advisory Committee, the Investment Committee and the Risk Management Committee. The Investment Committee manages and implements investment strategies and the Risk Management Committee sets up company-wide strategies and manages CIC's risk exposure. Both committees report directly to the Executive Committee. At the time of writing, the CIC is in the process of establishing an International Advisory Committee to advise on its operations. Its Board of Directors, including independent directors, is dominated by representatives from various government ministries and agencies.

As far as the actual management team is concerned, several of the members (Lou Jiwei, Gao Xiping, Xie Ping and Jesse Wong) have experience in managing public and private sector investments. Only two directors, Lou Jiwei

Figure 2.4: The Organisational Structure of the China Investment Corporation

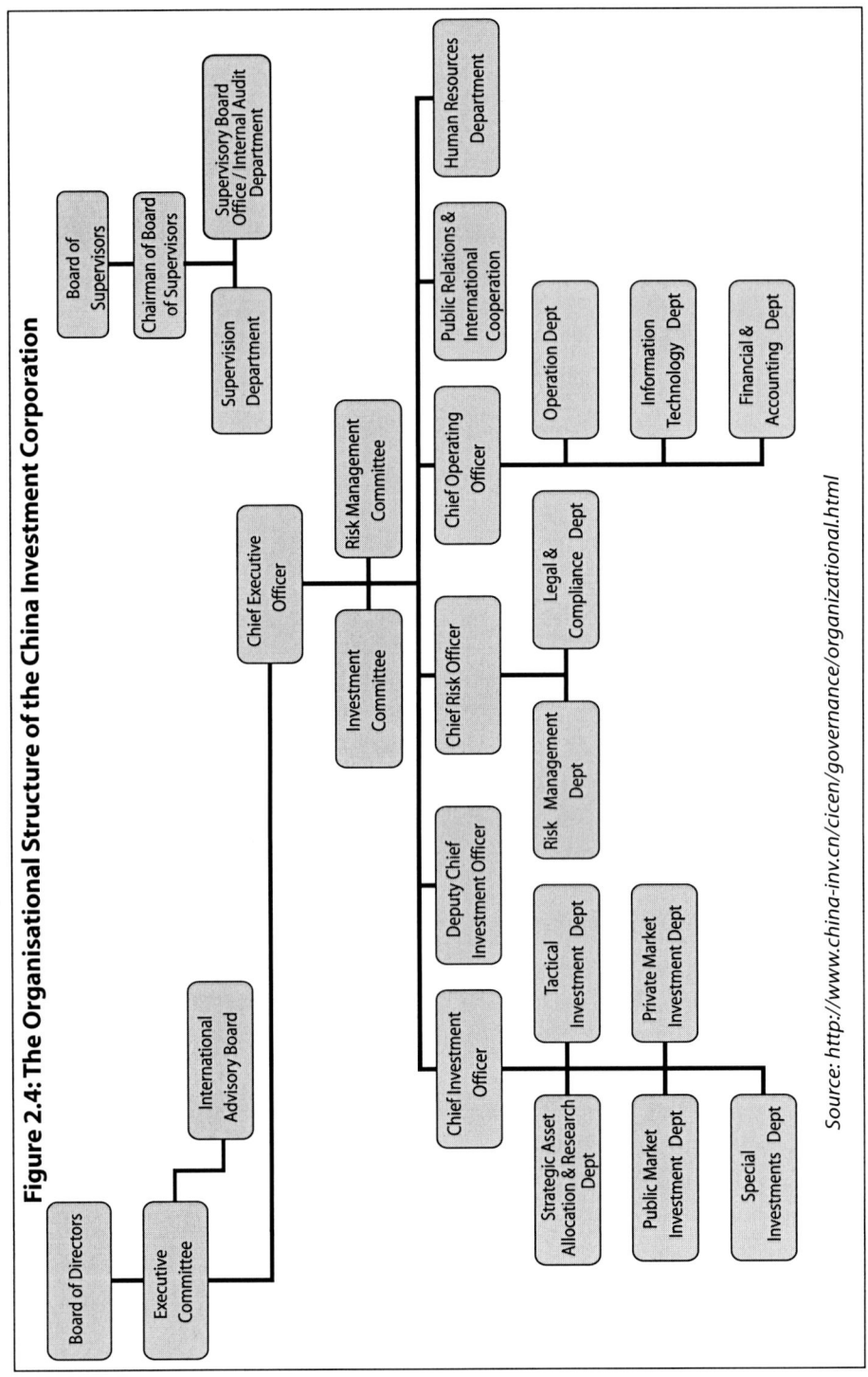

Source: http://www.china-inv.cn/cicen/governance/organizational.html

and Gao Xiping, are involved in the management. Within the management team, only Luo Jiwei has spent significant time in provincial posts and important parts of the state bureaucracy. Cognato (2008) argues that the composition of the management team and Board of Directors can help to protect the CIC from official interference; the CIC will thus not be pressured to support loss-making SOEs. However, unlike Abu Dhabi and Singapore, China is relatively inexperienced in running a SWF and it may take some time to form a team of fully experienced personnel.

2.2.5 Government Pension Fund – Global (GPFG)

The Norwegian Government established Norway's Petroleum Fund in 1990 to manage the country's petroleum revenues and the first capital was transfer to the Fund in 1996. The Petroleum Fund was renamed the Government Pension Fund – Global and the Government Pension Fund – Norway in 2006. The Government Pension Fund – Global is regarded as the SWF of Norway and it is managed separately from the Government Pension Fund – Norway. The Government Pension Fund – Norway invests in the domestic economy only while GPFG invests overseas. GPFG is owned by the Ministry of Finance while the management of the Fund is delegated to the Norges Bank. The GPFG is represented by an account held by the Norges Bank in the name of the Ministry of Finance. To manage the Fund, Norges Bank established Norges Bank Investment Management (NBIM) and is responsible for the actual operation of the Fund. Operating from offices in Oslo, London, New York and Shanghai, the Fund's objectives are to save and manage petroleum revenues to meet the needs of a rapid rise in public pension expenditure and to support the long-term management of the petroleum revenues. The Fund also acts as a stabilization fund to counter the effects of fluctuation on oil prices.

Unlike the other four SWFs in the previous sections, GPFG does not have a separate legal entity and it does not have a Board of Directors. Despite not being run as a separate legal entity, GPFG has the best corporate governance and transparency. The Fund has set out a very clear operational structure and is managed independently from its owner, the Ministry of Finance. However, the Ministry of Finance still has the overall responsibility to monitor and evaluate the Fund's operational management, plan the strategic asset allocation, set the ethnical guidelines and report to the parliament on GPFG's activities. The Ministry of Finance sets the limits on the risk and the strategic asset allocation with the advice of Norges Bank, the Ministry's advisory council, and external consultants. The Ministry is assisted by an ethical council to set the ethical guidelines for the Fund and advise on the exclusion of companies. The Ministry also uses external consultants for independent measuring and benchmarking of performance. Under the Pension Fund Act, the Ministry of Finance is the owner of GPFG but the Ministry of Finance reports to parliament on the Fund's annual performance and any significant changes in the Fund's investment strategy. Important changes such as changes in its mix of equities and bonds need parliamentary approval before implementation. The central bank, Norges Bank, is deemed to be the operational manager. The responsibilities of Norges Bank are to implement investment strategy, manage actively to achieve excess returns, run risk control and reporting, exercise the Fund's ownership rights and provide professional advice on investment strategy[15]. See Figure 2.5 on NBIM governance structure.

After the record losses of 2008 wiped out GPFG's 12 year of gains, NBIM named a new team of executives. Yngve Slyngstad who was previously the Fund's Head of Equity remained as CEO and Stephen Hirsh stayed as Deputy CEO. The Fund promoted Bengt Enge to chief investment officer, Trong Grande to chief risk officer, and Age Bakker to chief operating officer. In addition, Mark Clemens, formerly from Citigroup, joined as chief administrative officer and Jessica Irschick formerly from UBS joined as chief treasurers. (See Appendix 5 for NBIM Leader Group).

 The operation is divided into five divisions, Fixed Income, Equity, Corporate Governance, Real Estate Project and Chief Financial Officer. Under the Chief Financial Officer, there are Risk, Performance and Accounting, IT Infrastructure and Legal, Finance and Human Resources. In addition to running the GPFG, NBIM also manages the major share of Norges Bank's foreign exchange reserves and the Government Petroleum Insurance Fund.[16] According to the Norges Bank's official website, NBIM employed 249 permanent staffs as at 31 December 2009. See Figure 2.6 for NBIM's organisational structure.

---

15 Norway Government Pension Fund – Global presentation at The Business of Clean Energy at Alaska, 19 May 2009. http://alaskarenewableenergy.org/wp-content/uploads/2009/06/hege_eliassen.pdf
16 See Norges Bank, About NBIM, http://www.norges-bank.no/templates/article____69632.aspx

STRUCTURE, GOVERNANCE AND PROPOSED INTERNATIONAL GUIDELINES

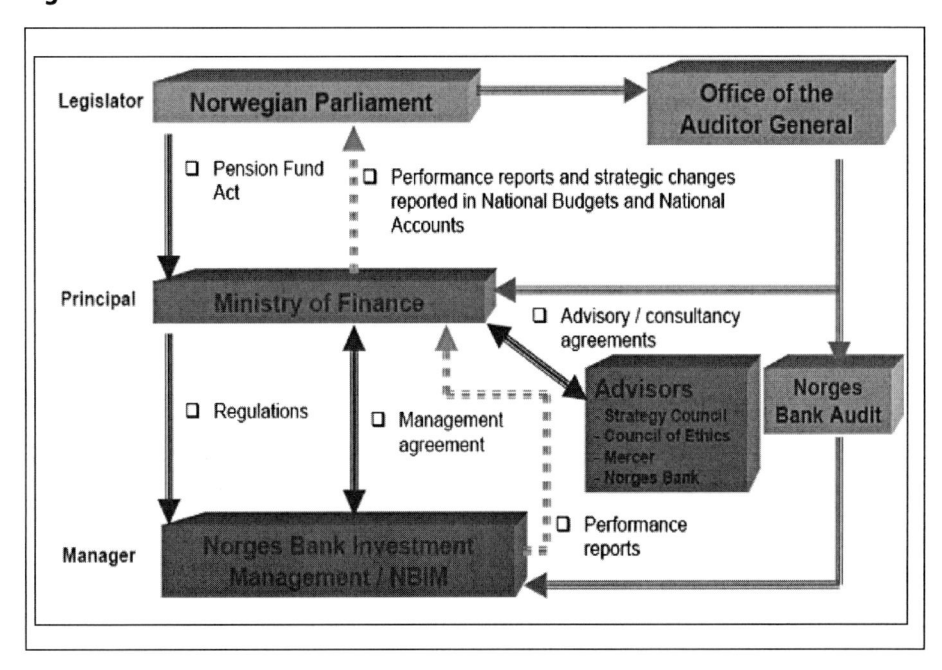

Figure 2.5: Government Pension Fund – Global Governance Structure

Source: The Norwegian Government Pension Fund & NBIM, Presentation to Central Bank of Chile Santiago, 3 October 2007.

The organisational structure of NBIM shows that the GPFG is managed separately from the government but there is still a formal connection to the government to ensure the Fund's accountability. The Norges Bank manages GPFG and reports the performance of the Fund on a regular basis while the Ministry of Finance provides annual reports on the management of the Fund to parliament. In addition, the Fund's Reports are available publicly and widely disseminated in English. Comparatively, GPFG, which does not have a separate legal entity, operates more independently than those SWFs which are established as separate legal entities. This accountability of GPFG to the parliament and the Norwegian people is a good practice not only in itself but also because the Funds acts as a fiscal tool to support the long-term management of the petroleum revenues and is integrated with Norway's state budget.

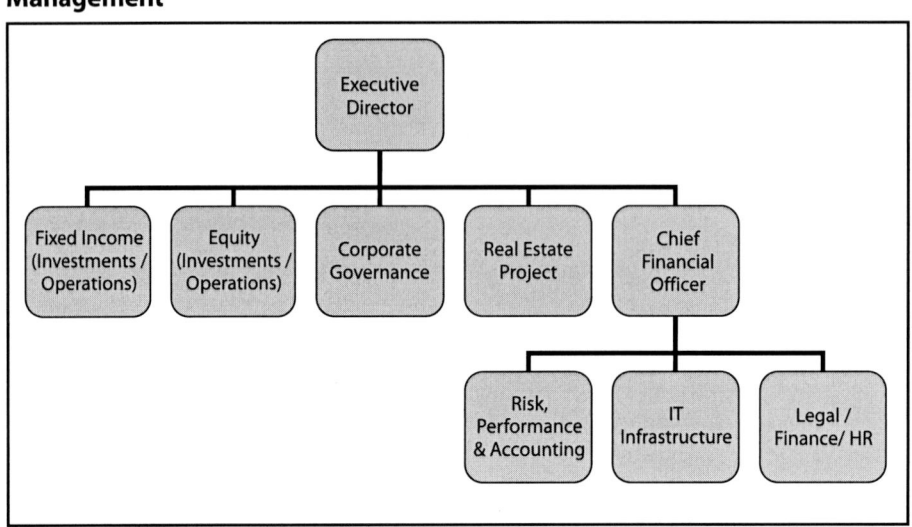

Figure 2.6: The Organisational Chart of Norges Bank Investment Management

Source: The Norwegian Government Pension Fund & NBIM, Presentation to Central Bank of Chile Santiago, 3 October 2007.

2.3 Current Governance and Transparency

SWFs are owned by sovereign states rather than by private corporations, therefore, the governance of these funds has generated great concerns among policymakers and market players. The issue of corporate governance is deemed to be more important in SWFs than in other types of investment vehicles because the shareholders of these funds are sovereign entities. The general fear is that the governments concerned will use their SWFs for political purposes and this makes policymakers in the West more determined to ensure that these funds are compliant with "best practice". It is important that the shareholders (governments in one way or another) do not play an active role in the operation of SWFs. The current problem is that the SWFs are not regulated by any international institution and they do not have to be transparent in their operations. In addition, the investments of these funds are widely diversified which makes it even more difficult to trace or check their corporate governance. Even if these funds make a statement on their corporate governance, the role of government is often ambiguous because government officials sit on the Boards of Directors. This makes it even harder to establish corporate governance in these funds. Aizenman and Glick (2008) conducted an empirical research to examine if a country with a lower level of national governance has a greater tendency to establish a SWF. They did not find any association between national governance and the presence of SWFs. However, they concluded that SWF countries tend to display better governance on average than other developing countries but they are characterised by relatively low performance on democracy.

GPFG, which is the most transparent SWF, has set up its corporate governance in a separate statement. The Fund is run by external fund managers and it does not hold any managerial role over the companies in which it has invested. Though GIC has announced that part of their Fund is managed by external fund managers, the role of government is ambiguous since most of its directors are government officials. As far as Temasek is concerned, there are seven independent Directors on its Board of Directors and information on its operations is published on the official website. Temasek first made its financial statements available to the public in 2004. However, there is no breakdown of some of the items, so there is still ambiguity in some of its operations. The CIC, as a newcomer in the SWF industry, has limited disclosure on its operations although its first annual report has recently been published. While only limited announcements on its investments are made in their official website, there is information on its Directors and Committee Members (see Section 2.2.4 on the CIC's organisation structure).

Doug Dowson and Edwin Truman constructed a scoreboard for SWFs.[17] They made use of systematic, regularly released public information to construct scores based on four criteria: the Structure of Fund, Governance of Fund, Accountability, and Transparency. To compute the score for Governance, they assessed the role of the government, the role of fund managers, decisions made by fund managers, guidelines for corporate responsibility and ethical guidelines in conducting their activities. In most SWFs, the role of government is neither defined nor clear. For SWFs in the West such as GPFG, Alaska's Permanent Fund and Wyoming's Permanent Mineral Trust, they gave scores of 80 or above for "Structure" because they have clear objectives and both the sources of funding and the use of funds are clearly laid out. The score on "Governance" reflects the roles of the government and fund managers and

---

17 From Truman (2008) A Blueprint for Sovereign Wealth Fund Best Practices. Peterson Institute for International Economics, Number PB08-3, April 2008.

the corporate governance of these funds. ADIA, the biggest SWF, scored zero for its "Governance", while GIC and Temasek scored 40 and 50 and CIC 50 respectively. The SWFs that have a score around 40 and 50 are ambiguous on the role of their governments in the operation of the funds. This ambiguity leaves open the possibility for government officials to influence investments for non-financial purposes but some of these SWFs which have a low score on "Governance" are entirely silent on their corporate structure and governance and do not appear to be planning to take action to remedy the situation. Only bigger SWFs such as ADIA, CIC and GIC have stepped in to reassure the public their SWFs are operated separately from the government.

For good governance, GPFG obtains a full score while Kuwait is the only non-western SWF that has a high score at 80. In addition, GPFG, Kuwait's Investment Authority and Wyoming's Permanent Mineral Trust have laid down ethical guidelines in their operational activities (refer to Truman's (2008) Scoreboard in Table 2.1).

Table 2.1: Truman's (2008) Scoreboard: A Summary o SWF Scoreboard (Percent of Maximum Possible Points)

COUNTRY	FUND	STRUCTURE	GOVERNANCE	ACCOUNTABILITY AND TRANSPARENCY
Algeria	Revenue Regulation Fund	56	40	11
Australia	Australian Government Future Fund	100	80	68
Azerbaijan	State Oil Fund of the Republic of Azerbaijan	88	60	89
Botswana	Pula Fund	69	60	54
Brunei	Brunei Investment Agency	31	0	25
Canada (Alberta)	Alberta Heritage Savings Trust Fund	94	60	79

STRUCTURE, GOVERNANCE AND PROPOSED INTERNATIONAL GUIDELINES

COUNTRY	FUND	STRUCTURE	GOVERNANCE	ACCOUNTABILITY AND TRANSPARENCY
Chile	Economic and Social Stabilisation Fund	94	60	82
China	China Investment Corporation	50	50	14
Iran	Oil Stabilisation Fund	50	20	18
Ireland	National Pensions Reserve Fund	100	100	86
Kazakhstan	National Fund for the Republic of Kazakhstan	88	60	84
Kiribati	Revenue Equalization Reserve Fund	69	60	7
Korea	Korea Investment Corporation	75	60	45
Kuwait	Kuwait Investment Authority	75	80	41
Malaysia	Khazanah Nasional	44	50	46
New Zealand	Superannuation Fund	100	100	100
Nigeria	Excess Crude Account	50	30	14
Norway	Government Pension Fund–Global	94	100	100
Oman	State General Reserve Fund	50	0	18
Qatar	Qatar Investment Authority	34	0	2

SOVEREIGN WEALTH FUNDS

COUNTRY	FUND	STRUCTURE	GOVERNANCE	ACCOUNTABILITY AND TRANSPARENCY
Russia*	Reserve Fund and National Welfare Fund	72	40	50
Singapore	Temasek Holdings	50	50	61
Singapore	Government of Singapore Investment Corporation	63	40	39
Timor-Leste	Petroleum Fund for Timor-Leste	100	40	96
United Arab Emirates (Abu Dhabi)	Abu Dhabi Investment Authority and Council	25	0	4
United States (Alaska)	Alaska Permanent Fund	100	80	100
United States (New Mexico)	Severance Tax Permanent Fund	100	50	86
United States (Wyoming)	Permanent Mineral Trust Fund	100	90	82
Venezuela	Macroeconomic Stabilisation Fund	50	0	18

Source: Edwin M. Truman, A Blueprint for Sovereign Wealth Fund Best Practices, Peterson Institute for International Economics, April 2008, p. 7.

* On January 30 the Russian Stabilization Fund was split into National Wealth Fund and Reserve Fund. http://mnweekly.ru/business/20080214/55309843.html

The transparency of SWFs is also a big concern for policymakers and market players. The huge cash flows from these funds are welcome but not the secrecy behind their operations. Most western policymakers fear that the funds will use the acquired foreign assets for political manipulation. Given the huge amounts of reserves held by SWFs as well as the size of the top ten SWFs, there is the possibility of herding behaviour by these funds or by other market participants who follow their lead. The fear of herding is aggravated by the lack of transparency in the SWF operation. State investors (including the central banks over their reserve management) traditionally always operate in secrecy,. The common reason given for this is the fear of speculative attacks on its currency. However, it is argued that this is no longer a valid reason given that these countries regularly report their foreign reserve holdings to the International Monetary Fund (IMF).

On the economic level, the availability of information on SWFs to the policymakers, international institutions (such as IMF) and other market users is important for analysis. The lack of this information may hinder economic decisions and mislead policymakers and lead to adverse effects on economic performance and planning. Whether the assets of SWFs are held directly or indirectly, they should be reflected in the government's net worth as they form part of a nation's wealth. According to an IMF report in 2008, there are significant gaps in the statistics on SWFs – details of SWF investments were not included in some members' balance of payments (BOP) and international investment position (IIP). Based on the response of 20 members of IWG, 65% of the SWFs included their data in BOP or IIP, 15% do not include their data in BOP or IIP and 20% did not specify on data availability.[18] In response to the international call for more transparency, Lou Jiwei, the head of the CIC said: "We will increase transparency without harming the commercial interest of CIC. That is to say it will be a gradual process. Transparency is really a tough issue. If we are transparent on everything, the wolves will eat us up."[19] After the Asian financial crisis, Asian central banks have accumulated massive foreign reserves to defend their currencies and these countries are reluctant to disclose their wealth, regularly citing avoidance of speculative attack on their currency as one of the reasons for non-disclosure.

---

18 IWG (2008) "Sovereign Wealth Funds – Current Institutional and Operational Practices," 15 September 2008. http://www.iwg-swf.org/pubs/eng/swfsurvey.pdf

19 Jamil Anderlini, "China wealth fund coming early of age," Financial Times, 20 December 2007. http://www.ft.com/cms/s/0/b8cca8a0-af2b-11dc-880f-0000779fd2ac.html

Very little information on SWF operations in terms of management structure, investment strategy and risk management is available to the industry as well as to individual SWFs. Although the organisational structure, investment objectives and general operational issues of some SWFs are posted on their websites, this information does not give the general public much knowledge of their operations. Similarly, informal market knowledge of the industry is insufficient. The SWF investment objectives and asset allocations are the main concerns of most host countries who fear that SWFs may be used to advance political motives through cross-border investments. For example, Dubai World's investment in the US ports was blocked for political reasons. Its investment objectives and investment strategy are particularly vague, with limited disclosure. In fact most SWFs have limited disclosure on their investments. Most of the funds state that their objective is to maximise return subject to an acceptable risk level. Unlike other types of funds such as pension funds, existing laws and regulations do not cover government investment vehicles except in so far as SWFs' overseas investments fall under the regulations for foreign direct investments of recipient countries. This lack of transparency is particularly evident in their asset allocations, investment transactions, risk management and use of derivatives. In addition, these funds are not required to publish their financial accounts and in most cases their returns are also unknown. This lack of transparency creates uncertainties in the financial markets and several attempts have been made to develop an index of transparency based on information available to the public.

Truman's (2008) Accountability and Transparency Indices (see Table 2.1) assess if an SWF can comply with the 14 elements identified. The 14 elements are classified into four categories: investment strategy implementation, investment activities, reports and audit. They examine how much information related to these categories is disclosed and assign a higher score for funds that have a higher level of disclosure. The Alaska Permanent Fund and GPFG scored a percent score of 100. It is not surprising to find that scores for Asian and Middle Eastern SWFs were significantly below average. The Qatar Investment Authority had the lowest score at 2, followed by ADIA at 4. China got 14 points while GIC had 39 points. With a score of 61 points, Temasek showed a higher level of disclosure compared to its counterpart GIC. Temasek has published its financial statements since 2004 but limited information was available on its operation prior to 2004. Since the computation of Truman's Scoreboard, SWFs such as ADIA, GIC and Temasek have increased their level of transparency. ADIA has disclosed its strategic asset allocation to the media and has hired

STRUCTURE, GOVERNANCE AND PROPOSED INTERNATIONAL GUIDELINES

Figure 2.7: Linaburg – Maduell Transparency Index, 4th Quarter 2008

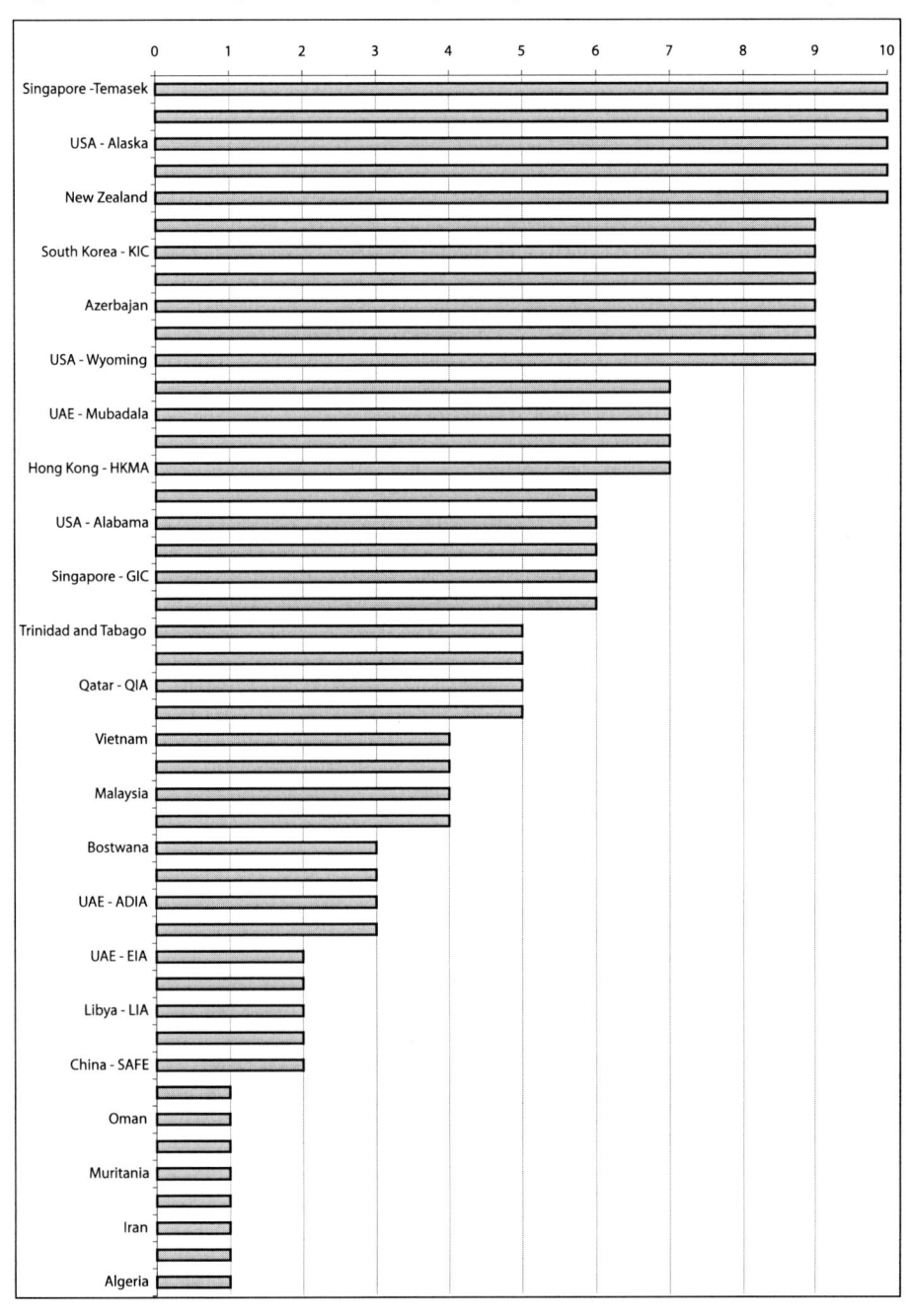

Fund	Score
Singapore - Temasek	10
USA - Alaska	10
New Zealand	10
South Korea - KIC	9
Azerbajan	9
USA - Wyoming	9
UAE - Mubadala	7
Hong Kong - HKMA	7
USA - Alabama	6
Singapore - GIC	6
Trinidad and Tabago	5
Qatar - QIA	5
Vietnam	4
Malaysia	4
Bostwana	3
UAE - ADIA	3
UAE - EIA	2
Libya - LIA	2
China - SAFE	2
Oman	1
Muritania	1
Iran	1
Algeria	1

Source: Sovereign Wealth Fund Institute (SWFI) (May 2009)

a public relations company to improve its corporate image, while GIC and Temasek have published their annual reports on their official websites (see Chapter 3 on their strategic asset allocations). However, most SWFs are not transparent in their operations and asset allocations. The Sovereign Wealth Fund Institute (SWFI) has also developed the Linaburg-Maduell Transparency Index to rate the transparency of SWFs. This index is constructed using ten principles that relate the degree of fund transparency to the public. The higher the level of transparency, the more points are allocated to a SWF. The index is updated when there is a change of information on the fund monitored (refer to Appendix 5 for details on the ten principles used to construct the Linaburg-Maduell Transparency Index).

Using this scale, Temasek attained the highest point in the transparency index in the fourth quarter of 2008. Temasek was ranked eleventh in the last quarter and has improved tremendously within a single quarter. This is due to their disclosure of more information to expedite their issuance of bonds. While the other Singaporean SWF GIC had an index of 6, Ireland's NPFR, the US's Alaska, GPFG, and New Zealand's Superannuation Fund scored 10 points in the third and fourth quarters of 2008 based on this Index. With the exception of UAE's Mubadala, Bahrain Mumtalakat Holding, Kuiwait Investment Authority and Qatar Investment Authority, most of the Middle East Funds ranked quite low in the transparency index, with an average index of less than 5. The CIC had an index of seven which is relatively high given that China's state-owned agencies are always criticised for a lack of transparency. It obtains the same number of points as the Hong Kong Monetary Authority which has been well-known for promotingthe country's openness as a financial market (refer to Figure 2.7 for the Linaburg – Maduell Transparency Index of SWFs in the fourth quarter 2008).

The role of government in the SWF is at the centre of corporate governance practice. This is of great importance as it provides an indication of how much influence a government should exert over a SWF operation. It is assumed that the higher the level of government involvement, the higher the possibility and risk that it will use the SWF for its political ambitions. Hence, the level of government involvement in SWF has been of great interest to many policymakers and international institutions. Table 2.2 indicates the level of government involvement in some SWFs. It shows that most governments are involved in the SWF either as members of the board or in the management team, as illustrated by Kuwait Investment Authority, the Qatar Investment Authority and Russia's RRF and NWF. It also reveals that the Middle Eastern and

Russian SWFs such as ADIA and QIA have strong government presences on their boards of directors, but there is no information on the role of government in the senior management. The Russian SWFs' board of directors and senior management is made up only of only government officials from the Ministry of Finance. In addition, the table shows that a high level of government involvement is associated with a low level of transparency.

Table 2.2: A Comparative Analysis: Governance

SWF	TYPE OF LEGAL ENTITY	ROLE OF GOVERNMENT IN THE SWF BOARD	ROLE OF GOVERNMENT IN SENIOR MANAGEMENT	REPORTING PROCEDURE	AUDIT PROCEDURE
ADIA	Government agency	Strong government presence	Limited information-strong government presence	No information beyond subject to supervision by the Abu Dhabi government	Internal Audit and Audit Committee
AGFF	Comprised of two bodies: an incorporated body and a prescribed agency	Totally independent	Independent	Annual report and quarterly portfolio updates available online	Internal Audit committee and external Australian National Audit Office
CIC	Incorporated	Five government officials on the board	Members of the executive committee do not have current government positions, but come form governmental background	Accountable to the State Council and published annual report	Internal Audit Department and National Audit Office
GIC	Incorporated	Mixed of government and independent members	Independent	Publishes publicly available annual reports as well as quarterly update reports to the Ministry of Finance	Auditor-General of Singapore

SOVEREIGN WEALTH FUNDS

SWF	TYPE OF LEGAL ENTITY	ROLE OF GOVERNMENT IN THE SWF BOARD	ROLE OF GOVERNMENT IN SENIOR MANAGEMENT	REPORTING PROCEDURE	AUDIT PROCEDURE
KIA	Government agency	Mixed of government and independent members	Mixed of government officials and independent members	KIA reports directly to the Kuwaiti Council of Ministries on an annual basis. This report is not available to any outside party	State Audit Bureau
LIA	Government agency	Four senior government officials on the Board of Trustees; 2/7 Directors hold current government positions	Independent	LIA reports to the People's Congress on an annual basis	The People's Supervision Authority and external audited by an international audit firm
GPFG	Integrated into the Ministry of Finance	Government appointed members	Independent – Norges Bank operates as Norway's central bank	Quarterly and annual reports to the Ministry of Finance which are made public through the fund's website	Deloitte AS as well as internal audits conducted by the central bank. Both parties submit reports to the supervisory board, then final audited by the office of the Auditor General.
QIA	Strong government presence	Strong government presence	Limited information- mix of government officials and ruling family	No information regarding reporting procedure	The State Audit Bureau

SWF	TYPE OF LEGAL ENTITY	ROLE OF GOVERNMENT IN THE SWF BOARD	ROLE OF GOVERNMENT IN SENIOR MANAGEMENT	REPORTING PROCEDURE	AUDIT PROCEDURE
RRF & NWF	All are Ministry of Finance officials	All are Ministry of Finance officials	Ministry of Finance	Reports to the government on a quarterly basis and publishes monthly fund updates to the public	Accounts Chamber of the Russian Federation
Temasek	Independent and highly diversified	Independent and highly diversified	Independent	Publishes annual report including a financial summary as well as highlights from the year's activities	Financial statements are externally audited by an international audit firm

Source: IRRC Institute and Risk Metrics Group (2009)

2.4 Current and Proposed International Standards

SWF investments are subject to various laws and regulations in the recipient countries. In 2007, the US Congress established new legislation for SWFs. Investments by SWFs in the US bank and bank holding companies that meet certain criterion such as having substantial control over voting shares or the board of Directors are subject to the Bank Holding Company Act and the Change in Bank Control Act.

International bodies, particularly those that involve cross-border investments, have proposed numerous standards on the regulations and guidelines to govern SWF operations. The Commission of the European Community has proposed a common approach to SWFs. The Organisation for Economic Co-operation and Development (OECD), which has developed a guideline for recipient countries towards investment from SWFs, gives emphasis to symmetry in market access, non-discrimination, transparency and predictability, proportionality of policy measures, and accountability. In principle, besides promoting transparency and the accountability of investments, the guidelines aim to encourage cross-border transactions on a fair and equal ground for both the SWFs and recipient countries. If the need for the protection of national security arises, the protection should not be greater than that required to avoid excessive protectionism by the recipient countries (refer to Table 2.3 for a brief summary of the OECD guideline). However, the OECD Guidelines are primarily addressed to its industrialised member states.[20] The Santiago Principles, which were proposed by the IWG, have more effects as they have a larger number of members.

Table 2.3: A Summary of the OECD Guidelines

AN OPTIMAL POLICY RESPONSE: PRINCIPLES FOR SOUND INVESTMENT POLICIES (FROM ODEC)	
PRINCIPLE	EXPLANATION
Symmetry of market access	Policymakers should work towards reducing asymmetrical cross-border investments whereby on the one hand economies may be benefiting from access to open markets in pursuing their foreign investments, and on the other hand, they may set up protectionist rules on inward investment.
Non-discrimination	Governments should adopt a non-discriminatory approach towards foreign investors. It is recommended that the same measure of standards be applied in the treatment of foreign investors as to local investors. Specific circumstance could be an exception should an individual investment pose a threat and undermine the national security.
Transparency and predictability	Transparency and predictability refer to investors' access to the codification and publication of investment rules, heads-up for upcoming changes, consultation for affected/interested parties, procedure fairness in treatment, protection of sensitive information. In short, increasing transparency leads to an increased level of predictability.

---

20 *Members of OCED: Australia, Austria, Belgium, Canada, Czech Republic, Denmark, Finland, Germany, Greece, Hungary, Iceland, Ireland, Italy, Japan, Korea, Luxembourg, Mexico, the Netherlands, New Zealand, Norway, Poland, Portugal, the Slovak Republic, Spain, Sweden, Switzerland, Turkey, the United Kingdom and the United States.*

PRINCIPLE	EXPLANATION
Proportionality of policy measures	While there is a need to protect national security, restrictions and conditions on transactions and investment should not be greater than required to safeguard national security. Newer restrictions should be avoided if existing measures are adequate to address present concerns.
Accountability	The role of the government is to provide law and order and create conditions conducive to investment. Accountability includes the due process of law and judicial review for investment-related procedures, periodic regulatory impact assessment and high-level decision making.

Source: Organisation for Economic Development and Cooperation, Sovereign Wealth Funds and Recipient Country Policies, OCED Investment Committee Report, Paris, April 4, 2008.

The International Working Group (IWG) of SWFs released its Generally Accepted Principles and Practices (GAAP), the Santiago Principles, in October 2008. Twenty-four principles and practices for better transparency, disclosure and governance in the operation of SWFs are represented. The objectives of GAAP are:

a) to encourage the free flow of capital and maintain the global financial system's stability;
b) to ensure that investment is based purely on economic considerations;
c) to comply with the policies and regulations of recipient countries; and
d) to provide a framework where SWFs can operate with transparency, sound governance and proper accountability.

Some of the principles aim at providing better information about the organisation structure, investment policy and investment process of SWFs. This is to ensure that the operations are free from government intervention and will not be used for political motives. As we have said the main investment objective of SWFs is risk-adjusted return maximisation. The financial statements of the SWFs should be audited up to international standards and relevant data should be communicated to shareholders with information about the macroeconomic data. There should also be a proper procedure for risk management and the general approach towards risk should be made available to the public. Another important issue is that SWF investment can have significant macroeconomic implications and hence its activities should be closely coordinated with domestic fiscal and monetary authorities. This calls for a clear operation structure with strategies that are independent and implemented in accordance with a clearly defined structure.

To guard against governments using an SWF to advance their political agenda, the GAAP has laid down specific principles to address the concern. GAAP 6 recommends the independent operational management of SWFs to ensure that all investment decisions and operations are based on economic and financial considerations consistent with their investment policies and objectives and free from political influence and interference. The Principle further recommends that in cases where SWFs are established as pools of assets without legal personality, the owner may exercise the functions of the governing body(ies) through one or more of its organisational units (e.g. a ministry or a parliamentary committee). For example, Norway delegates the operation of its SWF to the central bank. In addition, GAAP 16 recommends SWFs to disclose their governance structure so as to verify to outsiders that they are operated separately from the government. This is to reassure the recipient countries that SWF investments are based on economic and financial considerations and employ sound operational controls and risk management systems. GAAP 19 recommends SWFs to publicly disclose and explain a situation where the investment is not based on financial criteria. For example, GPFG does not invest in some companies for ethical reasons and they publicly disclose a list of companies in which the Fund will not invest. GAAP 21 recommends that if an SWF chooses to exercise its ownership rights, it should do so in a manner that is consistent with its investment policy and protect the financial value of its investments. To dispel concerns that SWFs would use voting rights to influence the companies they have invested in for non-economic or non-financial objectives, SWFs should have ex-ante disclosure of whether they will exercise their voting rights and how. SWFs should also make appropriate ex-post disclosures to demonstrate that their voting decisions continue to be based on economic and financial criteria.

Besides addressing the role of the government in SWFs, the GAAP Principles are also designed to ensure that investments are based on economic and financial considerations and consistent with the defined objectives of each SWF so that the investment activities will not destabilise the global markets. GAAP 18 recommends that SWFs have a clear and consistent investment policy with defined strategic asset allocation, and for the investment policy to be disclosed to the public. The defined strategic asset allocation should ensure that SWFs are not engaged in investments which will adversely affect the interests of the general public. The use of derivatives and leverage in the SWF's operation should be measured and managed appropriately. The use of leverage in SWF's operations and its disclosure is of the utmost importance after the disclosure of Dubai World's debt crisis and its affect on the financial markets. The possible default of Dubai's SWFs has brought attention to SWF operation and leverage, and the potential impact on financial markets if a large SWF falls. In particular, any fall or big change to the portfolios of big SWFs would have a significant impact on the stability of the financial markets (see Table 2.4 for a summary of the GAAP Principles).

Table 2.4: Summary of Generally Accepted Principles and Practices (GAAP) – The Santiago Principles

AN OPTIMAL POLICY RESPONSE: PRINCIPLES FOR SWF GUIDELINES (THE SANTIAGO PRINCIPLES)	
PRINCIPLE	EXPLANATION
Sound legal framework	The legal framework for the SWF should be sound in order to achieve its stated objective and support its operational effectiveness. This includes the legal soundness of SWF and its transaction and legal relationship between SWF and other state bodies should be publicly disclosed.
Clearly defined objectives	The SWF's objectives should be clearly defined and publicly disclosed.
Coordination with domestic fiscal and monetary authorities	Where the SWF's activities have significant direct domestic macroeconomic implications, those activities should be closely coordinated with the domestic fiscal and monetary authorities, so as to ensure consistency with the overall macroeconomic policies.

PRINCIPLE	EXPLANATION
Clear policies, rules, procedures, or arrangements regarding funding, withdrawal, and spending operations	There should be clear and publicly disclosed policies, rules, procedures, or arrangements in relation to the SWF's general approach to funding, withdrawal, and spending operations. This includes the source of SWF and withdrawals from the SWF while spending on behalf of the government is to be publicly disclosed.
Timely statistical reporting	The relevant statistical data pertaining to the SWF should be reported on a timely basis to the owner, or as otherwise required, for inclusion where appropriate in macroeconomic data sets.
Sound governance to facilitate accountability and operational independence	The governance framework for the SWF should be sound and establish a clear and effective division of roles and responsibilities in order to facilitate accountability and operational independence in the management of the SWF to pursue its objectives.
Setting of objectives, appointment of governing bodies, oversight by owner	The owner should set the objectives of the SWF, appoint the members of its governing body(ies) in accordance with clearly defined procedures, and exercise oversight over the SWF's operations.
Clear mandate, adequate authority and competency for governing bodies	The governing body(ies) should act in the best interests of the SWF, and have a clear mandate and adequate authority and competency to carry out its functions.

PRINCIPLE	EXPLANATION
Independent operational management	The operational management of the SWF should implement the SWF's strategies in an independent manner and in accordance with clearly defined responsibilities.
Clearly defined accountability framework and the publication of annual report with accordance with international accounting standards.	The accountability framework for the SWF's operations should be clearly defined in the relevant legislation, charter, other constitutive documents, or management agreement. An annual report and accompanying financial statements on the SWF's operations and performance should be prepared in a timely fashion and in accordance with recognized international or national accounting standards in a consistent manner.
Annual audit of operations and financial statements	The SWF's operations and financial statements should be audited annually in accordance with recognized international or national auditing standards in a consistent manner.
Clearly defined professional and ethical Standards	Professional and ethical standards should be clearly defined and made known to the members of the SWF's governing body(ies), management, and staff.
Dealing with third parties based on economic and financial grounds	Dealing with third parties for the purpose of the SWF's operational management should be based on economic and financial grounds, and follow clear rules and procedures.
Operations in host countries in compliance with all applicable regulatory and disclosure requirements	SWF operations and activities in host countries should be conducted in compliance with all applicable regulatory and disclosure requirements of the countries in which they operate.

SOVEREIGN WEALTH FUNDS

PRINCIPLE	EXPLANATION
Public disclosure of governance framework, and provisions for operational independence	The governance framework and objectives, as well as the manner in which the SWF's management is operationally independent from the owner, should be publicly disclosed.
Financial information to be publicly disclosed	Relevant financial information regarding the SWF should be publicly disclosed to demonstrate its economic and financial orientation, so as to contribute to stability in international financial markets and enhance trust in recipient countries.
Investment policy based on sound portfolio management principles	The SWF's investment policy should be clear and consistent with its defined objectives, risk tolerance, and investment strategy, as set by the owner or the governing body(ies), and be based on sound portfolio management principles. GAPP 18.1. Sub-principle. The investment policy should guide the SWF's financial risk exposure and the possible use of leverage. GAPP 18.2. Sub-principle. The investment policy should address the extent to which internal and/or external investment managers are used, the range of their activities and authority, and the process by which they are selected and their performance monitored. GAPP 18.3. Sub-principle. A description of the investment policy of the SWF should be publicly disclosed.
Investment decisions to maximise risk adjusted financial returns – or otherwise clear definition and public disclosure of other considerations	The SWF's investment decisions should aim to maximise risk-adjusted financial returns in a manner consistent with its investment policy, and based on economic and financial grounds. GAPP 19.1. Sub-principle. If investment decisions are subject to other than economic and financial considerations, these should be clearly set out in the investment policy and be publicly disclosed. GAPP 19.2. Sub-principle. The management of an SWF's assets should be consistent with what is generally accepted as sound asset management principles.

PRINCIPLE	EXPLANATION
No seeking or taking advantage of privileged information or inappropriate influence by government in competing with private entities	The SWF should not seek or take advantage of privileged information or inappropriate influence by the broader government in competing with private entities.
Respect to shareholder ownership rights	SWFs view shareholder ownership rights as a fundamental element of their equity investments' value. If a SWF chooses to exercise its ownership rights, it should do so in a manner that is consistent with its investment policy and protects the financial value of its investments. The SWF should publicly disclose its general approach to voting securities of listed entities, including the key factors guiding its exercise of ownership rights.
Framework for operational risk management	The SWF should have a framework that identifies, assesses, and manages the risks of its operations. GAPP 22.1. Sub-principle. The risk management framework should include reliable information and timely reporting systems, which should enable the adequate monitoring and management of relevant risks within acceptable parameters and levels, control and incentive mechanisms, codes of conduct, business continuity planning, and an independent audit function.GAPP 22.2. Sub-principle. The general approach to the SWF's risk management framework should be publicly disclosed.
Reporting of assets and investment	The assets and investment performance (absolute and relative to benchmarks, if any) of the SWF should be measured and reported to the owner according to clearly defined principles or standards.

PRINCIPLE	EXPLANATION
Regular review of GAPP implementation	A process of regular review of the implementation of the GAPP should be engaged in by or on behalf of the SWF.

Source: International Working Group of Sovereign Wealth Funds, Sovereign Wealth Funds – Generally Accepted Principles and Practices, Washington, October 11, 2008.

The OECD Guidelines and the Santiago Principles are founded on the principle of voluntary compliance. According to a report prepared by Riskmetric in October 2009, only a few SWFs have increased their level of disclosure a year after the Santiago Principles were proposed and a number of SWFs did not meet the standards. The report further identifies that the key hurdle to compliance is the subjective nature of the Santiago Principles since the interpretation of the requirements is entirely up to the SWFs. Despite this, the CIC published its first annual report for the year 2008 which gives an overview of its operations and performance without details of its investments. This indicates a good start for adopting international standards though the process is expected to be gradual and it is unlikely that we shall see SWFs adopting the Santiago Principles in the short-run.

In addition to the Santiago Principles, the US Treasury has separately produced a joint statement with ADIA and the GIC that sets out nine principles for SWF investment. These five principles for governing SWF operations stress the need to have greater disclosure, fair competition with the private sector, compliance with the rules of host countries, strong governance and internal structures and that the investment decision should be commercially motivated. The four principles for the host countries stress the need for non-discrimination against investors, respect for investors' decisions, availability of a predictable investment framework and the elimination of protectionism.[21] To show their commitments to proper governance and greater disclosure, ADIA has increased its exposure to the media and the GIC published its annual report for 2008/2009.

On the current indices for transparency and governance, the Asian and Middle Eastern SWFs rank very low as compared to their western counterparts. However, with the launch of the Santiago Principles in 2008, the situation has started to improve especially when SWF countries are more

---
21 *"Treasury Reaches Agreement on Principles for Sovereign Wealth Fund Investment with Singapore and Abu Dhabi,"* Press Release, U.S. Department of Treasury, 20 March 2008. http://www.treas.gov/press/releases/hp881.htm

involved in drafting the guidelines for SWF operation. This has shown the commitment of SWFs to establish a set of standardised principles to regulate their industry. These SWFs understand that by reassuring recipient countries and international communities that their investments are purely commercial, agency costs would fall.

In the next chapter we shall discuss the general investment policies of the SWFs (in so far as we know them), how investments are allocated by the funds and the direct foreign investment policies of SWFs.

Appendix 1: The Board of Directors of Abu Dhabi Investment Authority (ADIA)

MEMBER	POSITION HOLDING IN SWF	POSITION HOLDING OUTSIDE SWF
H.H Sheikh Khalifa bin Zayed Al Nehayan	Chairman	President of the UAE
H.H Sheikh Sultan bin Zayed Al Nehayan	Director	First Deputy Prime Minister of UAE
H.H Sheikh Mohammed bin Zayed Al Nehayan	Director	Crown Prince of Abu Dhabi Commander of UAE Armed Forces Next-in-line to President of the UAE
H.H Sheikh Ahmed bin Zayed Al Nehayan	Director and Managing Director	Chairman of the Zayed bin Sultan Al Nahyan Charitable and Humanitarian Foundation
H.H Sheikh Mansour bin Zayed Al Nehayan	Director	Member of Presidential Affairs Chairman of International Petroleum Investment Company (IPIC)
H.H Sheikh Mohammed bin Khalifa bin Zayed Al Nehayan	Director	Director of Abu Dhabi Food Control Authority
H.H Mohammed Habroush Al Suwaidi	Director	Chairman of Abu Dhabi Finance Department (Local Finance Ministry)
H.H Dr. Jua'an Salim Al Dhaheri	Director	NIL
H.H Saeed Mubarak Rashid Al Hajeri	Director	Chairman of Abu Dhabi Commercial Bank (ADCB) Board Member of the Higher Corporation for Specialized Economic Zones (HCSEZ) Board Member of Dubai Cable Company (DUCAB)

Source: http://www.adia.ae and various sources.

Appendix 2: The Board of Directors of Government of Singapore Investment Corporation Pte Ltd (GIC)

MEMBER	POSITION HOLDING IN SWF	POSITION HOLDING OUTSIDE SWF
Lee Kuan Yew	Chairman	Minister Mentor
Lee Hsien Loong	Deputy Chairman	Prime Minister
Dr Tony Tan Keng Yam	Deputy Chairman & Executive Director	Former Deputy Prime Minister Coordinating Minister for Security & Defence
Mr Lim Hng Kiang	Director	Minister of Trade & Industry
Mr Tharman Shanmugaratnam	Director	Minister of Finance
Mr Raymond Lim	Director	Minister of Transport Second Minister for Foreign Affairs
Dr Richard Hu Tsu Tau	Director of GIC and Chairman GIC Real Estate	Former Minister of Finance
Mr Ang Kong Hua	Director	Executive Director of NatSteel Ltd
Mr Peter Seah Lim Huat	Director	Chairman of Singapore Technologies Engineering Ltd
Mr Chew Choon Seng	Director	CEO of Singapore Airlines Ltd
Mr Hsieh Fu Hua	Director	CEO of Singapore Exchange Ltd
Mr Lim Siong Guan	Group Managing Director GIC	Chairman of Economic Development Board (EDB)

MEMBER	POSITION HOLDING IN SWF	POSITION HOLDING OUTSIDE SWF
Mr Ng Kok Song	Managing Director of GIC Group Chief Investment Officer	Member of the Board of Directors of Temasek Holdings
Mr Quah Wee Ghee	President GIC Asset Management	NIL
Dr Seek Ngee Huat	President of GIC Real Estate	Member of the Advisory Board of real estate programs at the National University of Singapore
Dr Teh Kok Peng	President of GIC Special Investments	Former Deputy Managing Director of the Monetary Authority of Singapore (MAS)

Source: http://www.gic.com.sg and various sources

Appendix 3: The Board of Directors of Temasek Holdings

MEMBER	POSITION HOLDING IN SWF	POSITION HOLDING OUTSIDE SWF
S Dhanabalan	Chairman	1996-1998: Chairman of Singapore Airlines Ltd 1999-2005: Chairman of DBS Group Holdings Ltd Former Cabinet Member
Kwa Chong Seng	Deputy Chairman	Chairman and Managing Director of Exxon Mobil Asia Pacific Pte Ltd Board of Directors of DBS Group Holdings Ltd
Ho Ching	Executive Director & CEO	1997-2001: President and CEO of the Singapore Technologies Group Formerly held various positions in Ministry of Defence
Kua Hong Pak	Director	Managing Director and Group CEO of ComfortDelGro Corporation Ltd Deputy Chairman of SBS Transit Ltd and VICOM Ltd Board of Directors of PSA International Pte Ltd, PSA Corporation Ltd, StarHub Ltd, Ringier Print (HK) Ltd and Cabcharge Australia Ltd

MEMBER	POSITION HOLDING IN SWF	POSITION HOLDING OUTSIDE SWF
Koh Boon Hwee	Director	Chairman of DBS Group Holdings Ltd Executive Chairman
Non Executive Chairman of Sunningdale Tech Ltd
Executive Director of Media Ring Ltd
Former Chairman of Singapore Airlines Ltd, SIA Engineering Co Ltd and Singapore Telecommunications Ltd, Executive
Former Chairman of the Wuthelam Group and Managing Director of Hewlett Packard Singapore.
Goh Yew Lin	Director	Managing Director of GK Goh Holdings Ltd
Independent Director of CIMB-GK Pte Ltd, Boyer Allan Management Ltd and various funds managed by Boyer Allan
Actively involved in the securities industry in Southeast Asia for 25 years until 2005
Chairman of the Yong Siew Toh Conservatory of Music
Deputy Chairman of the Singapore Symphonia Company Ltd
Board Member of the National University of Singapore
Simon Israel	Executive Director	Current Chairman of the Singapore Tourism Board and Asia Pacific Breweries Ltd
Former Chairman Asia Pacific, member of Executive Committee of Danone Group

MEMBER	POSITION HOLDING IN SWF	POSITION HOLDING OUTSIDE SWF
Teo Ming Kian	Director	Permanent Secretary of the Ministry of Finance and Permanent Secretary of National Research and Development in the Prime Minister's Office Chairman of MND Holdings Pte Ltd, Accounting and Corporate Regulatory Authority and Inland Revenue Authority of Singapore 2001-2006: Executive Chairman of the Singapore Economic Development Board
Marcus Wallenberg	Director	Chairman of Skandinaviska Enskilda Banken (SEB), SAAB AB and AB Electrolux Deputy Chairman of LM Ericsson Board of Director of AstraZeneca, Stora Enso, Foundation Asset Management, and the Knut and Alice Wallenberg Foundation Chairman of the International Chamber of Commerce Former President and CEO of Investor AB

Source: http://www.temasekholdings.com.sg and various sources

Appendix 4: The Board of Directors of China Investment Corp Ltd (CIC)

MEMBER	POSITION HOLDING IN SWF	POSITION HOLDING OUTSIDE SWF
Lou Jiwei	Chairman & CEO	Former Deputy Secretary-General of the State Council, Alternate member of the 17th CPC Central Committee
Gao Xiqing	Vice Chairman, President & CIO	Former Vice Chairman of the National Council of the Social Security Fund (2003 – 2007)
Zhang Hongli	Executive Director, Executive Vice President & COO	Former Vice Minister of Ministry of Finance
Zhang Xiaoqiang	Non-Executive Director	Vice Chairman of National Development and Reform Commission (NDRC)
Li Yong	Non-Executive Director	Vice Minister of Ministry of Finance
Hu Xiaolian	Non-Executive Director	Alternate Member of the 17th Communist Party of China Central Committee; Director of State Administration of Foreign Exchange
Liu Zhongli	Independent Director	Chairman of Chinese People's Political Consultative Conference, Sub-committee of Economy
Wang Chunzheng	Independent Director	Vice Minister of State Development and Reform Commission
Yu Erniu	Employee Director and the Human Resource Director of CIC	Former Deputy Director of the Personnel and Education Department of the State Ministry of Finance; Former Board of Director and Chairman of Remuneration Committee of the Bank of China Ltd

MEMBER	POSITION HOLDING IN SWF	POSITION HOLDING OUTSIDE SWF
Jin Liqun	Chairman of Board of Supervisors	NIL
Linghu An	Supervisor	Deputy Auditor General of the National Audit Office
Wang Huaqing	Supervisor	Secretary of Discipline Inspection of the China Banking Regulatory Commission (CBRC)
Fan Fuchun	Supervisor	Vice Chairman of the China Securities Regulatory Commission (CSRC)
Cui Guangqing	Employee SupervisorHead and Managing Director of the CIC Supervisory Board Office / Internal Audit Department	Board of Supervisors of Central Huijin Investment Ltd

Source: http://www.china-inv.cn/cicen/

Appendix 5: Leader Group of Norges Bank Investment Management (NBIM)

MEMBER	POSITION HOLDING IN SWF	OUTSIDE SWF
Yngve Slyngstad	Chief Executive Officer	He was previously 1998-2007 Head of Equities / Chief Investment Officer Equities, Norges Bank Investment Management (NBIM) 1996-1998 Chief Investment Officer, Asian Equities, Storebrand Asset Management
Stephen A. Hirsch	Deputy Chief Executive Officer	He was previously a Portfolio Manager in Norges Bank in 1998.
Bengt O. Enge	Chief Investment Officer	His last position was as Global Head of External Management. He previously worked with Frank Russell Company in London as a Research Analyst in Fixed Income Managers Research.
Jessica Irschick	Chief Treasurer	She was Chief of Staff to the CEO of the Investment Bank in UBS.
Trond Grande	Chief Risk Officer	He joined NBIM in 2007 as Global Head of Risk Management, and has previously held a dual role as Deputy COO and Global Head of Risk Management.
Mark Clemens	Chief Administrative Officer	He was from Citigroup in New York where he was global Chief Administrative Officer with responsibility for the Compliance & Control division.

STRUCTURE, GOVERNANCE AND PROPOSED INTERNATIONAL GUIDELINES

MEMBER	POSITION HOLDING IN SWF	OUTSIDE SWF
Age Bakker	Chief Operating Officer	He has previously held positions in teaching and in the investment management industry. He has worked at Storebrand Kapitalforvaltning in Norway for 14 years, and his last position was Chief Operating Officer.
Dag Dyrdal	Chief Strategic Relations Officer	He was the CEO and entrepreneur of two London-based enterprises within trading methodologies and reputation analysis.
Jan Thomsen	Chief Compliance Officer	He is from Orkla ASA where he was Chief Risk Officer.

Source: http://www.norges-bank.no/templates/article____75363.aspx

CHAPTER 3
Sovereign Wealth Fund Investment Activities

Writing this chapter has proved more challenging than initially thought because SWFs have kept a low profile concerning their investment activities and have always tried to avoid media attention. Attempts to categorise these funds are almost impossible. So in this chapter, various SWF transactions are analysed to explain their investment strategies and to provide a possible rationale for their asset allocation. The transactions quoted come from the Monitor Sovereign Wealth Fund 2008 Annual Report, Deutsche Bank Research, as well as various research and news articles.

Prior to the 2007-2008 subprime crisis, investments by SWFs were viewed unfavourably by recipient countries; some were even speculating about the motive behind these cross-border investments. There were fears that these SWF investments were politically motivated and targetted strategic industries so that they would be in conflict with the national interest of recipient countries. Summers (2007) and Gieve (2008) stress a different danger – that of an expanding government role in global capital markets which would encourage state capitalism rather than a free market. The surge of SWFs in the international market has raised concerns about this reversal of the move towards privatisation.

During the first half of 2008 the Asian and Middle Eastern SWFs went on a shopping spree for western financial institutions, attracting considerable international attention. Indeed during the early days of the subprime crisis, these SWFs were seen as "white knights" for some of the western financial institutions that needed capital just to keep themselves afloat. Some cash strapped financial institutions such as Barclays Bank actively courted these funds as an alternative to accepting government bailout money.

The main role of government in SWFs should be to determine the objectives of the funds and their governance structure; so far there is no reported case of direct government involvement in specific investments. To avoid SWFs using their investments for political motives, Willem Buiter[1] suggests that SWFs should only be allowed to invest in non-voting equity shares. But the fear of the use of SWFs for political motives seems to be quite unfounded. Most SWF countries hold substantial amounts of US government securities; they could sell off these securities at any moment. They do not need to use SWFs to destabilise other economies.[2]

Most SWFs are found to behave either as sophisticated investment houses (e.g. ADIA and GIC) or opportunists (e.g. CIC). However, since getting their fingers burnt, the CIC has been less aggressive in its overseas acquisitions and announced in late 2008 that it will keep away from western financial institutions.

This chapter examines general SWF investment policies, their investments by region and sector, their choices of investment strategies, the policies of recipient countries on cross-border investments, and discusses some of the more controversial investments made by SWFs or government-related agencies. The section on investment policies will examine SWFs from different regions and how these SWF policies are different from other types of investment vehicle. Next, the SWFs' investment activities from 1995 to June 2009 are analysed using Deutsche Bank's Report. This is followed by a discussion on the factors that affect SWF investment strategies and the types of strategies available to these funds. The next section examines the investment policies SWFs face in recipient countries and highlights the change in local policies due to the emergence of SWFs. The final section provides examples of controversial investments made by SWFs and government-related corpporations and briefly discusses the rationale for these investments.

3.1 Investment Policies

Governments typically invest excess funds in low-risk, marketable assets such as treasury bills that are readily available to monetary authorities to meet the

---

[1] Willem Buiter. "Taming sovereign wealth funds in two easy steps." Maverecon – Willem Buiter's Blog, 22 July 2007. http://maverecon.blogspot.com/2007/07/taming-sovereign-wealth-funds-in-two.html

[2] Kavaljit Singh, "Sovereign wealth funds some frequently asked questions," The Corner House, October 2008. http://www.thecornerhouse.org.uk/summary.shtml?x=562749

needs of balance of payments. In general, SWFs are a heterogeneous group of investors with varying risk appetites. Some target safe assets such as sovereign debt, blue chip stocks and investment rated corporate bonds while others operate more like an investment house tending to go for investments with varying risks and seeking to diversify their investments into a wider range of assets so as to earn an overall higher return. Those SWFs with a higher appetite for risk include in their portfolios real estate, investments in distressed companies and private equity firms. Like hedge funds and investment banks, most SWFs do not disclose investment allocations and performance, but the lack of transparency and disclosure, coupled with unregulated pools of capital, mean that SWF investment policies are more likely to attract international attention. The most important question is: are these funds politically motivated or merely returns motivated?

Why is it attractive to create a fund to manage a country's wealth? Firstly, equity prices have risen more quickly than oil prices over recent decades, and it has been more profitable for oil-producing countries to extract their oil and invest the proceeds in the equity market.[3] Secondly, investment in non-oil assets allows oil-producing countries to hedge against future volatility in oil prices. To countries that hold huge foreign reserves, returns on government debts are lower than returns on equity and they would want to look for higher returns. Asian central banks have been stockpiling US treasuries over the years, particularly after the 1997-1998 Asian crisis, but the returns of the US treasuries have been the lowest in history. So Asian central banks have been providing "cheap savings" to the US. Given this low rate of return, it has been more attractive to invest in other classes of assets. Figure 3.1 shows the returns on government bonds from developed countries. From 2004 to 2007, the returns on world equity have performed better than government bonds. Firstly, equity offers higher rates of return than government bonds (except during a financial crisis). Although equity returns plunged during the subprime crisis, they have picked up quickly and suppressed the returns on bonds. Secondly, the fear of a fall in US dollar due to large US deficits has made some countries seek alternative investments for their reserves. Thirdly, the average returns on a diversified portfolio of assets are likely to be higher than those of a single asset. This follows one of the tenets of Modern Portfolio Theory that for uncorrelated assets the average return will be higher for the same average risk.

---

3 "Sovereign wealth funds, Asset backed insecurity," *The Economist*, 17 January 2008. http://www.economist.com/businessfinance/displaystory.cfm?story_id=E1_TDVPPQNR

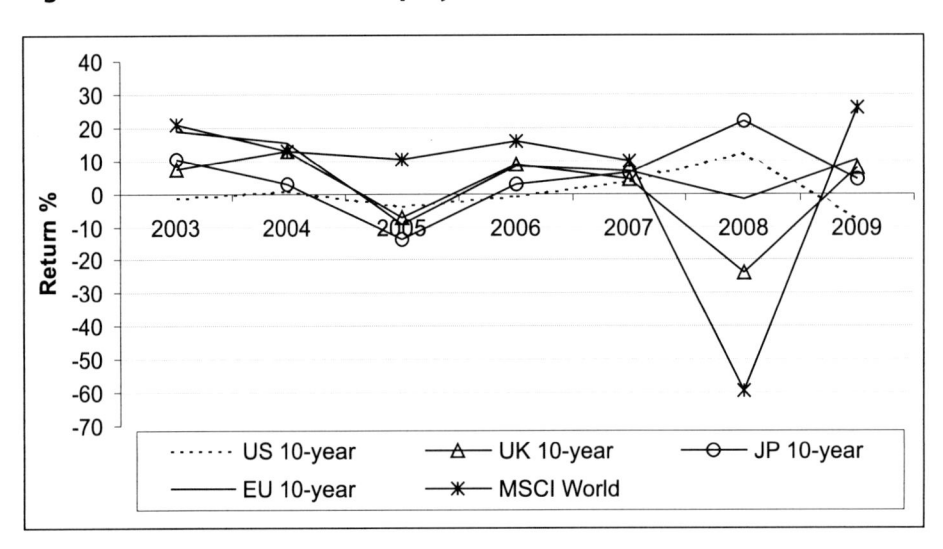

Figure 3.1: Returns (in USD) of Equity and Government Bonds

```
40
30
20
10
 0
-10    2003    2004    2005    2006    2007    2008    2009
-20
-30
-40
-50
-60
-70
```
Return %

······· US 10-year   —△— UK 10-year   —◦— JP 10-year
——— EU 10-year   —✱— MSCI World

Source: Datastream, Thomson

As discussed in Chapter 1, SWFs are established for different objectives and these objectives affect their investment strategy. The revenue from oil is invested and passed on as savings for future generations or stabilisation funds would be mainly commodity-based and hence, would have investments which are negatively correlated with the commodity prices that fund them. These funds have to hedge against falling energy prices. For example, the Kazakhstan National Fund has to hedge against oil and gas price volatility since the country derives its revenue from those commodities. Its initial objective was revenue stabilisation, but the objective changed when the country had accumulated enough reserves to stabilise its government revenues, and with increasing commodity prices, the Fund diversified and took on a higher risk profile. Similarly, ADIA was initially set up as a stabilisation fund to provide income for future generations. However, with increasing oil prices, the Fund has accumulated a vast income and it is now estimated to be the world's largest SWF. ADIA has been diversified into many areas including real estate, infrastructure and financial institutions, and it has been used to promote domestic and regional economic development. With investments in domestic markets and growth industries, it serves the objectives of creating national wealth and supporting industrial policy. As far as Temasek is concerned, it invested heavily in the domestic economy in sectors such as port management, airlines, banking and telecommunications in the early days.

However, over the years, Temasek has diversified its investment overseas into a wider range of industries to obtain higher returns. The Korea Investment Company has specifically indicated that one of its objectives is to develop the country as the financial hub of North East Asia. The SWF supporting economic development is expected to invest in local ailing domestic companies. Some SWFs play a role in acquiring intellectual property, technology and capabilities to improve their domestic economy. CIC and Temasek have both explicitly stated that one of their roles is to help domestic companies venture into international markets.

In this chapter, the policies of several SWFs are briefly discussed but those of ADIA, CIC, GIC, GPFG and Temasek are omitted to avoid repetition because these five will be examined in depth in Chapter Four. Examples from these five Funds may also be cited to explain why SWFs invest in certain sectors. Furthermore, the investment policies of certain funds that have varying degrees of transparency are examined. These range from the Canadian and Australian SWFs which have laid down very clear investment policies and published annual reports to Brunei's SWF which reveals very limited information to the public. However, these examples aim to give readers a general glimpse of SWF investment policies and are by no means comprehensive. In the following analysis funds from developed countries are examined first, then funds from Asian and Middle Eastern countries.

The Canadian Alberta Heritage Fund was created in 1976 and the Fund is managed as an endowment fund to maximise long-term returns on saving from non renewable resources for current and future generation of Albertans. The Fund's target five-year benchmark annualised return is 4.5% above the Canadian Consumer Price Index. It sets its target asset allocation as follows: 50% in Canadian and global equities, 30% in inflation sensitive and alternatives[4] and 20% in money markets and fixed income. However the actual asset mix as at 31 March 2009 was 43% in equities, 29% in inflation sensitive and alternatives and 28% in money markets and fixed income. The higher investment in money markets and fixed income reflects the Fund's commitment to maximise returns at a prudent level of risk. This cautious approach is necessary, as any shortfall in the Fund's performance will affect the government's fiscal policy. The Fund's value has declined by 18.1% from 31 March 2008 to 31 March 2009. Due to the uncertainty in the global market, the Ministry of Finance and Enterprise has approved the new asset mix from

---
4   Inflation sensitive and alternatives are investments in real estates, infrastructure, real return bonds, timberlands and hedge funds.

1 April 2009 to allow the Fund's management more flexibility to adjust the asset allocations to match market condition. The new asset mix is 35-70% for equities, 15-45% for money markets and fixed income and 15-40% for inflation sensitive and alternatives. The Fund is also very clear on how it measure its performance by comparing each asset class with a market based benchmark such as comparing investments in US equities to S&P 1500 Index[5].

The Australian Government Future Fund is set up to meet the public sector's superannuation liabilities. The Fund targets an average real return of 4.5 to 5.5% per annum over a rolling ten-year period. They have set their long-term asset allocation as follows: 35% in equities, 30% in tangible assets, 20% in debts and 15% in alternative assets. The Fund limits it holding in individual foreign companies to no more than 20% while holdings in domestic companies are not higher than an amount that would trigger a takeover. Despite setting out a long-term asset allocation portfolio, the Australian Government Future Fund focuses on the effective management of market-related risk and takes a flexible approach to asset allocation. In 2007-2008, the Fund adopted a more conservative approach and reduced their equity holding in favour of debt securities.

Most Asian SWFs have their investment objective set to seek a high return at a certain risk level. Of them all, Brunei Investment Authority is the least transparent about its investment activities with no disclosure of its investment policy even though it is one of the oldest established funds. Other than occasional media reports about the Fund's overseas investments, no information is available. Malaysia's Khazanah Nasional plays an active role in Government Linked Corporations (GLCs) and its domestic investments cover industries such as automotive manufacturing, banking, property development and telecommunication.[6] It aims to catalyse the transformation of GLCs to increase shareholder and strategic values. However, its policy on cross-border investment is unclear even though the first overseas office was set up in Beijing in 2008. As for the Timor-Leste Petroleum Fund, it is required to hold 90% of its investment in US treasuries, other government debts and US dollars. The Fund's investment policy may change given the low return of US treasuries, and the need to generate higher returns to rebuild the economy. With the Fund announcing its first loss due to the falling US dollar and low

---

[5] For more detail on market based benchmark used by Canada Alberta Heritage Saving Trust Fund Annual Report 2008-2009.

[6] See Khazanah Nasional official website for list of companies which Khazanah Nasional holds substantial stake. http://www.khazanah.com.my/portfolio.htm

US interest rates in 2008,[7] it plans to hire fund managers to help diversify its investment out of US treasuries.

The source of funds for Middle Eastern SWFs is revenues from oil and other commodities. They invest in assets such as bonds that they can use as a hedge against the price volatility of their commodities. The Kuwait Investment Authority seeks to achieve a rate of return on its investment that exceeds the composite benchmark.[8] As far as the Qatar Investment Authority is concerned, its investment policy is to build a diversified portfolio in terms of assets and geographical locations and it adopts a flexible investment strategy. The Fund invests mainly in international markets and focuses on revenue diversification, seeking to minimise risk from the volatility of energy prices. The Qatar Investment Authority invests in different asset classes such as listed securities, real estate and private equity, and lately it has been an active investor in financial institutions. Dubai World does not set out its investment policy, but holds a diverse investment portfolio which includes port management, property development, retail, leisure and tourism, with its Dubai Port World one of the world's largest port operators. Most Middle Eastern SWFs do not disclose much information on their investment policies and there is limited information about investment allocations. However, publicly available information indicates that they behave like investment houses, aiming at high returns and adopting a long-term approach to investment policies. In late 2009, the debt problem of Dubai highlighted the problem of Middle Eastern SWFs in financing their overseas investments with a high level of leverage.[9] These funds have been secretive in their investments and according to media reports, they have been very aggressive in their overseas investments.

Comparatively speaking, western SWFs are more transparent in their investment and asset allocation policies. Such behaviour is very distinctive, especially for Canada and Australia. Both the Canadian and Australian SWFs are similar in creating a steady flow of income in the long-term but in the short-term, the former aims at increasing its holding of equities while the latter aims to increase its holding of debt investment. As for the Middle Eastern SWFs, they are keen to buy established companies in the OECD, particularly those with a global brand. Asian SWFs have mixed strategies, with the Malaysian

---

[7] Neil Chatterjee and Yvonne Cheong, "East Timor wants to diversify $3bln state fund," Reuters, UK, 24 May 2008. http://uk.reuters.com/article/idUKSP29816520080524

[8] Mr Bader M. Al Saad, "Overview on the Kuwait Investment Authority and Issues related to SWFs," key note speech at First Luxemburg Foreign Trade Conference, 9 April 2008.

[9] Jennifer Hughes, Patrick Jenkins and Roula Khalaf, "Dubai shockwave hits global market," Financial Times," 27 November 2009. http://www.ft.com/cms/s/0/7896cac2-db93-11de-9424-00144feabdc0.html

SWF investing heavily in domestic companies and East Timor SWF investing only in sovereign debts and US currency. When the Asian and Middle Eastern SWFs went on a buying spree in the US and Europe, French President Nicholas Sarkozy complained about their political motives and suggested that France should set up its own fund in order to protect its strategic industries from foreign SWFs. France's SWF was created in 2008 with a capital of 20 billion Euros to protect companies considered to be strategic by the government from potential "foreign predators". Therefore, we are likely to see the French SWF investing in domestic companies rather than making cross-border investment.

Studies in the investment activities of SWFs have compared SWF investment strategies with those of hedge funds and private equity firms. Hedge funds have traditionally gone for more risky assets than SWFs and invested like an opportunist betting on events. Comparatively speaking, hedge funds are more aggressive in their investment approach. Although SWFs are less aggressive in their strategy, they do invest in actual hedge funds. For example, GIC has invested in a property related hedge fund in the USA. Some SWFs have worked closely with private equity firms as co-investors, but there are still significant differences between them. Unlike hedge funds and private equity firms, SWFs typically do not require leverage, and hence are financially flexible in their choice of investment. SWFs have no explicit liabilities and hence can assume a long-term investment horizon and afford higher risks. Although Temasek of Singapore issued bonds in 2005[10] and Dubai World announced in August 2009 that it had a debt of $59 billion,[11] most SWFs do not raise capital in the international market. Basically, because SWFs have a longer investment horizon they are more focused on long-term returns. They are also more diversified in their investment allocation in terms of asset classes. However, some SWFs appear to be active private equity investors. ADIA and Qatar Investment Authority have substantial private equity stakes in Ferrari and Carlyle Group. Qatar Investment Authority has been actively seeking to buy controlling stakes in a company that has recently attempted a buyout of Sainsbury PLC through Delta Two. It is difficult to estimate the size of SWF holdings in private equities because such information is even less well-documented than their equity investments in global listed equities. GPFG is more similar to an endowment fund which invests in safe assets with

---

10 Conrad Tan, "Temasek plans 10-year US$ bond issue," *Singapore Business Times*, 20 October 2009. http://app.mfa.gov.sg/pr/read_content.asp?View,13781

11 Stefania Bianchi, "Dubai World $60B liabilities add to Emirates' debt woe," *Dow Jones Newswires*, 20 August 2009. http://www.zawya.com/pdfstory.cfm?storyid=ZW20090820000043&l=102357090820

a long-term horizon. The Fund is a long-term savings fund set up to cope with an ageing population, hence a conservative approach is adopted with regard to its asset allocation. Its increased holdings of public listed equities during the subprime crisis should not be interpreted as a change of policy from conservative to aggressive. It was due to the falling value of equities and the Fund's view that these firms were value for money (see Table 3.1 for the losses of the big SWFs). ADIA is estimated to have incurred the biggest loss during the subprime crisis, followed by Kuwait Investment Authority and GPFG.

Table 3.1: Estimated Losses of SWFs

NAME OF FUND	ESTIMATED LOSSES 2007 – 2008 USD $BN
Abu Dhabi Investment Authority (ADIA)	183
SAMA Foreign Holdings	46
Government of Singapore Investment Corporation (GIC)	41.6
Norway Government Pension Fund – Global (GPFG)	92
Kuwait Investment Authority (KIA)	94
China Investment Company Ltd.	4.2
Hong Kong Monetary Authority Investment Portfolio	9.6
Temasek Holdings	39
Qatar Investment Authority (QIA)	27

Source: Various news reports.[12]

In sum, most SWFs invest in fixed income and equities in the global market. Since most Middle Eastern SWFs do not publish their strategic asset allocation (SAA), the only information available is these funds' investments in the global market. Table 3.2 provides a summary of SWFs' strategic asset allocation.

---

12 Gulf's SWFs (http:topnews.ae/content/2811-sum-350-bln-lost-gulf-sovereign-funds-reports-un) ; GIC (http://online.wsj.com/article/SB125418236117447877.html) ;Temasek (http://online.wsj.com/article/SB124350003544761935.html); Norway's Government Pension Fund – Global (http://news.bbc.co.uk/2/hi/business/7937360.stm); CIC (http://www.marketwatch.com/story/chinas-cic-reports-21-loss-on-global-assets-2009-08-07)

Table 3.2: Investment Strategy and Strategic Asset Allocation of SWFs

FUND	CAPITAL SOURCE	INVESTMENT STRATEGY AND STRATEGIC ASSET ALLOCATION (SAA)
ADIA/ ADIC	Oil	An important global investor (refer to Chapter 4 for SAA)
Norway's GPFG	Oil	Allocated all over the world with 40% stocks and 60% global fixed income assets
KIA	Oil	Local, regional and global financial markets
GIC	Non-commodity	Invest in all global assets (refer to Chapter 4 for SAA)
Temasek	Non-commodity	Invest in global assets (refer to Chapter 4 for SAA)
CIC	Non-commodity	Investment portfolio focuses on domestic and international financial institutions and commodities
Russia Oil Stabilization Fund	Oil	Mainly invest in fixed income assets with 44% in USD, 46% in Euros and 10% in sterling pound
Hong Kong Investment Portfolio (HKMA)	Non-commodity	Two types of assets: sustaining and investing ones
Australia's GFF	Non-commodity	Invest domestically and globally
Brunei Investment Agency	Oil	Invest in global securities, financial assets and real estate, with no published SAA.
KIC	Non commodity	Global asset allocation, with no published SAA
Chile ESSF	Copper	66.5% government bonds and 30% money market instruments, 3.5% in inflation-indexed sovereign bonds; containing USD, Euro and Yen

FUND	CAPITAL SOURCE	INVESTMENT STRATEGY AND STRATEGIC ASSET ALLOCATION (SAA)
Chile Pension Fund	Copper	66.5% government bonds and 30% money market instruments, 3.5% in inflation-indexed sovereign bonds; containing USD, Euro and Yen
Botswana's Pula Funds	Diamonds	Invest in stock and fixed income instruments in industrial countries, not in emerging markets.
Iran	Oil	Invest global market, with no SAA
New Zealand Superannuation Fund	Non Oil	Invest in domestic and global market: 45% equity, private markets 20%, commodities 5%, fixed interest 17% (as at 30 Nov 2009)
Qatar Investment Authority	Oil	Invest in global market, with no SAA
Venezuela	Oil	No SAA
Mubadala	Oil	Invest domestic, regional and global, published list of companies with substantial holdings
Alaska Permanent Reserve Fund	Oil and minerals	Stock 38%, cash 2%, bonds 22%, real estate 12%, others 11%, infrastructure 3%, private equity 6%, absolute return strategies 6%

Source: IMF (2007); author updates from public information from websites

3.2 Investments by Region and by Sector

Investment abroad allows SWFs to achieve diversification from their domestic economy and achieve a potentially higher rate of return in international markets. In addition, this avoids the crowding out effect of government investments, enables the government to avoid competing with domestic companies for domestic assets and offers an escape from diminishing returns in domestic assets. An added advantage for some countries is the avoidance of asset bubbles where all the capital is poured into a single country. Firms in the US and EU have been the targets of SWFs due to their developed liquid capital markets with a wide selection of investments. Furthermore, these developed markets have the capability to absorb large volumes of funds and SWFs can achieve diversification without upsetting the financial stability of these markets. Geographical diversification offers benefits, but some of the SWFs still invest heavily in domestic economies due to informational advantage and their familiarity with the domestic markets. For example, Malaysia's Khazanah Nasional invests heavily in its domestic market. While industry diversification avoids the volatility in any one industry, especially if a country itself relies heavily on a particular industry, some SWFs choose geographical diversification but not industry diversification because they are familiar with the target industry. Temasek, for instance, has made substantial investments in overseas ports and shipping companies through Temasek Linked Corporations (TLCs), showing that the Fund is interested investing in industries which offer a comparative advantage. Singapore is the world's busiest port for container shipping and indeed Temasek itself was partly responsible for building up Singapore's port.

Deutsche Bank Research shows that from 1995 to June 2009, 31% of SWF investments were concentrated in Asia, 30% in the EU, 20% in the US and 4% in the Middle East (see Figure 3.2 on SWF investments by region).[13] Investments in Asia are made mainly via intra-regional investments, while regional investments in the Middle East are less frequently reported. SWF investments in Asia reflect the long-term growth potential of the region, with China being the most sought after investment location especially by Singapore's SWFs. Other Asian economies such as Hong Kong, Indonesia, Malaysia, Thailand and Taiwan have also attracted investments from SWFs. India's recent economic performance has also attracted interest from ADIA which used to invest only in developed markets. Countries in the EU and the US have always been popular choices for SWFs because of their developed and liquid financial markets which offer a wider selection of investments.

---

13 Steffen Kern, "Sovereign wealth funds – State investments during the financial crisis," Deutsche Bank Research, July 2009.

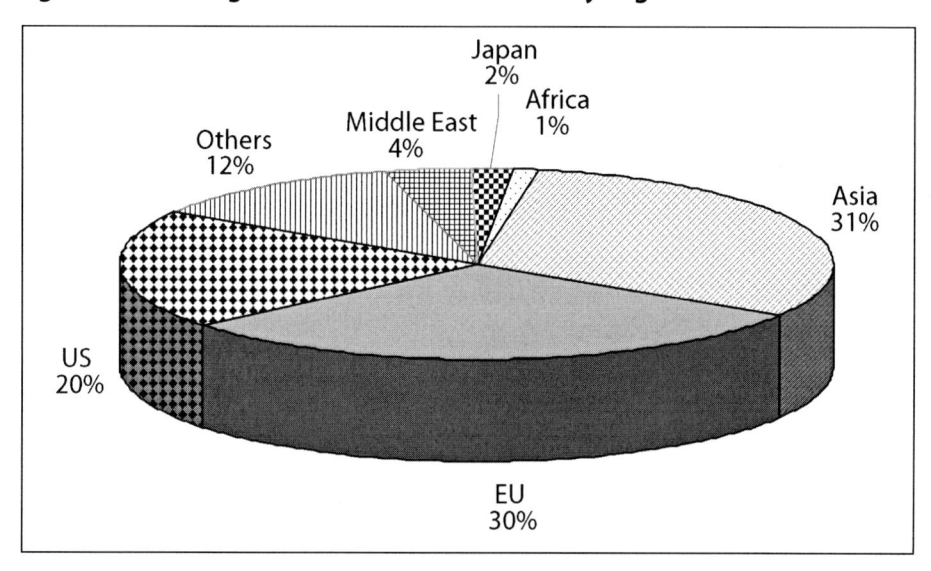

Figure 3.2 Sovereign Wealth Fund Investments by Region

- Japan 2%
- Africa 1%
- Middle East 4%
- Others 12%
- US 20%
- EU 30%
- Asia 31%

Source: Deutsche Bank Research, Sovereign Wealth Funds – State Investments during the Financial Crisis, July 2009, p. 15. (Data based on publicly reported transactions between 1995 to June 2009)

From 1999 to June 2009, the UK was the main destination for SWF investments in the EU, attracting 49% of the EU share (see Table 3.3). This is due to the fact that London is an international financial centre where overseas SWF offices are based. The Dubai International Financial Centre invested $1,648 million in London Stock Exchange Plc in August 2007, while the Qatar Investment Authority invested $1,400 million in J. Sainsbury, a major supermarket chain in June 2007. SWF investments in the rest of the EU have a more balanced distribution: 15% in Denmark, 12% in France, 6% in The Netherlands and less than 5% for the rest of the EU member states.

Table 3.3: Sovereign Investments in EU Member States

COUNTRY	USD BILLION	% OF EU TOTAL
United Kingdom	28.0	49
Germany	8.2	15
France	6.6	12
The Netherlands	3.4	6
Italy	2.5	4
Denmark	2.4	4
Spain	1.1	2
Sweden	1.0	2
Portugal	1.0	2
Austria	0.8	1
Finland	0.5	1
Greece	0.5	1
Malta	0.3	0
Bulgaria	0.1	0
Slovakia	0.0	0
Total	56.4	100%

Source: Deutsche Bank Research, Sovereign Wealth Funds – State Investments during the Financial Crisis, July 2009, p. 16. (Data based on publicly reported transactions between 1995 to June 2009)

Prior to 2008, Middle Eastern funds ADIA and Kuwait Investment Authority invested primarily in OECD countries while Asian funds Temasek and Khazanah Nasional were more domestically focused. However, this trend has changed since the 2007-2008 subprime crisis. According to the Monitor SWF Annual Report 2008, most of the SWF transactions took place in the first quarter of 2008.[14] It also reports that the domestic investments account for 40% of the transactions undertaken in the third and fourth quarters of 2008. In 2008 26% of all the reported investments were made in domestic markets compared to 17% in 2007. This trend indicates that the SWFs have slowed down their activities due to the global economic downturn and the uncertain future in the developed markets. To some SWFs such a move is necessary to help domestic firms which are having difficulties in raising capital. For example, China's CIC has been actively involved in reviving domestic firms and invested

---

14 Monitor Group and Fondazione Eni Enrico Mattei "Weathering the Storm, Sovereign Wealth Funds in the Global Economic Crisis of 2008, SWF Annual Report 2008," April 2009. http://www.monitor.com/Portals/0/MonitorContent/imported/MonitorUnitedStates/Articles/PDFs/Monitor-FEEM_SWF_Weathering_the_Storm_04_2009.pdf

$20 billion to recapitalise the Agricultural Bank of China, whereas the SWF of France, which was set up specifically to help local firms, has taken an 8% stake in Valeo SA, France's second largest car parts maker. Likewise, the Russian ex-president Putin encouraged the investment of excess oil reserves in domestic companies.

Currently many SWFs are highly exposed by investments in financial institutions, real estate and energy. The largest investment went to the finance sector, $78 billion (42% of the total SWFs investments) was being invested in the finance sector from 1995-2009. Most of these investments were made by large SWFs in western financial institutions in 2007-2008. ADIA invested in Citigroup, CIC in the Blackstone Group and Morgan Stanley, GIC in UBS and Citigroup, Temasek in Merrill Lynch and Standard Chartered PLC, Dubai International Financial Centre in Deutsche Bank and the Qatar Investment Authority in Barclays Bank and Credit Suisse. The second largest investment went to industry (14%), followed by services (13%), real estate (11%), commodities (10%), technology (9%) and defence (1%). See Figure 3.3.

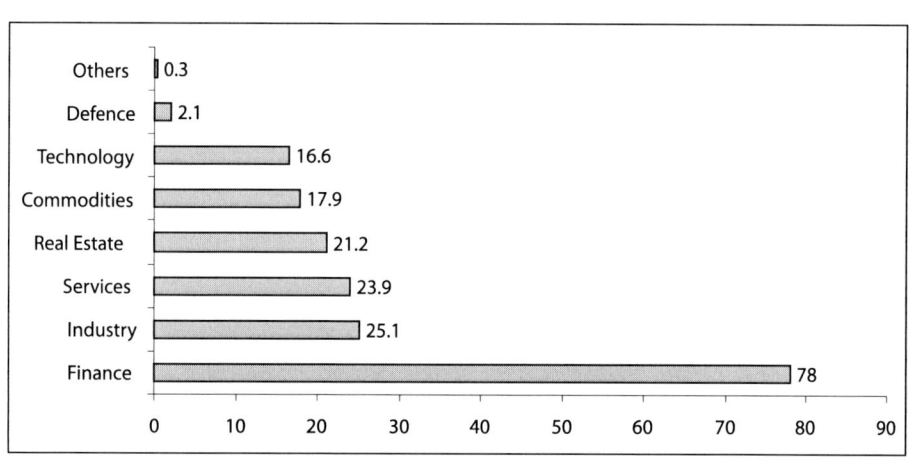

Figure 3.3: Sovereign Investments by Target Sector (in US Dollars)

Sector	Value
Others	0.3
Defence	2.1
Technology	16.6
Commodities	17.9
Real Estate	21.2
Services	23.9
Industry	25.1
Finance	78

Source: Deutsche Bank Research, Sovereign Wealth Funds – State Investments during the Financial Crisis, July 2009, p. 17. (Data based on publicly reported transactions between 1995 to June 2009)

It appeared to be a good bargain when SWFs invested in western financial institutions, which had enabled them to obtain a piece of the global investment banking sector at a lower price. However, the drastic fall in the share prices of these banks has caused some SWFs to suffer the biggest loss in their history. Temasek was reported to have lost one-third of its asset value, while the CIC's loss has aroused public concern in its home country. Qatar Investment Authority and International Petroleum Investment sold their stakes in Barclays PLC in April and June 2009 respectively. Temasek also sold its stakes in Merrill Lynch and the Bank of America in 2008 and 2009. The Deutsche Bank Report in July 2009 estimates that typical equity portfolios held by SWFs may have lost 45% between the end of 2007 and early 2009 resulting in an overall reduction in SWF value by 18%.

While SWF investments in investment banks have been widely reported in the media, investments in private equity funds have gained relatively less attention. In 2006, ADIA bought a 9% stake in Apollo Management, a US-based private equity firm. In the subsequent year, CIC invested in the private equity firm Blackstone and in 2008 it invested in a new private equity fund managed by JC Flowers & Company, headed by a former Goldman Sachs investment banker. Around the same time, GIC invested $2.5 billion in a new equity fund managed by Texas Pacific Group. In April 2008, GIC invested $1.5 billion in the main investment vehicle of the Benetton family while Istithmar World took a majority stake in Gulf Stream Asset Management for an undisclosed sum. Buying stakes in private equity funds has enabled the SWFs to tap into the expertise of these funds and at the same time allows knowledge transfer. These funds have explicitly shown their ambitions in developing their countries into financial centres and investing in private equity funds creates a win-win situation for both. Butt et al. (2007) argue that the recent activities of SWFs in private equity firms indicate a convergence of SWFs and private equity firms.

Investments in the financial sector are attractive to SWFs for a number of reasons. Firstly, the recent subprime crisis allowed the SWFs to pick up global brand investment banks at attractive terms. Prior to the crisis, the price of getting a stake in an investment bank would seem too high and unattractive, particularly in an economic boom. Secondly, investment in financial institutions is generally a popular choice among international investors, given that the sector is well-regulated and likely to provide stable returns even in gloomy times. The only exception was in 2007-2008 when the subprime crisis was caused by financial institutions. In the past, financial institutions have been able to survive well in economic gloom and were able to pick up more quickly than other sectors when the economy recovered. Thirdly, some of the SWFs investing in financial institutions are already familiar with this sector as they already held large stake in domestic financial institutions and some have established their countries as financial hubs. For other SWFs, investing in financial institutions provides an opportunity to "buy into" the skills and experience that will help their own countries to become global financial hubs. Some top management personnel in ADIA are from western financial institutions and were personally persuaded by the managing director to join ADIA (see Chapter Two). The recent investments of SWFs in financial institutions may have appeared to be opportunist behaviour, but the stakes taken up were small. The fact that they invested at the time when uncertainty prevailed suggests that the investments were made for the long-term. However, when shares of these banks plunged, some SWFs sold off their stakes in these investments and suffered a loss. Looking back, SWFs have been able to stabilise the banking sector during the crisis and managed to save the banking sector from short-term liquidity problems and avoid the stringent rules associated with bailouts with public money.

One of the largest real estate investments was made by Abu Dhabi Investment Council[15] which bought a 90% stake in the Chrysler Building in New York for $800 million. Other investments in real estate by Middle Eastern funds are concentrated in the Gulf region, except for ADIA's investments in UK shopping malls. GIC Real Estate Pte Ltd is actively involved in real estate around the world. Direct property investments involve offices, retail stores, residential apartments and hotels. Recently GPFG has announced a plan to reduce part of its holdings in fixed income and invest 5% of the total Fund in real estate. Australia indicates that their SWF will look for property and infrastructure investments to cover future pension payouts due to poor performance in equity markets.[16]

Table 3.4 shows a breakdown of SWFs investments in terms of region and industry. The target sectors for SWFs in the EU are finance ($23bn), industry ($10.3bn) and services ($8.7bn), while the target sectors in the US are finance ($21.7bn) and real estate ($6.7bn). Most SWFs investments in Asia are intra-regional investments with the highest proportion in industry ($20.4bn), followed by technology ($10.4bn), commodities ($9.6bn), finance ($8.9bn), real estate ($5.1bn) and services ($2.9bn). Temasek is active in its intra-regional investments and has bought stakes in telecommunication, banks in Indonesia and telecommunication and real estate in Thailand. Recently CIC

---

15 Abu Dhabi Council (ADIC) was established in 2007 and took over local subsidiaries previously owned by ADIA. ADIC invests globally but has a strong focus in Abu Dhabi's economy. For list of local subsidiaries, see http://www.adcouncil.ae/AboutUs/InvestmentStrategy/tabid/63/Default.aspx

16 "Australia's wealth fund hunting for more property bargains," reported by James Grubel, edited by James Regan, Reuters, 21 October 2008. http://www.reuters.com/article/rbssTechMediaTelecom-News/idUSSYD11899720081021?sp=true

has invested in commodity industries such as mining. Comparing the three regions, investments in finance dominates investments in the EU and US, most of which were taken during the 2007-2008 subprime crisis. Industry and commodities top the list of investments for SWFs in Asia where most are direct investment in these sectors. Only 2% of the total investments are in defence as most SWFs want to avoid political backlash. According to Deutsche Bank Research in 2008, the Dubai International Capital holds 3.12% of shares in EU-based EADS which was acquired in 2007. The 2% does not include Temasek's investment in Singapore Technologies part of whose businesses includes defence.

Table 3.4: EU, US and Asia Investments: Sovereign Investments in EU, US and Asia by Target Sector

TARGET SECTOR	EU	US	ASIA	TOTAL USD BILLION	% OF GLOBAL TOTAL
Finance	23	21.7	8.9	53.6	36
Industry	10.3	1	20.4	31.7	21
Real Estate	5.6	6.7	5.1	17.4	12
Commodities	6.2	0.5	9.6	16.3	11
Technology	0.7	3.6	10.4	14.7	10
Services	8.7	0.5	2.9	12.1	8
Defence	2.1	0.8	0	2.9	2
Others	0	0	0.3	0.3	0
Total	56.6	34.8	57.6	149	100

Source: Deutsche Bank Research, Sovereign Wealth Funds – State Investments during the Financial Crisis, July 2009, p. 18-20. (Data based on publicly reported transactions between 1995 to June 2009)

Miracky et al. (2008) show that SWFs do take majority stakes, but mostly in domestic companies or emerging markets, and the sectors involved are not politically sensitive. Generally speaking, SWFs have tried to avoid holding majority stakes in overseas acquisitions so as not to upset recipient countries. For example, the Kuwait Investment Authority originally bought a 27.1% stake in British Petroleum in 1988 but later reduced its stake by half. Middle Eastern SWFs such as ADIA and Kuwait Investment Authority generally do not hold large stakes in public companies but Dubai World and its subsidiaries (Istithmar and Dubai Ports) do tend to hold large stakes in some strategic investments. Qatar Investment Authority and Dubai International Financial Centre Investments collectively held a 52% stake in the London Stock Exchange as at September 2007 but the combined stake had been reduced to 35.7% as at 31 December 2008.[17] GPFG does not hold a large stake in its equity investment. Mirackey et al. (2008) point out that where SWFs do take controlling stakes in companies most of these are in emerging markets. It also points out that Asian SWFs are more likely to take controlling stakes than Middle Eastern SWFs. In 2008, Malaysia's Khazanah Nasional took eleven controlling stakes, eight of which were in domestic companies; Temasek took nine controlling stakes, seven in domestic companies. Most of these deals are in the emerging and domestic markets. The publicity generated by the SWFs has forced some SWFs to take smaller stakes in their investments. For example, ADIA agreed to take less than 4.9% stake in Citigroup and has no right or control over its management.

The political debate on SWFs has witnessed a shift with SWFs moving from investing in sensitive sectors to ones with less political involvement, but nonetheless investment in consumer goods and manufacturing is still fairly limited. From 2007 SWFs started to invest in the energy sector and in 2008, Mubadala entered a joint venture with Petrofac Ltd to provide a full range of engineering, design, procurement and construction services for onshore oil and gas, refining and petrochemical projects in the UAE. In the same year, GIC paid for an 11% stake in a US firm, AEI Services. AEI's business is in power distribution, natural gas transportation, distribution and services, and retail fuel. SWFs are also active in developing alternative energy. Khazanah Nasional entered a joint venture with Beijing China Sciences General Energy and Environment Company to develop municipal waste-to-energy projects in China, and the Qatar Investment Authority made an investment in Fisker Automotive, an American hybrid sports car manufacturer.

The Sovereign Wealth Fund Institute has created a Consensus Demand Meter to track what the SWFs are demanding in the next three quarters starting from December 2009. A score of 10 means that the sector is attractive to most SWFs while a score of 1 means most SWFs are likely to have lower exposure in that sector. See Figure 3.4 on demand by sectors.

---

17 London Stock Exchange Annual Report 2008, p95. http://www.investis.com/lse/finperformance/reports/results/ar08/LSE_AR08_web.pdf

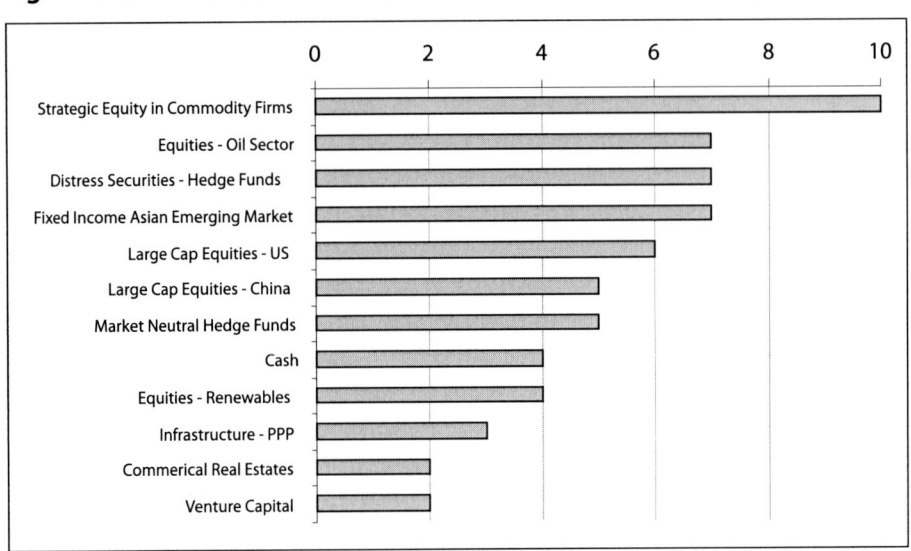

Figure 3.4: SWF Institute – Consensus Demand Meter Q4 Y2009 (December)

Category	Value
Strategic Equity in Commodity Firms	~10
Equities - Oil Sector	~7
Distress Securities - Hedge Funds	~7
Fixed Income Asian Emerging Market	~7
Large Cap Equities - US	~6
Large Cap Equities - China	~5
Market Neutral Hedge Funds	~5
Cash	~4
Equities - Renewables	~4
Infrastructure - PPP	~3
Commerical Real Estates	~2
Venture Capital	~2

Source: Sovereign Wealth Fund Institute (February 2010)

Figure 3.4 shows that Strategic Equity in commodity firms has the highest expected demand in the next three quarters. This reflects SWFs' strategies to capitalise on higher demand for and expected higher returns on commodities in the near future. CIC has been actively investing in this sector in 2008 and 2009. The sectors that have the second highest demand are Equities – Oil Sector, Distress Securities – Hedge Fund and Fixed Income – Asia Emerging Markets. Demand for equities in the oil sector has been reflected in CIC and GPFG's investments in oil companies (See Chapter 4 on CIC's and GPFG's investments). Prior to the subprime crisis, investment in distress securities was an attractive investment for private equity firms and investment banks but with the crisis, these institutional investors do not have the capital to invest in high risk assets. Hence this created the opportunity for SWFs to invest in the sector without many competitors. This sector appeals to the SWFs particularly because it involves high risk and high return and would compromise only a small portfolio for the larger SWFs. Fixed income in Asia Emerging Markets is attractive to SWFs because returns on bonds issued by developed countries have been falling. The recent debt problems of Greece and Spain have also made investments in bonds issued by developed countries risky. These high budget deficits in developed countries have increased the credit risk of these bonds. Interestingly demand for Commercial Real Estates is low. This contradicts the announcements made by Australia Future Fund and GPFG to include a real estate sector in their portfolios. This also suggests that ADIA, CIC and GIC's reported increasing investments in the real estate sector has either not materialised or has not been captured by the Consensus Demand Meter (See Chapter 4 on investments in real estate by ADIA, CIC, GIC and GPFG).

In general, SWFs are moving from a passive investment strategy towards a more aggressive one. Just from the publicly announced transactions, we can see that the Asian and Middle Eastern SWFs are becoming more aggressive and investing directly in industries in some countries. These SWFs used to adopt the investment approaches of western SWFs and invested most of their capital in listed companies in developed markets. However, more direct investments are now taken by Asian and Middle Eastern SWFs. Middle Eastern funds such as Qatar Investment Authority and Mubadala have been making direct investments in a variety of industries. Asian funds such as Temasek and Khazanah have been making direct investments in domestic markets and become more aggressive in the region. ADIA and GIC have been active investors in OECD countries for years and will continue to be so though part of their investments are likely to shift to emerging markets due to the rapid growth in these markets. The SWFs have the majority of their liquid assets in OECD countries and the less liquid assets in emerging markets. The investments in emerging markets have a much longer investment horizon because these are mostly direct investments. As the developed capital markets are more liquid they allow the SWFs to divest in the shortest possible time to meet any cash flow needs of their governments (this does not mean that they are investing for short-term but that they have to meet the government's liquidity need in crisis or in recession). In short, there is a shift of investments from developed markets to emerging markets due to the higher returns especially when the future of the developed markets looks more uncertain after the subprime crisis. This is confirmed by a survey carried out by Financial Dynamics and International in 2009 which interviewed senior executives from a number of world-leading SWFs. Brazil, China and Central America were found to be the most attractive regions for SWF investments.[18] SWFs can adopt a more aggressive approach in the emerging market than in the developed market as SWFs face less regulation and criticism in the emerging market. SWFs are also

---

18 "Sovereign wealth funds remain cautions toward current market valuations and re-iterate their status as passive long term investors," Press Release, Financial Dynamics International (FD), a member of FTI Consulting Inc15 February 2009. http://www.fd.com/admin/upload/uploaded_files/Survey_of_leading_SWFs.pdf

likely to take direct investments in emerging markets because these markets do not have a liquid capital market which makes financial investment less viable. Furthermore, the emerging markets are less worried about SWFs taking controlling stakes in their companies.

SWFs tend to choose to invest a part of the funds in safe assets such as government bonds and blue chip equities, part in riskier assets such as real estate and listed/unlisted shares, and some in the riskiest assets such as distressed companies. However, only a few of the top SWFs invest in distressed companies. Most appear to have a preference for fixed income and listed equities and benchmark their performance to financial indices such as the MSCI World Index. For example, Korea Investment Corporation benchmarks performance of its fund against the MSCI World Index for equity and Lehman Global Aggregate Index for fixed income.[19]

Summing up the above investment policies and activities, the main objective of the heterogeneous SWFs can be divided into two broad categories: income transfer and wealth creation. GPFG, Timor-Leste Petroleum Fund and Australian Government Future Fund operate like endowment funds which are invested in long-term, safe and liquid assets. These funds need to maintain a steady flow of income in order to meet future pension obligations. The passive investment approach by Timor-Leste Petroleum Fund is due to its stated objective to use returns to build the country and it cannot afford to incur losses on its capital. With an objective of wealth creation or accumulation, funds such as ADIA, CIC and GIC have a more diversified portfolio of assets with varying degrees of risk, and they invest in medium- to long-term assets focusing on risk-adjusted returns. These funds would also benchmark their returns with the market returns. Occasionally we can see these funds behaving like opportunists, buying global brands in OECD countries and investing in distressed companies. Over time the funds with income transfer may change their initial objective to wealth creation when they need to look for higher returns to cover the increasing burden of their ageing population.

Apart from these studies by financial institutions, other researchers have also observed the investment patterns of SWFs. Bernstein et al. (2009) study the data from SWFs' private equity investments and observe the following patterns in SWF investments: (i) it is more likely for SWFs to invest in home countries when domestic equity prices are higher, and overseas when foreign prices are higher; (ii) the Asian SWFs invest at significantly lower price earnings

---

19 Guan Ong, "Sovereign wealth funds and Asia's future investment landscape," Speech at Merrill Lynch Rising Stars Conference, Ritz Carlton Millenia, Singapore, 16 May 2008.

(P/E) ratios when investing in domestic market and at higher P/E ratios when investing overseas; the Middle Eastern SWFs are the opposite; (iii) a year after their investment, SWFs see the industry P/E ratios of their home investments drop while they see a positive change in P/E for their overseas investments; (iv) SWFs with government involvement in governance have a greater likelihood of investing at home while those relying on external managers are less likely to do so.

Balding (2008) observes that SWFs allocate their investments in different classes of assets in the same manner as other financial institutions. Most of the investments are made in fixed income securities, commercial real estate and domestic equities, whereas investments in western financial institutions in 2007-2008 were considered minor activities for these funds. Chhaochharia and Laeven (2008) find that SWFs tend to invest in industries that are underrepresented in their home country to diversify risk and in countries that share the same culture. This suggests that investment decisions are not entirely based on economic and financial considerations.

3.3 The Choice of Investment Strategies

The above sections provide an overall picture of SWFs' investment policies and activities. The activities show that the SWFs shift from conservative to high-risk investments, and with this shift more than one investment strategy is needed to manage a portfolio. Most SWFs rely on external fund managers to implement asset allocations in unfamiliar markets. SWFs may have the expertise to invest in fixed income securities through directors and managers who are from the government sector but they have limited expertise in managing riskier assets such as equities, real estate and investments in distressed companies. The choice of investment strategy is important for an SWF to preserve (or increase) the national wealth and to achieve the objectives of the fund. This section discusses some of the proposed investment strategies and approaches for SWF investments.

Given that different SWFs have different portfolio choices with different objectives, it is impossible to say if something exists that could be called the best investment strategy or approach. Mercer Investment Consulting has identified four factors which affect SWFs' choice of investments: time horizon, competitive advantages, beliefs and philosophies and timing considerations. The first factor concerns the investment horizon of the SWFs and how this affects their choice of investments. Saving funds have a longer-term investment horizon than stabilisation funds which take a short- to medium-term investment horizon. SWFs with a long-term investment horizon tend to take responsible considerations such as sustainable investments into their investment policy. These SWFs have begun to invest or show an interest in investing in industries such as clean energy. This is an appropriate choice because of their long-term investment horizon and their ability to meet the industry's high capital outlay over the long term. The second factor is the SWFs' competitive advantages. The SWFs need to assess their strengths and identify their comparative advantages in order to achieve sustainable advantage over their investments. For example, GIC's strength in real estate investments has enabled the Fund to build a huge portfolio of real estate in many countries (see Chapter 4). A third factor is the SWFs' own beliefs on asset and security pricing which help to determine their choice of investments. For example, the Australian Government Future Fund believed in a cautious approach during the subprime crisis, so the Fund reduced its holdings of equity. While GPFG believed in increasing its investment in equities during the subprime crisis. Finally, the history of a fund can affects its attitude towards risk. Funds with a shorter history are less likely to take on high-risk investments due to a lack of expertise and investment track record.

Besides investment horizons, Das et al. (2009) suggest the following additional factors: risk constraint, asset classes and their correlation, asset liability management, currency composition, liquidity requirements and legal and regulatory constraints as the other determining factors for a strategic asset allocation. Risk constraint is based on the ultimate stakeholders' willingness and ability to take risks. A new SWF's risk tolerance level may be zero due to its desire to preserve capital but over time when wealth has been built up, the risk level may increase. The correlation of asset classes is of particular importance, and especially for commodity-based SWFs where the sensitivities of these asset classes to changes in commodity prices needs to be considered. For oil-based funds, a balanced portfolio will require assets that are inversely related to oil prices. The correlation of assets within a portfolio also needs to be examined to ensure that risks are diversified. In addition, a proper understanding of asset classes and the risks associated with them are important. This has been highlighted in GPFG's 2008 losses where the risks of its assets were underestimated (See Chapter 4). The choice of currency composition depends on the objectives and the liability structure of the SWF and, as a general rule, funds should avoid investment in assets in the currency to which their own currency is pegged, otherwise, the additional exchange rate risk is added to the central bank's balance, and in addition no hedging of currency risk is achieved. CIC appears to add exchange rate risk to its central bank balance sheets when purchasing US denominated assets. However, such a move could be due to China's policy to gradually diversify out of the US dollar. GPFG has a good policy where its benchmark portfolio is constructed using an international currency basket (See Chapter 4 for details). Such a policy ensures that returns on investments are in international purchasing power and exchange rate risk has limited effect on the Fund's real returns. In cases where the SWF has an outflow which is certain, then the required amount could be invested in liquid assets which match this outflow. Legislations may mandate that the fund is allowed to invest in certain class of assets (e.g. Leste-Timor) and not allowed to invest domestically (e.g. Korea Investment Corporation).

The 2007 IMF Global Financial Stability Report presents the different strategies for asset allocation of different SWFs. Stabilisation funds are used to insulate a commodity-exporting country from shocks in commodity prices by allocating their funds to low-risk, liquid assets to meet contingent financing requirements. This type of fund invests in short-term and medium-term fixed income. A stabilisation fund needs to hedge against the risk inherent in a fund which is meant to cover, for example, the price of oil. When the contingent financing need is met, the fund can aim for high-risk and high-return investments. SWFs such as saving funds which have long-term objectives can afford to invest in higher risk assets if they can tolerate short-term volatility and have a longer investment horizon. These funds can invest in equities and other long-term assets. The asset allocations of pension reserve funds with explicit liabilities for their assets are designed to preserve solvency.

Targeting the commodity-based SWFs, Gintschel and Scherer (2008) develop a framework for partially hedging the market risk of oil reserves through allocating the financial assets for oil-based SWFs appropriately. Taking into account the aggregate wealth of financial assets and oil reserves, they show that in the absence of short-sale constraints, an investment decision can be separated into two steps: determining (standard) efficient portfolios and determining a hedge portfolio with zero investment which are unique for all efficient portfolios. The positions in the hedge portfolio depend on the oil sensitivities of the covariance matrix of the assets under consideration. They found that if the market values of oil reserves and financial funds are equal, risk reduction is lowered to 50% (10% if short sales are not allowed) from the original levels, translating into a certainty equivalent return of

3.26% per annum (48 basis points if short sales not allowed). They also show that the hedge potential is substantial and produces certainty equivalent returns exceeding those of active portfolio management. In oil-based SWFs, the financial assets partially act as hedge instrument against oil price volatility. Using the hedge portfolio, the variance of aggregate wealth is reduced between 20% and 50%, depending on the partition and the relative importance of the oil assets, compared to standard efficient portfolios. Scherer (2009) extends the above model to a multi-period framework and shows that oil-based SWFs should hold considerable amount of long-term US government bonds to hedge against the negative effects of oil price shocks and against deteriorating short rates.

SWFs have to incorporate risk management in their investments because their investment portfolios are normally exposed to riskier assets compared to central banks. Figure 3.5 shows the level of risk associated with SWFs based on their asset allocation. The Asian and Middle Eastern SWFs invested in higher risk assets than GPFG and Australian Government Future Fund. Though some of these funds have outlined their risk management in the official website, no detail on risk management methodology is mentioned. Taking into account that SWFs operate like a corporate, Asset Liability Management (ALM) would suit the risk management purpose of SWFs.

Figure 3.5 shows that most Asian and Middle Eastern SWFs have higher exposure to risk while GPFG and Australian Government Future Fund has lower risk exposure. Their risk exposure will increase when they increase investments in real estate to pursue a higher return. However, since SWF are handling a nation's wealth, most of their investments are expected to be in safe liquid assets such as government bonds and investment grade corporate bonds, blue chip stocks with only a smaller portion of the investments in risky asset such as private equity, hedge funds and distressed companies. In particular, the new SWFs, with the exception of CIC, normally have a lower risk tolerance level due to their objective to preserve capital and their lack of experience in investing in riskier assets. Therefore, the overall risk exposure of SWFs is significantly lower than that of private equity firms and hedge funds.

Most SWFs give a brief outline of their risk management process without much information on how they manage the risks in their portfolios. The debt problem of Dubai World has highlighted the importance of managing an SWF's balance sheet. In cooperation with Deutsche Bank, the EDHEC Risk and Asset Management Research Centre suggests the use of the Asset Liability

SOVEREIGN WEALTH FUND INVESTMENT ACTIVITIES

Figure 3.5: SWF's Level Of Risk Associated With Their Asset Allocation

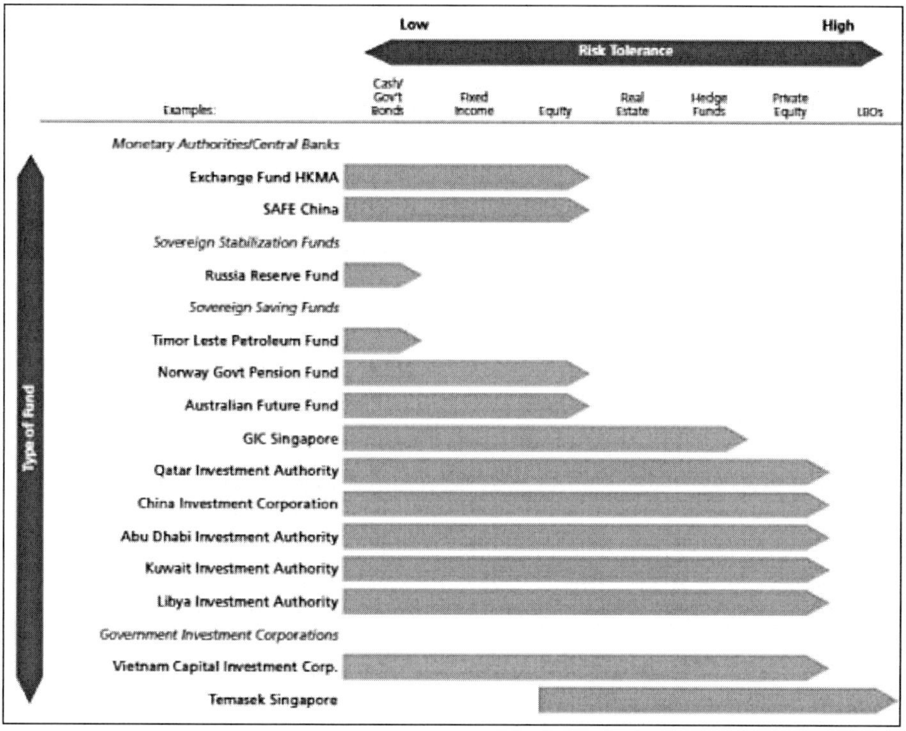

Source: Pascuzzo(2008)

Management (ALM) framework to analyse the optimal investment policy of an SWF in which the SWF's risk appetite is dependent on the patterns of inflow and outflow of funds.[20] GIC appears to be adopting such an approach. In an interview with the *Financial Times*, Tony Tan of GIC revealed that GIC look at risk first, how much money can GIC afford to lose and when the risk is manageable and within their risk limits then they will look at what is a reasonable rate of return.[21] The ALM approach has been used for a few decades by financial institutions and has been widely adopted by the pension fund industry. Financial institutions apply ALM to manage the risks by matching the financial features of the assets (e.g. the characteristics of interest rate)

---

20 The Deutsche Bank "Asset-liability management techniques for SWF management" Research Chair, 1 January 2009. http://www.edhec-risk.com/ALM/DB_Research_Chair
21 "Transcript: Tony Tan of Singapore's Government Investment Corporate," Interview with Tony Tan, Deputy chairman and executive director of GIC at Davos 25 January 2008, Financial Times, 3 February 2008. http://www.ft.com/cms/s/0/7b0549f4-d0f1-11dc-953a-0000779fd2ac.html?nclick_check=1

with financial feature of liabilities and hedge the risks when the risk cannot be matched. On the other hand, pension funds use ALM to match the cash inflow and cash outflow in order to avoid liquidity risk.

In analysing the SWF's investment strategy, the ALM framework examines where the money comes from and how it is going to be used and the risks that may arise due to the mismatch between the assets and liabilities. Even though some SWFs do not have an explicit or implicit liability such as pension obligations, they still need to make provision for contingent liability because as the government investment vehicle the SWF needs to provide the funds for that government to smooth out its spending or when there is a revenue shortfall during a recession. In times of financial crisis, the SWF fund may also be used to bail out domestic firms. In an IMF working paper, Cassard and Folkerts-Landau (1997) comment that the risk tolerance of the sovereign may prove tricky to estimate and there is no single measure for such risk. Generally speaking, the risk tolerance of a government ultimately depends on the size of the public debt, its currency composition and its maturity. Although the SWF can be operated as a separate legal entity from the government, it is still subject to the sovereign risk of the country. The ALM framework allows the SWF to design an investment portfolio that is dependent on its risk appetite. However, the existing ALM framework cannot be adopted completely because an SWF is an investment vehicle which needs to take in risks from public and private sectors, so the existing ALM framework has to be adjusted to reflect these hybrid features. The ALM requires a thorough analysis of the sensitivities of the assets and liabilities (including contingent liability) of the SWF to the financial and political variables that affect its performance. The advantage of using ALM is that the SWF is able to manage simultaneously its investment portfolio and the risk of the fund. In contrast, the hedge portfolio suggested by Gintschel and Scherer (2008) only manages the market risk of oil reserves. The application of ALM looks promising but a stabilisation fund with the main objective of hedging against the risk of commodity price fluctuations due to a country's high reliance on commodity may want to consider Gintschel and Scherer's (2008) approach.

The political risks faced by SWFs can be analysed in terms of the domestic political risk and the political risk of recipient countries. Wu (2008) comments that the demand for greater transparency and accountability from SWFs has increased the political risks faced by SWFs. This is indeed true given that most hostility to SWFs' investments comes from policymakers. For overseas investments, they can be subject to changes in regulations in the recipient countries. Since the emergence of SWFs, some countries have tightened and increased their regulations on foreign investments (see Chapter Two). When analysing the political risk faced by SWFs, one needs to take into account the type of investments made. For example, SWFs with direct investments inevitably have higher risk than those with financial investments. As far as Singapore is concerned, GIC faces less political risk than Temasek which often faces a political backlash from other countries as a result of its direct investments. The next section examines these investment policies in recipient countries.

3.4 The Investment Policies of Recipient Countries

SWF investment activities have been at the centre of political debates recently, and the reactions of recipient countries have been mixed. Western economies have concerns about the political motivation of these investments and this has led to calls for protectionism, and raised the possibility of some governments implementing reciprocal treatment. Any form of protectionism could result in a reversal of the trend towards globalisation, and would have significant adverse effects on the economies of the parties concerned. However, governments who understand the benefits of SWF investments to the international financial markets have called for more transparency in investment policies. For example, the setting up of SWF offices in London is welcomed, and Japan indicates its positive attitude towards SWF investments by waiving the tax on interest accrued on their holdings in the country. Normally overseas investors face a 15% tax on interest income.[22]

Most countries have specific policies for foreign direct investments. The OECD has developed a Foreign Direct Investment (FDI) Restrictiveness Index which measures the openness of recipient countries to foreign investment, with "0" representing full openness and "1" prohibition of FDI. This index covers nine sectors and 11 sub-sectors. Countries in Europe appear to be most open while developing countries in Asia are least open (see Figure 3.6).

---

22 Investors from countries with which Japan has bilateral tax accords pay a lower tax of 5-10%.

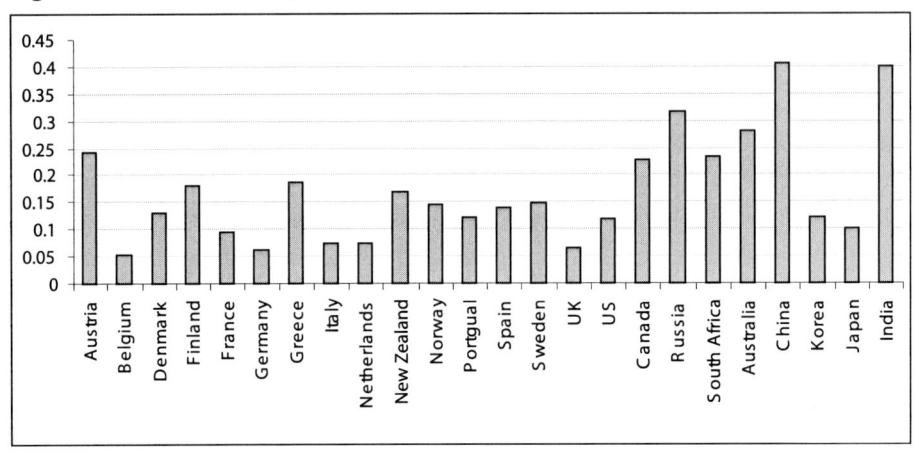

Figure 3.6: OECD's FDI Openness and Restrictiveness Index

Source: OECD December 2006

The OECD has also developed an index which covers the restrictions in terms of industries. Most countries display a similar pattern in terms of industry restrictions. The sectors which receive most restrictions are electricity, transport, telecommunications and finance. The sectors that receive least restriction are manufacturing, tourism, construction and distribution. In terms of differences between OECD and non-OECD countries, transportation and tourism are relatively less restricted in non-OECD countries while electricity, distribution and finance are relatively more restricted in non-OECD countries.

Following debates by western politicians on the possibility of using SWFs for political purposes, some countries have set up new policies to screen SWF investments in their countries, for example, Australia's Foreign Acquisitions and Take-overs Act, Act No. 92 of 1975. According to the Act, the screening process requires all important investments by foreign governments or agencies to be reported to the Australian Government and they are then examined by the Foreign Investment Review Board (FIRB). FIRB plays an advisory role and it is the treasury which holds the power to reject a proposal which is deemed contrary to the national interest. In February 2008, a set of principles was established, specifying the main factors that would determine whether a particular investment by a foreign government and its agencies was consistent with Australia's national interest. EU members such as Germany and France are the harshest critics of SWFs and have been calling for action against SWF investments in strategic industries. The German Chancellor, Angela Merkel argues, "One cannot simply react as if these are completely normal funds of privately pooled capital."[23] Although Germany has not specified which strategic industries are included, in its new regulations for foreign investments any foreign investment leading to a stake higher than 25% needs to be reviewed by the Federal Ministry of Economics and Technology. Currently no other EU member state has tightened its policies and screening procedures for foreign investments, but the EU has called for a common approach to address the issue of foreign investments.[24] In particular, Joaquín Almunia, Commissioner for Monetary and Economic Affairs, called for SWFs to be more transparent in their investment policies and asset allocations.[25]

Russia recently passed the Federal Law of the Russian Federation on Foreign Investments in Companies Having Strategic Importance for State Security and Defence. The law specifies 42 activities of strategic significance for national defence and state security and sets the trigger values for different sectors necessitating government approval. The USA passed the Foreign Investment and National Security Act in 2007, tightening the Committee on Foreign Investment in the US (CFIUS)'s review and investigation process and codifying the practices relating to the acquisition of US businesses by foreigners. Increased clarity and transparency in the review process can avoid political embarrassment as in the the Dubai Port World affair. Appendix 7 provides details on the policies on foreign investments in some significant countries.

3.5 Controversial Investments Made by SWFs and Government-related Corporations

Some of the investments made by large SWFs such as CIC, GIC and KIA in OECD markets have created a great deal of concern for politicians. Some of the

---
23 Carter Dougherty, "Europe looks at controls on state-owned investors," The New York Time, 13 July 2007. http://www.nytimes.com/2007/07/13/business/business/worldbusiness/13iht-protcet.4.6652337.html?_r=1
24 Lars-Hendrik Röller and Nicholas Véron, "Safe and Sound: An EU approach to sovereign investment," Bruegel Policy Brief Issue 2008/08, November 2008. http://aei.pitt.edu/9581/01/BruegelPolicyBrief_071108-1.pdf
25 "Transcript: Highlights of the FT's interview with Joaquín Almunia, European Commissioner for economic and monetary affairs," Financial Times, 27 September 2007. http://www.ft.com/cms/s/0/88cfdb64-6cf9-11dc-ab190000779fd2ac.html

transactions have caught media attention either because they are deemed to be in a strategic industry, or the recipient country considered the stake to be high. There was no opposition when ADIA invested $7.5 billion in Citigroup, but when China's state-owned oil enterprise CNOOC attempted to acquire Californian oil firm Unocal in 2005 and the UAE's DP World took over P&O's business in US, a fierce debate broke out over the ownership of strategic industries by these two countries. Interestingly, most of the unsuccessful bids for overseas companies resulted from US politicians' opposition, but there was little disquiet in the London Stock Exchange about having Arab countries as major shareholders.

The following section discusses some of the most notable and controversial investments made by SWFs and government-related agencies.

The Kuwait Investment Authority (KIA) investment in British Petroleum

In 1988 Kuwait Investment Authority (KIA) bought a 21.7% stake in British Petroleum (BP) when the British government privatised the oil company. The purchase created a political upheaval in the UK and the British Government ordered the stake to be reduced. The UK's Monopolies and Mergers Commission decided that the KIA shareholders could exercise considerable influence over BP and the SWF could use the fund to advance the political interest of its government. Eventually, KIA had to sell its stake at a loss and reduced its holding in BP to 9.9%. The Kuwait Oil Company has a long history with BP dating back to the time when Kuwait was still a British colony. It was set up by the Anglo-Persian Oil Company (APOC) which is now BP and it was only in 1975 that Kuwait took over the ownership of the Kuwait Oil Company from the British. At the time when KIA invested in BP, the move was regarded as complementary to Kuwait's oil business rather than an investment that could be used for strategic reasons.

Singapore Temasek's investment in the Shin Corporation

Singapore Temasek paid for a 96% stake in the Shin Corporation, a telecommunications firm owned by the Prime Minister Thaksin Shinawatra's family in 2006. The sale of Shin Corporation, the largest telecom group in

Thailand, to a foreign government led to strong opposition from the public and the investment was extremely controversial. The protest centred on the $1.9 billion tax-free profits made by the Shinawatra family and led to the subsequent ousting of Thaksin Shinawatra as the country's Prime Minister in September 2006. Temasek has maintained that they followed the Thai and Singaporean tax rules while investing in Shin Corporation and the non-payment of capital tax was a domestic issue. Another issue raised was that Shin Corporation, as a huge firm with sizeable interests in telecommunication, satellite, media and aviation, should not be sold to foreigners. The Thai government also argued that Shin Satellite, which formed part of the sale, would pose a security threat to the country if it was foreign owned. Due to the huge political upheaval created by the investment, Temasek has made a statement that it will avoid investing in "iconic" firms in future and plans to reduce its stake in Shin Corporation.[26]

So far this is the only SWF which has drawn so much political attention, largely because the sale also highlighted the problem of corruption in Thailand's politics. Temasek's purchase of telecom companies in the region has met with opposition from Indonesia, and the move to buy Shin Corporation was part of its strategy to invest in the region's top telecom companies including Australia's Optus and Indonesia's Indosat. The Shin Corporation investment aroused mass public attention because the company was owned by the Prime Minister's family and involved the non-payment of capital gains tax; so it is unlikely that the opposition was prompted by issues related to the country's security.

Purchase of P&O by Dubai Port World (DPW)

DP World, which is controlled by the government of Dubai, bought P&O, a British company in 2006 P&O is one of the world's largest shipping and port operators, managing ports in New York, New Jersey, Philadelphia, Baltimore, New Orleans and Miami. The purchase of P&O allows DP World to control the facilities of these six major ports as well as 16 other ports. The deal was approved by the Committee on Foreign Investment in the United States (CFIUS) but met with opposition in Congress, where concern was expressed about US port security. Politicians in the US were locked into a fierce debate on the sale of key US national infrastructure to a company controlled by

---

26 Amy Kazmin, "Singapore state investment arm plans to cut stake in Shin Corp," *Financial Times*, 18 June 2008. http://www.ft.com/cms/s/0/06c48e42-3cd0-11dd-b958-0000779fd2ac.html

an Arab government. The deal was approved by CFIUS and there was no opposition until a shareholder of DP World was linked to the hijackers of September 11. This started a fierce debate over the security implications of DP World's control of US's ports, and created huge public anxiety. There was fierce lobbying by politicians to stop the deal and eventually DP World was blocked from operating US ports.

The incident has also caused the CFIUS's procedure for reviewing foreign investments in the US to come under fire.[27] In addition, the saga brought embarrassment to the Bush administration when the deal was approved, and eventually DP World was forced to sell the US port operations to a US company, AIG Global Investment. This has also led to a clearer and more transparent review process in CFIUS. When US politicians were locked in the fierce debate over the Arab ownership of US ports, they did not examine DP World's role as the world's third largest port developer and operator, operating terminals in Australia, China, the Dominican Republic, Germany, India, Saudi Arabia, Venezuela and the UAE and involved in a port development project in South Korea. Purchasing P&O was a strategy by DP World to enter the North America market. Reviewing DP World's track record, one can see that the shareholders of the company have no role in its management.

The Chinese National Offshore Oil Corporation's (CNOOC) bid for Unocal

CNOOC, an energy company controlled by the Chinese government, announced its cash bid for Unocal in June 2005. This roused strong opposition from some US politicians, and the US House of Representatives voted for President, George W Bush, to review the bid based on the grounds that the investment would be a threat to US security. There was speculation that CNOOC was the proxy of the Chinese government which was seeking to control strategic energy assets valuable to the US. The debate against CNOOC's bid centred on security issues while completely overlooking CNOOC's operations. The security issue raised was that Unocal operated on 10 platforms which were near or had access to US military bases, and the technology owned by the company for deep sea exploration and drilling had dual-use potential. Some observers have argued that CNOOC's motives were

---

27 Randall Beisecker and James Martin, "DP World and US port security," NTI Issue Brief, March 2006. http://www.nti.org/e_research/e3_75.html

not purely economic as the cash offer of $18.5 billion was deemed to be too high compared to Chevron Texaco's offer of $17 billion. In the end, CNOOC withdrew its bid as a result of the political tension in the US and Unocal was subsequently sold to US-based Chevron Texaco. Market observer such as Oppenheimer analyst Fadel Gheit think that CNOOC could have acquired Unocal if they had better mastered the art of negotiation.[28] At the same time, Mubadala's successfully purchased an 8% stake in Advanced Micro Devices (AMD), a US semi-conductor company, by keeping a low profile, taking a stake under 10% and not seeking a seat on the AMD board.

Little attention was paid to the economic reasons why CNOOC was determined to purchase Unocal. Firstly, CNOOC is the third largest national oil company in China and focuses on the exploitation, exploration and development of crude oil and natural gas, and the company is facing foreign competition in its domestic market after China's entry into the WTO. Buying an established US oil company would have strengthened its domestic market share and gained entry into the North America market. Secondly, much of Unocal's valuable oil and natural gas assets were in Indonesia, Thailand and Burma, so the purchase of Unocal would have allowed CNOOC to gain access to oil and gas resources in this region. Thirdly, Unocal had the latest technologies for oil exploration and drilling which interested the Chinese who want to develop strategies for downstream investment in oil and energy.

---

28 "Why China's Unocal bid runs out of gas," BusinessWeek, 4 August 2005. http://www.businessweek. com/bwdaily/dnflash/aug2005/nf2005084_5032_db016.htm

Appendix 7: Investment Regimes of Selected Countries

Australia

CRITERIA	SUMMARY
Process	Foreign Investment Review Board (FIRB) screening
Legal basis	Foreign Acquisitions and Takeovers Act 1975 (FATA)
Objectives	To protect national interests
Review criteria	Adverse implications for national security Impact on economic development Consistency with specific foreign investment legislation, including sectoral rules
Trigger values	15% in shares or voting rights for single investors 40% in aggregate in shares or voting rights for two or more investors
Review body	FIRB reviews and advises The Treasurer takes final decision
Sectoral focus	No sectoral focus
Documentation	Specified on case-by-case basis
Duration	30 D review by The Treasurer
Appeal	No
Possible decisions	Approval Conditional approval Decline
Other legal provisions	Specific foreign investment legislation exists for certain sectors, including transport and telecommunications. The Treasurer issued additional guidelines for Foreign Government Investment Proposals on Feb 17, 2008, establishing additional criteria for the admission of investments by foreign governments and their agencies. The six guidelines include: (i) An investor's operations are independent from the relevant foreign government. (ii) An investor is subject to and adheres to the law and observes common standards of business behaviour. (iii) An investment may hinder competition or lead to undue concentration or control in the industry or sectors concerned. (iv) An investment may impact on Australian Government revenue or other policies. (v) An investment may impact on Australia's national security. (vi) An investment may impact on the operations and directions of an Australian business, as well as its contribution to the Australian economy and broader community.

Canada

CRITERIA	SUMMARY
Process	ICA review
Legal basis	Investment Canada Act, 1985
Objectives	To ensure net benefit to Canada
Review criteria	Level and nature of economic activity, including employment, resource processing, domestic sourcing and exports Significance of Canadian participation in company and industry Productivity, industrial efficiency, technological development, innovation and product variety Competition Competitiveness in world markets National industrial, economic and cultural policies
Trigger values	CAD 295m for WTO investors CAD 5m for direct investments by non-WTO investors investing in culture, transportation, financial services and production of uranium CAD 50m for indirect investments by non-WTO investors' investing in culture, transportation, financial services, production of uranium
Notification	Compulsory
Review body	Industry Canada led by Minister of Industry Canadian Heritage led by Minister of Canadian Heritage
Sectoral focus	No sectoral focus Separate trigger values for investments in culture, transportation, financial services and production of uranium
Documentation	Information about investors, investment, the Canadian business to be acquired, its assets, investors' plan for the Canadian business Reasons to undertake the investment
Duration	45 Day review 30 Day extension In practice, average 52 Day for Industry Canada filing, 75 Day for Canadian Heritage filing
Appeal	No
Possible decisions	Approval Conditional approval Decline
Other legal provisions	Ownership restrictions in financial sector Max. 25% foreign ownership in air carriers Max. 33% foreign ownership in telecommunications companies Competition Policy Review Panel mandated to suggest new measures to protect national interests

China

CRITERIA	SUMMARY
Process	Foreign investment review
Legal basis	2006 Regulations for Mergers and Acquisitions of Domestic Enterprises by Foreign Investors
	Catalogue for the Guidance of Foreign Investment Industries
	Various regulations by relevant ministries
	Various guiding opinions by relevant ministries
Objectives	National security and economic interests
Review criteria	National security
	National economic security
	Protection of critical industries, as specified in the Catalogue for the Guidance of Foreign Investment Industries
	Protection of famous trademarks and traditional brandsIn practice, a number of other factors is understood to influence the review process, including negative public attention on relevant officials, bureaucratic infighting, differences in priorities between local and central-level governments, political calendar, regulatory ambiguity and lack of procedural transparency.
Trigger values	Not specified
Notification	Compulsory
Review body	Ministry of Commerce
Sectoral focus	Catalogue for the Guidance of Foreign Investment Industries specifies 67 industries in which foreign investments are restricted, and 34 industries in which foreign investments are prohibited in the areas of farming, fisheries, mining, manufacturing, power, water, gas, communication, transportation, storage, post, telecommunication, wholesale trade, retail trade, banking, insurance, real estate, leasing, commercial services, scientific research, technical services, irrigation, environment, public utilities management, education, public health, sports, social welfare, arts, entertainment and other industries
Documentation	Not specified
Duration	Not specified
Appeal	No
Possible decisions	Approval
	Conditional approval
	Decline
Other legal provisions	Total of more than 200 laws involving foreign investment, including: 2007 Antimonopoly Law, State Council Opinion on Revitalising the Industrial Machinery Industry, Guiding Opinion Concerning the Advancement of Adjustments of State Capital and the Restructuring of State-Owned Enterprises, Equity Joint Ventures Law, Foreign Contractor Joint Ventures Law and Foreign Capital Enterprises Law

France

CRITERIA	SUMMARY
Process	Foreign investment review
Legal basis	Law 2004-1343 Decree 2005-1739
Objectives	Public order Public safety National defence
Review criteria	Activities likely to jeopardise public order, public safety or national defence interests Research in, and production or marketing of, arms, munitions, or explosive powders or substances Preservation of industrial capacities on French territory (R&D, know-how and other IP assets, production capacity), continuity of supplies, compliance with contractual commitments contained in certain existing contracts (e.g. public procurement contracts or contracts in specific industry sectors) EU companies: Only those operations leading to the effective transfer of a sensitive activity Non-EU companies: Full review generally applied
Trigger values	Review to be conducted if investor acquires "control" of a firm whose corporate headquarters are located in France, acquires a branch of a firm whose corporate headquarters are located in France, or acquires more than one-third of the capital or voting rights of a firm whose corporate headquarters are located in France
Notification	Compulsory
Review Body	Ministry of Economy, Finance and Employment Other ministries consulted
Sectoral focus	11 sectors as specified in 2005 Decree, including gambling and casinos, private security, research, development, or production of means to stem the unlawful use, in terrorist activities, of pathogens or toxins, equipment designed to intercept correspondence and monitor conversations, testing and certification of the security of information technology products and systems, production of goods or supply or services to ensure the security of the information systems, dual-use items and technologies, cryptology equipment and services, activities carried out by firms entrusted with national defence secrets, in particular under the terms of national defence contracts or of security clauses, research, production, or trade in weapons, ammunitions, powders, and explosives intended for military purposes or war materials

CRITERIA	SUMMARY
Documentation	Location where the investor is a legal entity, details on the individuals and public legal entities that have ultimate control over the investing organisation, identity of the primary known shareholders holding more than 5 per cent of the capital or voting rights, board members' names and addresses, identity of the fund manager, if applicable, investment target's business activity, investment target's last fiscal year revenues, shareholder structure before and after the contemplated deal
Duration	60D limit after receipt of full documentation Extension possible
Appeal	Yes
Possible decisions	Approval Conditional approval Decline
Other legal provisions	National sector-specific restrictions, e.g. in media, finance, aerospace State monopolies in energy, railway passenger transport, coal mines, explosives and postal services Issuance of golden shares by government possible EU Capital Requirements Directive (Art. 19) and Reinsurance Directive (Arts. 19 and 19a) provide for prudential rules for ownership of financial institutions, based on suitability of owner from prudential perspective and financial soundness of acquirer. Based on the criteria, competent authorities (i.e. supervisors) can reject acquisitions of financial institutions in the EU.

Germany

CRITERIA	SUMMARY
Process	AWG foreign investment review
Legal basis	2008 Draft Thirteenth Law Amending the Foreign Trade Act and the Foreign Trade Decree 2004 Amendment to Foreign Trade Act 1961 Foreign Trade Act
Objectives	Public order Public security
Review criteria	Real and sufficiently great danger to public order or public security that touches upon the fundamental interests of German societyOnly applicable to foreign investors from outside the EU and the European Free Trade Association
Trigger values	25% of aggregate of coordinated voting rights, direct, indirect holdings
Notification	Voluntary
Review body	Ministry of Economics and Technology Subject to final approval by Federal Government Informally, other ministries and services can be consulted on individual basis
Sectoral focus	No sectors specified
Documentation	To be specified by Ministry of Economics and Technology
Duration	90D for decision to initiate the review process 60D for conduct of review
Appeal	Yes
Possible decisions	Transaction considered approved unless Federal Government decides otherwise within specified time frame Conditional approval Decline
Other legalprovisions	Competition Law (Gesetz gegen Wettbewerbsbeschränkungen) EU Capital Requirements Directive (Art. 19) and Reinsurance Directive (Arts. 19 and 19a) provide for prudential rules for ownership of financial institutions, based on suitability of owner from prudential perspective and financial soundness of acquirer. Based on the criteria, competent authorities (i.e. supervisors) can reject acquisitions of financial institutions in the EU.

Japan

CRITERIA	SUMMARY
Process	Foreign investment review
Legal basis	1991 Amendment to Foreign Exchange and Foreign Trade Act of 1949
Objectives	National security Public order Public safety Economic interests
Review criteria	Threats to national security, public order, public safety, or the economy Specific, unpublished criteria used to determine when an investment poses a significant threat
Trigger values	10% share in listed company Any share in unlisted company Establishment of branch, factory, business offices Change in corporate objectives of companies with higher than 33% foreign ownership Certain loans to domestic companies
Notification	Ex-ante mandatory notification for transactions in sensitive industries, with countries with no reciprocal investment agreement, for capital transactions subject to permission by Ministry of Finance, and dual-use items and items used for the maintenance of the defence industrial base Post-factum mandatory notification in non-sensitive industries within 15D after transaction
Review body	Ministry of Finance
Sectoral focus	National security (aircraft, weapons, nuclear power, spacecraft, and gunpowder) Public order (electricity, gas, heat supply, communications, broadcasting, water, railroads, passenger transport), public safety (biological chemicals, guard services) Smooth management of the economy (primary industries relating to agriculture, forestry and fisheries, oil, leather and leather products manufacturing, air transport, and maritime transport)
Documentation	Percentage of shares to be acquired Business plan of the investing company, and the reason for the transaction Information related to foreign control, such as the number of foreign board members and the foreign company's reputation
Duration	30D limit 120D maximum extension
Appeal	Yes
Possible decisions	Approval Conditional approval Decline
Other legal provisions	Sector-specific restrictions on foreign ownership and management, including broadcasting, telecommunications and tobacco industries

The Netherlands

CRITERIA	SUMMARY
Process	No review process
Legal basis	Financial Supervision Act of 2006
Objectives	Competition Financial market oversight
Review criteria	NA
Trigger values	NA
Notification	NA
Review body	NA
Sectoral focus	NA
Documentation	NA
Duration	NA
Appeal	NA
Possible decisions	NA
Other legal provisions	Mandatory anti-trust review for domestic and foreign investments Sector-specific rules in financial markets empowering the Netherlands Central Bank to block transactions on grounds of financial stabilityCertain sectors publicly-owned and controlled and therefore closed to foreign investments, including electricity and water grids, railway passenger services, national airports, central banking, certain postal and transportation services

Russia

CRITERIA	SUMMARY
Process	Foreign Strategic Investment Law (FSIL) review process
Legal basis	Federal Law on Foreign Investments in Companies Having Strategic Importance for State Security and Defence, No. 57-FZ, as effective from May 7, 2008
Objectives	National defence State security
Review criteria	National defence State security
Trigger values	Acquisition of control (>50% share), including appointment of >50 of the board of directors or management board, in a strategic company Assumption of managing company functions or any other transactions leading to establishment of control in respect of a strategic company Acquisition by a foreign state, international organisation or organisation under their control of >25 percent or other blocking right in a strategic company Prohibition on foreign states, international organisations or organisations under their control from acquiring control of a strategic company Additional restrictions on investment in companies engaged in geological survey or exploration and development of a subsoil area of federal significance
Notification	Compulsory for investments leading to shares in a company in a strategic sector of 5% or more
Review body	Federal Antimonopoly Services (FAS) Final decision taken by a governmental commission, chaired by the Prime Minister
Sectoral focus	FSIL law specifies 42 sectors considered to have strategic significance for national defence and state security, falling into eight categories: (i) nuclear materials, devices, waste, (ii) coding and cryptographic equipment, (iii) weapons and military equipment andtechnology, (iv) aviation and space, (v) television, radio broadcasting, printed mass media, (vi) natural monopolies designated as such by the Federal Antimonopoly Service, (vii) telecommunications,(viii) geological survey and exploration and development of subsoil areas of federal significance
Documentation	Detailed documentation as specified in FSIL law

CRITERIA	SUMMARY
Duration	14D assessment by FAS to initiate the review process
30D evaluation of the transaction by FAS
30D review by governmental commission
180D extension option in unspecified cases
No time specification for national security review
Appeal	Yes
Possible decisions	Approval
Conditional approval
Decline
Other legal provisions	Foreign investments in Russian enterprises are subject to additional rules and restrictions as defined by the following laws: Law on the Subsoil, Law on the Continental Shelf, Law on Joint Stock Companies, Law on Limited Liability Companies, Law on Investigation Activities, Law on Foreign Investments, Antimonopoly Law, Law on Communications

United Arab Emirates

CRITERIA	SUMMARY
Process	No review process
Legal basis	Agencies Law of 1981 Companies Law of 1984
Objectives	NA
Review criteria	NA
Trigger values	NA
Notification	NA
Review body	NA
Sectoral focus	NA
Documentation	NA
Duration	NA
Appeal	NA
Possible decisions	NA
Other legal provisions	49% cap on foreign ownership in any UAE company, as specified in 1984 Company Law Foreign companies can import goods into the UAE only via a local agent, as specified in 1981 Agencies Law Limits imposed by government procurement laws, including the Government Tenders Law 51% ownership floor on any industrial project, plus citizenship rules for management Various restrictions on landownership Various sector-specific limitations, especially 40% cap on foreign ownership in oil and gas-related industries, as well as restrictions in sectors such as telecommunications, insurance, travel services Preferential treatment for investors from member state of the Gulf Cooperation Council (GCC) In addition, strong, non-codified, informal restrictions on foreign investments in sensitive industries, including energy, defence, water, power generation, used to further national security, economic, labour-market-related and business interests

United Kingdom

CRITERIA	SUMMARY
Process	No formal review process
Legal basis	Enterprise Act of 2002
Objectives	Public Interest
Review criteria	Public interest National interest Control of classified and sensitive technology
Trigger values	No trigger values applicable
Notification	Notification rules of Office of Fair Trading and Competition Commission
Review body	Secretary of State for the Department of Business, Enterprise and Regulatory Reform (DBERR) makes Public Interest Intervention Office of Fair Trading reviews and submits recommendations Competition Commission reviews and submits recommendations
Sectoral focus	Secretary of State can make Public Interest Intervention, and intervene in any investment transaction, including a transaction only involving British parties, which he considers harmful to the public interest
Documentation	Specified on case-by-case basis
Duration	120D after a Reference has been provided by the Competition Commission
Appeal	Yes
Possible decisions	Approval Conditional approval Decline
Other legal provisions	Government golden share and 29.5% cap on foreign shareholding in British Aerospace PLC and Rolls Royce PLC Foreign-controlled company may not be granted defence procurement contracts Citizenship requirements for certain companies engaged in classified work Veto over disposal of assets for certain companies Restrictions on foreign investment activity in certain sectors. Under OECD Code of Liberalisation of Capital Movements, UK reserves right to restrict foreign investment in air transport, broadcasting, maritime transport Limitations to OECD National Treatment Instrument in aerospace, maritime transport, government defence procurement contracts

United States of America

CRITERIA	SUMMARY
Process	CFIUS review
Legal basis	Exon-Florio Amendment to the Defense Production Act of 19502007 Foreign Investment and National Security Act (FINSA)
Objectives	National security
Review criteria	Potential national security-related effects on US-critical infrastructure, including major energy assets Potential national security-related effects on US-critical technologies Whether the transaction is a foreign government-controlled transaction Review of the current assessment of (i) the acquiring country's adherence to non-proliferation regimes, (ii) the relationship of the acquiring country with the United States, specifically on its record on cooperating in counter-terrorism efforts, (iii) the potential for transhipment or diversion of technologies with military applications, including an analysis of national export control laws and regulations Long-term projection of US requirements for sources of energy and other critical resources and material Potential effects of the transaction on sales of military goods, equipment, or technology to any country identified by the Secretary of Defence as posing a potential regional military threat to the interests of the United States
Trigger values	No trigger values CFIUS investigation triggered if (I) the lead agency responsible for negotiating mitigation agreements and other conditions and for monitoring compliance with mitigation agreements recommends an investigation and CFIUS agrees, or (II) whenever a review resultsin a determination that (i) the transaction threatens national security and the threat has not been mitigated, (ii) the transaction is a foreign government-controlled transaction, or (iii) the transaction would result in control of critical infrastructure, CFIUS determines that the transaction could impair national security, and the impairment has not been mitigated
Notification	Voluntary

CRITERIA	SUMMARY
Review body	Committee on Foreign Investment in the United States (CFIUS) reviews and submits recommendation to the president. CFIUS composed of Treasury (chair with other department as lead agency on case-by-case basis), Homeland Security, Defence, State, Justice, Energy, Labor (non-voting), Director of National Intelligence (nonvoting) The president takes final decision
Sectoral focus	No sectors officially specified
Documentation	Specified on case-by-case basis
Duration	30D review 45D investigation 15D Presidential review
Appeal	No
Possible decisions	Approval Conditional approval Decline
Other legal provisions	None

Adapted from Deutsche Bank Research, SWF and Foreign Investment Policies – An Update 22 October 2008.

CHAPTER 4 Case Studies

Chapter Three provided an overview of the investment policies of SWFs, their investments by countries and by sectors, choice of investment strategies and the regulations that these funds face in their overseas investments. In this chapter, investments of five of the largest SWFs, ADIA, CIC, GIC, Temasek, and GPFG are examined in greater detail (see Chapter Two for an explanation why these five SWFs have been chosen).

Of the five, UAE's ADIA is the biggest SWF in asset value and has been the most active in terms of its investment and its quest to build itself into an international investment house. Norway's GPFG is the second largest SWF in asset value and has been widely praised for its corporate governance and its transparency in its operations. China's CIC is the newest fund to join but has the potential to become the largest SWF in asset value due to China's huge foreign reserves. The other two funds being studied are GIC and Temasek. Even though both are from Singapore, they are operated in very different ways. Temasek is smaller than GIC but its model is being followed by CIC and other potential SWFs like the Japanese SWF. Of these four Asian and Middle Eastern SWFs, Temasek provide better disclosure and is the most transparent among the four in its asset allocations although there is still no detailed breakdown on the value of its investments and the percentage of holdings except for large investments. GPFG is hailed as the most transparent SWF and should be the benchmark for all SWFs. Nevertheless, it is unlikely that many SWFs will adopt Norway's disclosure policy and investment strategies. The information on ADIA, CIC, GIC, Temasek and GPFG cited in this chapter is from media sources such as press releases and speeches as well as from academic research and the SWFs' own annual reports.

In aiming to provide a better understanding of the investment activities and strategies of these five major funds, ADIA, CIC, Temasek, GIC, and GPFG, this chapter summarises them and compares them for differences and similarities. Less information was available for ADIA and CIC, the former being less transparent in its investments, the latter being a newer fund. The main focus has to be on Temasek's and GPFG's investment activities and their strategies because of the five funds studied, Temasek and GPFG are the most transparent and have a long history. More importantly, Temasek is consistently recommended as the model for other SWFs. On the other hand, GPFG investment strategy would suits new and potential SWFs who aim to be financial investors. It is hoped that this study will provide insight for those countries who would like to model their SWFs base on existing SWFs. This chapter also aims to provide clarity to parties who are concerned that the big SWFs use their financial muscle to wield political influence.

4.1   Abu Dhabi Investment Authority (ADIA)

The Emirate of Abu Dhabi has four investment funds: the Abu Dhabi Investment Authority, Mubadala Development Company, the International Petroleum Investment Company (IPIC) and the Abu Dhabi Investment Council (ADIC). Among these four funds, ADIA is the biggest and regarded as the representative SWF of Abu Dhabi. ADIA was set up in 1976 to manage the country's oil revenues and its operation is based on a strategy of secrecy, with an understanding that the Fund was established to save the Emirates' oil revenues. No one knows the exact value of the Fund, but most studies estimate it to be in the range between $500bn to $875bn. As cited in the *Financial Times*, the ADIA Chairman Sheikh Khalifa told a Lebanese newspaper that the $800bn figure 'does not reflect the truth and size of the Emirati investment abroad'.[1] The same view was endorsed by Seznec (2008) who estimates that the assets of all SWFs in Abu Dhabi are between $300-$400 billion with ADIA holding not more than $300 billion.[2] Mubadala Development, which was created in 2002 and tasked with the development of Abu Dhabi, is more open in its operations and has been actively forming

---

1   Andrew England, "Abu Dhabi plays down size of wealth fund," Financial Times, 30 June 2008. http://www.ft.com/cms/s/0/153e4632-466e-11dd-876a-0000779fd2ac.html
2   Jean-Francois Seznec, "The Gulf Sovereign Wealth Funds: Myths and Reality," Middle East Policy, 15(2), p102, 2008.

partnerships with overseas companies to develop Abu Dhabi. Mubadala released its first annual report in April 2009 revealing the Fund's loss in 2008,[3] the first of its kind by a Middle Eastern SWF. IPIC invests in oil-related projects for the Emirates. The newest fund, ADIC, was assumed to have been set up to take over the domestic portfolio of ADIA, but no public information is available except for the Fund's purchase of a 90% stake in the Chrysler Building in New York. The managing director of the Abu Dhabi Investment Council, Khalifa al-Kindi, said in an interview with the *Financial Times* in April 2007 that ADIC would work in tandem with ADIA and there would be some overlap between the two,[4] thus clarifying the situation as to whether ADIC is to take over ADIA's domestic and regional investments or not.[5] Instead ADIC will focus on investments in the Middle East and also invest internationally.

Despite the lack of information on ADIA, its establishment generates much interest from policy-makers and the finance industry. It is the largest SWF in the world and has always kept a low profile until the announcement of its 4.9% stake in Citigroup. This stake was kept below 5% to avoid the need to report to regulators. Most of ADIA's investments are small and do not require disclosure and hence it is impossible to grasp fully its investment strategy. Setser and Ziemba commented in the RGE December 2007 report that due to the secretive nature of the Middle Eastern funds, any analysis is subject to a high margin of uncertainty.[6] Therefore, instead of analysing the investment strategy of ADIA, this section examines the Fund's investment activities based on the RGE Monitor Reports, news articles and information from the Sovereign Wealth Fund Institute (SWFI).

4.1.1 An Overview of ADIA Investments

ADIA is described as a sophisticated investment house, investing in diversified classes of assets but it is less strategic than Mabudala Development. ADIA maintains that the Fund seeks limited stakes in companies with no control – a strategy that is considered non threatening.[7]

---

3 Andrew England, "Abu Dhabi sovereign fund releases first report," Financial Times, 23 April 2009. http://www.ft.com/cms/s/0/cffb43ca-3039-11de-88e3-00144feabdc0.html

4 Simeon Kerr and Roula Khalaf, "Abu Dhabi gets new investment body," Financial Times, 26 April 2007. http://www.ft.com/cms/s/0/a5a56964-f45b-11db-88aa-000b5df10621.html

5 "Abu Dhabi to replace ADIA by ADIC – UAE," MENAFN.com, 23 October 2009. http://www.menafn.com/qn_news_story_s.asp?StoryId=1093131494#

6 Brad Setser and Rachel Ziemba, "Understanding the New Financial Superpower - The Management of GCC Official Foreign Assets," RGE Monitor, December 2007. http://www.menafn.com/qn_news_story_s.asp?StoryId=1093131494#

7 Simeon Kerr and Roula Khalaf, "Abu Dhabi fund hire media expert," Financial Times, 19 January

ADIA first disclosed its strategic asset allocation in an interview with *Business Week* in 2008[8] (See Table 4.1 on ADIA asset allocation). The Fund mostly invests in stocks in developed markets (45-55%), a pattern which most Middle Eastern SWFs followed until the recent subprime crisis. The second largest allocation is government bonds (12-18%), followed by stocks in emerging markets (8-12%). It was also reported in the same interview in June 2008 that ADIA had increased its indexed funds from 45% to 60% of the portfolio after finding that passive investments in indices outperformed some of ADIA's highly paid fund managers. S&P indices were used for equity investment in US and MSCI indices were used for equity investments in rest of the world. For the fixed income investments, ADIA uses its own customised form of various indices such as Barclays Corporate Bond Index, the JP Morgan Government Bond Index and the Barclays Inflation linked Bond Index.[9] At the same time, the number of hedge funds in its portfolio was halved. These activities tie in with Seznec's (2008) observation that it is not credible to imagine SWFs' investment strategies to be similar to those of hedge funds which make huge returns with higher risks. In his view, the Middle Eastern SWFs will not take over strategically sensitive companies in the West but will take advantage of good deals whenever the opportunity arises.[10] Another observation concerning ADIA's asset allocation is that the Fund focuses on returns in contrast to endowment funds which hold a small percentage of assets in low risk assets such as bonds. It is estimated that ADIA is one of the world's largest investors in private equity.[11]

2008. http://www.ft.com/cms/s/0/bb85a726-c633-11dc-8378-0000779fd2ac.html
8   Emily Thornton and Stanley Reed, "Inside the Abu Dhabi Investment Authority," BusinessWeek, 6 June 2008. http://www.businessweek.com/globalbiz/content/jun2008/gb2008065_742165.htm
9   Interview with HH Sheikh Ahmed Bin Zayed Al Nehayan, Managing Director of ADIA. Interview was conducted by Micheal Backfisch, Middle East Bureau Chief of Handelsbatt.
10 Jean-Francois Seznec, "The Gulf Sovereign Wealth Funds: Myths and Reality," Middle East Policy, 15(2), p105, 2008.
11 Sudip Roy, "Sovereign wealth funds: The new rulers of finance," Euromoney, December 2007.

Table 4.1: ADIA Asset Allocation

ASSET CLASS	PERCENTAGE OF PORTFOLIO(ADIA'S ASSET ALLOCATION RANGE)
Stocks in developed markets	45-55
Stocks in emerging markets	8-12
Small-cap stocks	1-4
Government bonds	12-18
Corporate and other bonds	4-8
Alternative investments	5-10
Real estate	5-10
Private equity	2-8
Infrastructure	0-4
Cash	0-5

Source: Data from ADIA, reported in Business Week, 6 June 2008.

With regard to the currency composition of ADIA assets in 2006, Ziemba from RGE Monitor estimated that 45% were in the USA, 40% in Europe, 10% in emerging markets and 5% in Japan.[12] However, this composition may have changed after the subprime crisis and ADIA has recently changed its investment pattern. In an interview with Micheal Backfisch from *Handelsbatt* in January 2010, ADIA disclosed that it distributes its assets in different regions as follows: US – 35 to 50%, Europe – 25 to 35%, Asia – 10-25% and Emerging Market – 15 to 25%.[13]

After the 9/11 attack, Middle Eastern SWFs have generally begun diversifying some of their investments into Europe and the emerging markets. In an interview with the *Financial Times*, Saeed Mubarak al-Hajeri, Executive Director of the Emerging Markets Department at ADIA, said that compared to other similar funds, ADIA has higher exposure to emerging markets, and the equity alone accounts for 14% of the Fund's equity portfolio. However, none of the investments is a controlling stake. In giving a brief idea of ADIA's investment horizon, he stated that its short-term is seen as 15 years and the Fund will be in the market for the next 50 years. It also has interests in the growing economies of China and India, particularly in China's insurance and oil and gas sector pre-IPO investments. In India, ADIA is interested in financial institutions and infrastructure assets. It was also revealed in the same news

---
12 Rachel Ziemba ," What are the GCC Funds Buying? A Look At Their Investment Strategies," RGE Monitor, June 2008.
13 See Note 9.

report that ADIA has limited exposure in the Middle East and it has never invested in local stock markets,[14] but the limited exposure in the region may change following the subprime crisis. There is speculation that Abu Dhabi has been called upon to invest in the region to help its neighbours. According to the *Financial Times* in December 2008, a banker said that there is debate among Abu Dhabi officials about whether more money should be spent domestically.[15]

4.1.2 ADIA's Recent Investments

ADIA appears to be the least aggressive among the Middle Eastern SWFs in its investment activities, or it is simply keeping a much lower profile compared with its counterparts in the Gulf region. However, since its highly publicised purchase of a 4.9% stake in Citigroup at $7.5 billion, ADIA has had to be less secretive about its investment activities and there have been numerous news reports on its activities and speculations about the Fund's investments. Below are some examples of ADIA's investments.

The Australian media reported that ADIA had teamed up with Lease's APPF and jointly owns 1 O'Connell Street in Sydney. In 2008, ADIA bought a small stake in the Australian-based construction giant Leighton Holdings and a 19.9% stake in the AMP New Zealand Office Trust. It was also speculated that they teamed up in 2007 to buy Central Plaza Two and Three office towers in Brisbane for $454.2 million.[16] ADIA has also entered Brazil's real estate market by investing in two towers in Rio de Janeiro[17] and this makes future collaborations between the two countries possible. This coincides with Brad Setser's comment in his blog in July 2007 about ADIA having a better business model than China. He wrote, 'Turning an oil surplus into Brazilian and Turkish equities has been a better business model over the past five years than turning a "manufacturing workshop to the world" surplus into US bonds'.[18] This is indeed the case for most countries in the Middle East where

---

14 Roula Khalaf, "Abu Dhabi focuses on investment in emerging areas," *Financial Times*, 23 March 2006. http://www.ft.com/cms/s/0/81b31f9e-b9fe-11da-9d02-0000779e2340.html
15 Andrew England, "Abu Dhabi braces for slowdown," *Financial Times*, 17 December 2007. http://www.ft.com/cms/s/0/524f6304-cc64-11dd-9c43-000077b07658.html
16 Turi Condon, "Abu Dhabi sovereign fund's $280m office deal," *The Australian*, 11 September 2008. http://www.theaustralian.news.com.au/story/0,,24326605-25658,00.html?from=public
17 "ADIA enters Rio realty with investments in 2 office towers," *Emirates Business 24-7*, 21 October 2009. http://www.business24-7.ae/Articles/2009/10/Pages/20102009/10212009_b0083a2fe43f4cd38-be06ef79a36e856.aspx
18 Brad Setser, "Abu Dhabi Investment Authority Investment secrets revealed," *Brad Setser's Blog: Follow the money*, 7 July 2007. http://blogs.cfr.org/setser/2007/07/07/abu-dhabi-investment-authority-secrets-revealed/

petrodollars are invested in higher return assets rather than in low-yield US treasuries.

Aside from investing in financial institutions and real estate, ADIA is also keen to invest in infrastructure. It appointed a new head for its infrastructure program in 2007 and has since invested in infrastructure funds and finance as well as service firms in India (see Table 2 on ADIA's investments). ADIA's latest major investment in UK involved a 15% stake in Gatwick Airport in 2010.[19] There is also a possibility that ADIA will invest in the British energy market, as the UK Prime Minister Gordon Brown told reporters that Britain and Qatar are planning a new joint energy fund to invest in British energy firms, and that talks with ADIA about investment opportunities in Britain are moving forward.[20] In a news report published in *Emirates Business* in October 2009, a key person from a Saudi bank said that ADIA may begin investing in the local bond market in an attempt to help the region and to facilitate the development of this market.[21] ADIA investments in the region are to help to revive the regional economy and provide liquidity to other states within the UAE.

Table 4.2: ADIA Investments

COMPANY	COUNTRY	% OWNERSHIP	COMMENTS
Egyptian Financial Group Hermes Holding Company	Egypt	8.3%	
Suez Cement Company	Egypt	7.6%	
Citigroup	United States	4.9%($7.5 bn)	
Toll Brothers	United States		
Ares Management LLC	United States	~20%	
Infrastructure Leasing & Financial Services Limited	India	10%	

19 Pilita Clark, "Abu Dhabi Fund purchases 15% stake in Gatwick," Financial Times, 5 February 2010. http://www.ft.com/cms/s/0/93ec80ee-11f5-11df-b6e3-00144feab49a.html
20 David Clarke, "UK's Brown to open energy markets to overseas investors," Reuters, 22 June 2008. http://uk.reuters.com/article/idUKCLA24069220080622
21 "ADIA may invest in UAE bonds, says Saudi Bank," Emirates Business 24/7, 21 October 2009. http://www.business24-7.ae/Articles/2009/7/Pages/18072009/07192009_6aaa3adf7f72484997d9ce7d43f5e9b8.aspx

COMPANY	COUNTRY	% OWNERSHIP	COMMENTS
Apollo Management LP	United States	9%	
Lion Breweries Development	New Zealand	50%(NZ$126m)	Haumi Developmenta
1 O'Connell St Office Tower	Australia	50%($320m)	
Central Plaza Two and Three Towers	Australia	($454.2m)	
111 Eagle Street Tower	Australia		
Oracle Shopping Centre	UK	50%	
Tiphook	UK		Open market
Pilkington	UK		Open market
Apollo Management Plc	US	9%	
Alliance Boots	UK		Buyout with Kohlberg Kravis Roberts
Gatwick Airport	UK	15%	
Ares Management	US	20%	
TXU Corp (now called Energy Future Holding)	US		Co-invest with TPG
Infrastructure Leasing and Financial Service Limited	India	10%	

Source: Sovereign Wealth Fund Institutes October 2009, Updates by author from various news articles.

Note: The list only contains part of ADIA's investment where public information is available. The investments listed were at time of news release and information may be different now.

4.1.3 Summary of ADIA Investment Activities

ADIA aims to build a portfolio that would diversify Abu Dhabi's economy and provide returns from its commodity exports for future generations. Most of its investments are seen as "value added". Some of them aim to enhance the country's industrial policy such as their stake in Ferrari. After the investment in Ferrari, Ferrari Theme Park and Formula One Grand Prix were developed in Abu Dhabi to help develop tourism in the region.

ADIA was secretive about its investment strategies until its investment in Citigroup. It has been described by many financial experts as one of the most sophisticated investment houses in the global market. Looking at the various investments that ADIA has made, their approach resembles that of private equity company or an endowment fund. Previously they held small stakes in companies to avoid disclosure, and used financial indices to track their investments. Such an approach is very similar to that of universities' endowment funds in the USA. However, their recent investment in real estate and private equity firms, and their taking of large stakes in pre-IPOs are similar to the practices of private equity firms. ADIA does not disclose its investment activities but notably they are active in developed markets in the US and the UK. As financial investors, they buy and sell shares directly in these markets using their investment arms in those countries.

4.2 China Investment Corporation (CIC)

CIC is part of the Chinese government's effort to improve the returns on its massive foreign reserves and to absorb some of the nation's excess liquidity. CIC's investment strategy is of great interest to many parties due to its potential to grow into the biggest SWF in the world. Its 2008 annual report stated that slightly over 50% of its registered capital had been allocated to global investment with the balance in domestic investment. However, it has no clear investment policy, and the ambiguities and lack of clarity of its investment strategy can be best summed up by the remark made by Jesse Wang, CIC's Chief Risk Officer in an interview:

> "We mainly do farming, but occasionally we go hunting, and we don't rule out the possibility of making a few other investments if good opportunities come up."[22]

Unlike other SWFs, the CIC's funding comes indirectly from the country's foreign reserves through bonds issued by the Ministry of Finance. Since it is obliged to pay interest on its capital, it is under pressure to invest in high

---
22 "China's CIC on the prowl for direct investment," reported by Eadie Chen, Langi Chiang and Simon Rabinovitch, edited by David Hulmes, Reuters, 3 March 2008. http://www.reuters.com/article/idUS-PEK13379020080303

return investments. The Chairman of CIC, Lou Jiwei, has estimated that CIC needs to earn $40 million a day to meet its funding costs, and this high interest obligation pressurised CIC into making more risky investments.[23] However, in a new agreement with the Ministry of Finance in 2009, the initial $200 billion will be treated as an asset rather than a debt and CIC will no longer be obliged to pay interest to the state, but only needs to pay regular dividends instead.[24] In addition, the performance of CIC will determine whether the Fund will receive further capital injections from its government. Despite the lack of transparency and detail on their website, CIC has a tradition of revealing to the public what they will and will not invest in through press releases before a deal is sealed. To analyse CIC's investment strategy (or investment behaviour), the following sections examine what it will and will not invest in, what they have actually invested in and the role CIC plays in its own domestic economy. CIC has also taken control of Central Huijin Investment (Central Huijin)[25] which holds a majority stake in China's state-owned banks, playing a central role in their recapitalisation.

4.2.1 What CIC Will Not Invest In

Before CIC went into business in September 2007, Chinese officials informed the press what CIC would not invest in so as to pacify western governments' fear that it would use the capital for political motives. CIC was quick to reassure the West of their purely economic intentions. In late 2007, China's Vice-Minister of Finance, Li Yong, confirmed that the CIC would not invest in overseas airlines, telecommunication or oil companies.[26] Chief Investment Officer, Gao Xiqing also said in a conference in Beijing in June 2008 that CIC were looking for clean energy and environmentally friendly investments and would not invest in tobacco, weapon and gambling industries.[27]

---

23 Jamil Anderlini, "CIC Raises Global Spending Power," *Financial Times*, 23 April 2008. http://www.ft.com/cms/s/0/f0a42942-1164-11dd-a93b-0000779fd2ac.html
24 Ouyang Xiaohong and Liu Peng, "CIC No Longer to Pay Interest to the State," *Economic Observer*, 26 August 2009. http://www.eeo.com.cn/ens/homepage/briefs/2009/08/26/149395.shtml
25 Central Huijin Investment Ltd (Central Huijin) was established on 26 Dec 2003 as a state owned investment company of China.
26 Yan Liang, "China Investment Corporation Unveils Investment Plan," *Xinhua News*, 7 November 2007. http://news.xinhuanet.com/english/2007-11/07/content_7029738.htm
27 Jamal Anderlini, "China wealth fund promises to shun tobacco, guns and gambling," *Financial Times*, 14 June 2008. http://www.ft.com/cms/s/0/311e6310-39ac-11dd-90d7-0000779fd2ac.html

4.2.2 What CIC Will Invest In

According to CIC's official website, their investment strategy is to maximise returns, and their investments are not restricted to any particular sector, geographical location or asset class. In his maiden interview with CBS, Gao Xiqing said that CIC had US$200 billion to invest and that the 180 employees in their Beijing headquarter were looking for investments in the West with a long term and prudent investment policy, but not seeking control over companies in which they invested[28]. Jesse Wang, Chief Risk Officer of CIC, has also stressed that CIC is a passive investor with an emphasis on returns.[29] In a forum in November 2007, Lou Jiwei said that the majority of CIC investment would be in publicly traded securities, although they will also seek direct investment. China's Vice Minister of Finance, Li Yong, said one-third of CIC capital would be used to invest in global financial markets.[30] CIC has defended itself as being one of the most transparent SWFs and according to Jesse Wong the Fund is aiming at conservative 5-6% returns which would be slightly above its funding cost of about 4-5%.[31]

In April 2008, Gao Xiqing announced that CIC would increase its international spending because less cash was needed for domestic investments. The amount of cash allocated to international investments increased to $90 billion from an initial estimated amount of $67 billion (about a third of its total capital). Most of this 30% increase would be invested by external fund managers in non-renminbi-denominated equities, fixed income, hedge funds, private equities and possibly commodities.[32] CIC started its global search for fixed income fund managers who could beat the benchmark returns in early 2008.[33] In 2008, CIC also shifted its investment interest to Asian markets such as Japan and one-third of its foreign investment portfolio will be in Asia.[34]

---

28 "China Investment An Open Book? 60 Minutes: Sovereign Wealth Fund's President Promises Transparency," CBSNEWS, 6 April 2008. http://www.cbsnews.com/stories/2008/04/04/60minutes/main3993933.shtml
29 Jason Dean and Andrew Batson ,"China Investment Fund May Tread Softly," The Wall Street Journal (Eastern Edition) New York, 10 September 2007.
30 Wang Hongjiang, "China's Sovereign Wealth Fund Seeks to be a Stabilizing Presence in Global Markets," Xinhua News, 30 November 2007.
http://news.xinhuanet.com/english/2007-11/30/content_7173963.htm
31 Robin Kwong, "China Sovereign Wealth Fund Rebuffs Critics," Financial Times, 2 April 2008. http://www.ft.com/cms/s/0/da22412a-0117-11dd-a0c5-000077b07658.html
32 See note 20
33 "China Investment Corp Seeks Fixed-income Product Managers," Asia Pulse, 4 February 2008.
34 Chris Oliver, "China's Sovereign Wealth Fund Favors Japanese Investments," Marketwatch, 21 February 2008. http://www.marketwatch.com/story/chinas-sovereign-wealth-fund-favors-japan-investments-nhk

4.2.3 What CIC Has Been Investing In

Even prior to CIC starting up operations, it was already in talks to buy Blackstone, a private equity firm. The agreement for the purchase was facilitated through China Jianyin Investment Ltd, a wholly-owned subsidiary of Central Huijin. The agreement was to purchase less than 10% of non-voting shares in the Blackstone Group for $3 billion.[35] When CIC was set up in September 2007, it took control of both investment companies.[36] Blackstone lost nearly 30% of its value following listing, and the market value is still less than what CIC paid prior to its listing.

On 19 December 2007, Morgan Stanley announced that CIC would pay $5bn for approximately 9.9% of the company on the same day that it announced its fourth quarter loss. Unlike Blackstone which was a pre-IPO stake, the Morgan Stanley stake has been structured to limit CIC's potential loss and its convertible bonds with a 9% return are convertible to stock after a tie-up period. In addition, CIC bought stakes in the state-owned China Railway and in Visa prior to their IPO. CIC's losses in Blackstone and Morgan Stanley may have prompted CIC to adopt a different approach after the subprime crisis. They have opted to invest in index funds and funds managed by professional fund managers such as Legg Mason Inc, Goldman Sachs Group Inc and Invesco Aim Advisors Inc.[37]

CIC has come under local criticism after making losses in overseas investment through to its purchase of foreign financial institutions. The harsh criticism came at a time when China's stock market had hit rock bottom, and many Chinese were unhappy that CIC used capital to invest overseas when the money could have been used to prop up domestic companies. CIC has invested in shares in pre-listed companies but they have not invested in listed Chinese companies. Coupled with domestic opposition, CIC has taken a more cautious approach following huge losses in western financial institutions and has publicly announced that it will stop investing in western financial institutions. Besides the huge losses on its investments, there are concerns about uncertainty over changes in US policies on SWF investment.[38]

---

35 Yan Liang, "China's forex investment company to invest $3 bln in private equity giant Blackstone," Xinhua News, 22 May 2007. http://news.xinhuanet.com/english/2007-05/22/content_6132682.htm
36 Xin Zhiming, "$200 Billion Investment Firm Starts Operation, "China Daily, 1 October 2007. http://www.chinadaily.com.cn/china/2007-10/01/content_6149456.htm
37 "CIC revealed US equity holdings,"Chinadaily, 8 February 2010. http://www.chinadaily.com.cn/bizchina/2010-02/08/content_9442687.htm
38 Raphael Minder, Geof Dyer and Jamal Anderlini, "China sovereign wealth group to stop investing in

This cautious strategy has paid off since the huge loss was reversed and CIC incurred only a small loss of 2.1% for its overseas portfolio and positive return of 6.8% for its entire portfolio. The return of 6.8% was attributable to the excellent performance of Central Huijin.[39] As of 31 December 2008, CIC's portfolio consists of cash funds 87.4%, fixed income security 9.0%, equities 3.2% and other assets 0.4%.[40] CIC revealed that it held $9.63 billion worth of US equities as at 31 December 2009.[41] This amount is small in comparison to the size of the fund.

The rebound in global stock markets in mid-2009 has renewed CIC's interest in overseas acquisition, and it has been buying stakes in foreign-owned energy and resources companies. In March 2009, CIC Deputy Manager Wang Jianxi said in the Chinese People's Political Consultative Conference (CPPCC) that it was a good opportunity for CIC to make international investments, but they would remain a passive investor.[42] In September 2009, CIC bought a stake in the Kazakhstan oil and gas company JSC KazMunaiGas Exploration Production for $939 million. In the following month, the Fund paid $300 million for a 45% stake in Nobel Oil Group, a Russian oil company.[43] It was also revealed in a report in the *Financial Times* that CIC is the fourth largest-investor in US oil exchange-traded funds.[44] CIC's investments in commodities have paid off in 2009 and Lou Jiwei has disclosed that CIC is in talks with Brazil and Mexico who produce iron ore and silver respectively.[45] CIC's ventures into resources companies appears to be part of the Chinese government's wider policy to invest in resources for future growth. However, speculation of a future price hike could also be one of the factors for CIC's investment in resources companies to achieve higher returns, this being in line with CIC's objective to compete with its counterparts in China.

---

western banks," Financial Times, 4 December 2008. http://www.ft.com/cms/s/0/1f527f24-c1a4-11-dd-831e-000077b07658.html
39 Jamal Anderlini, "China wealth fund outperform peers," Financial Times, 7 August 2009. http://www.ft.com/cms/s/0/60489da6-8378-11de-a24e-00144feabdc0.html
40 CIC Annual Report 2008, p.35.
41 See Note 37.
42 Deng Shasha, "China's Sovereign wealth fund sees "good opportunity" for internal investment," Xinhua News, 11 March 2009.
http://news.xinhuanet.com/english/2009-03/11/content_10992451.htm
43 Mu Xuequan, "China sovereign fund buys 45% in Russian oil," Xinhua News, 16 October 2009. http://news.xinhuanet.com/english/2009-10/16/content_12251556.htm
44 Chris Flood, "Chinese fund fillip for oil and gold ETFs," Financial Times, 10 February 2010. http://www.ft.com/cms/s/0/29fd1c38-15e3-11df-b65b-00144feab49a.html
45 "CIC planning more resource investments", Chinadaily, 28 January 2010. http://www.chinadaily.com.cn/bizchina/2010-01/28/content_9390095.htm

CIC has recently ventured into property investment when the Fund bailed the shareholders of UK's Song Bird Estates. By providing the needed cash for Songbird Estate to repay its bank loan, CIC owns about 19% of the company.[46] The investment has resulted in CIC's first venture into overseas real estate investment. Given that real estate investment is an inflation indexed investment and would provide substantial return in the long run, CIC is likely to increase real estate in its portfolio when the opportunity arises. The Fund is actively searching for opportunity to invest in commercial real estate investments in the USA.[47]

4.2.4 CIC's Investments in its Domestic Market

CIC's investment strategies are partly constrained by its commitment to take over Central Huijin. Having Central Huijin in the CIC portfolio could prove to be a liability as this company was set up to recapitalise China's state-owned banks and thus CIC took over this task. In addition, CIC was committed to provide capital to the Agriculture Bank of China and the China Development Bank.[48] An additional $2.7 billion was invested in China's Everbright Bank prior to its IPO in the Hong Kong stock market and China's A-share stock market in 2008; the purchase of a 70.92% stake was made through Central Huijin.[49] CIC clearly plays an important role in the banking sector in China, having control over many large state-owned commercial banks. According to research by Altbach and Cognato (2008), CIC's banks hold 58% of all bank assets and 59% of all loans in China.[50] There is no report on how the foreign currency injected into the domestic banks will be used but given Chinese firms' aggressive acquisitions in overseas markets, CIC's injections of cash are likely to be used by these banks to acquire stakes in foreign banks.

CIC also holds a 43.35% stake in China's largest investment bank, International Capital Corporation (CICC), the investment being held under China Jianyin Investment Limited.[51] CICC has been involved in all the high-

---

46 Daniel Thomas, "China aids Songbird rescue," Financial Times, 29 August 2009. http://www.ft.com/cms/s/0/eb5e6d10-9432-11de-9c57-00144feabdc0.html
47 Henny Sender, "US property attracts opportunistic investment," Financial Times, 11 January 2010. http://www.ft.com/cms/s/0/a52fabae-fe51-11de-9340-00144feab49a.html
48 "China to shift $20 billion as Capital for Policy Bank," The New York Times, 1 January 2008. http://www.nytimes.com/2008/01/01/business/01bank.html?_r=1
49 Mao Lijun, "Central Huijin bails out Everbright bank," Chinadaily, 8 November 2007. http://www.chinadaily.com.cn/china/2007-11/08/content_6239074.htm
50 Eric G. Altbach and Micheal H. Cognato, "Understanding China's New Sovereign Wealth Fund," NBR Analysis, The National Bureau of Asian Research, 19(1), p24, 2008.
51 CICC website, 18 October 2009. http://www.cicc.com.cn/CICC/english/about/page2.htm

CASE STUDIES

profile outward investments of most of the state-owned enterprises such as PetroChina and CNOOC. The other shareholders of CICC are Morgan Stanley, GIC and two other Chinese firms. CIC holds an 85.5% stake in China Reinsurance as a result of taking over Central Huijin while the remaining 14.5% is held by the Ministry of Finance.[52] The most recent domestic investment by CIC was the tie-up with a Canadian company in a coal mine in Mongolia. In recent years, China's state-owned enterprises have been the biggest investors in the commodities industries, and these investments are made due to the availability of opportunities rather than out of strategic investment decisions. They have also increased direct investment in companies instead of just being a financial investor.

4.2.4 Summary of CIC's Investment Strategy

Looking at the various investments made by CIC since its inception, one may question whether it has any investment strategy. It is difficult to determine whether CIC's lack of cohesive strategy is due to the teething problems of a new fund or a power struggle within the state bureaucracy, or both. CIC was created as a new investment vehicle to manage China's foreign exchange reserves and to soak up excess liquidity. The Chinese government needs to counter the excess net inflow of foreign exchange in order to prevent inflation and asset bubbles in its domestic market, and CIC provides this facility.

Despite the lack of clear strategy, CIC has performed well for a relatively new SWF and is expected to report good performance for the financial year 2009. However, CIC still has much to learn when investing overseas and it will take some time for it to develop a clearer strategy, which it does not appear to have at present. A *Financial Times* reporter wrote: 'Such a concentration of the country's wealth in one entity has inevitably drawn intense interest, not just from every fund manager on the planet but also from powerful forces within the state bureaucracy.'[53] An example of CIC's lack of strategy is that Li Yong initially said it would not buy into oil companies, but in October 2009 CIC bought a 45% stake in a Russian oil company and CIC has recently invested in the coal mining industry in the domestic market. CIC's inclusion of commodities in its portfolio makes one wonder whether it is attracted by the expected higher commodity prices or is playing a part in the Chinese

---
52 "CIC takes over supervision of China Reinsurance's Management Team," Wall Street Journal, 19 June 2009.
53 Jamal Anderlini, "China Wealth Fund's Early Coming of Age," Financial Times, 20 December 2007. http://www.ft.com/cms/s/0/b8cca8a0-af2b-11dc-880f-0000779fd2ac.html

government's strategic move to accumulate natural resources. A report from the *Financial Times* described CIC investment activities in the commodity sector as playing the role of "piggy bank for China Inc global expansion".[54]

In addition, following its losses from investment in US investment banks, CIC adopted a different strategy in its US equity investments. Instead of direct investments, CIC invests in index funds and funds managed by professional fund managers. This allows CIC to gain wider exposure to the US market without having to do the due diligence itself. This investment strategy suits a new SWF which does not have expertise in the sector. The switch from direct investment to being a financial investor will also reduce political backlash from the West.

As a new fund, it has little experience in fund management and has previously been constrained by its capital structure. The high financing cost of the capital indirectly forced CIC to invest in higher risk investments in order to make returns to finance its interest payment to the Ministry of Finance. However, the new agreement made in February 2009 removes this constraint and CIC only needs to pay a dividend on a regular basis instead of the high interest. This change in capital structure changes CIC's initial investment plans so they are no longer under pressure to meet the high interest payments. However, CIC faces competition from other state investment funds such as SAFE which is responsible for investing China's foreign reserves in the domestic and overseas markets.

CIC is following Temasek's model by playing a strategic role in the country's industrial development. At the same time, it faces calls to help local state-owned enterprises to venture into overseas investment in order to build these companies into multinational firms.[55] Arthur Kroeber, a consultant from Dragonomics in Beijing, commented that due to integrating Central Huijin as part of its operations, CIC 'looks to be more an instrument of China's industrial policy than a true international investment fund'[56] (see Table 4.3 on CIC's investments). The CIC portfolio includes major Chinese banks and global brands. Its overseas investments involve US and Russian companies, but given that CIC is created to diversify away from US dollar and to hedge the currency risk in the balance sheet of the country's central bank, it is likely

---

[54] Jamil Anderlini, "CIC accepts role as piggy bank for China Inc," Financial Times, 4 March 2009. http://www.ft.com/cms/s/0/47cc33ea-08e5-11de-b8b0-0000779fd2ac.html

[55] Li Yanzhen,"Li Rongrong: Zhongtou gongsi jiang bangzhu yangqi jiada haiwau touzi lidu,"Xinhua News, 13 September 2007. http://news.xinhuanet.com/newscenter/2007-09/13/content_6713982.htm

[56] Richard Mcgregor, "China moves from hunter to gatherer," Financial Times, 21 August 2007. http://www.ft.com/cms/s/0/4c348b7a-5000-11dc-a6b0-0000779fd2ac.html

for the Fund to invest in non-US dollar denominated assets in the future. If CIC concentrates its overseas investments in US companies, it will defeat the purpose of using the Fund to hedge against the US currency risk.

Following initial teething problems and changes in its capital structure, CIC seems likely to develop a clearer and more coherent investment strategy. However, this coherence will depend on whether the Fund is being used as a political tool within China. Before CIC was launched, there were political issues relating to the control of CIC as a result of the power struggle between the Ministry of Finance and the People's Bank of China. It was finally decided that CIC would report to the State Council directly, yet it is still viewed as being linked to the Ministry of Finance. CIC is under pressure to perform well on its investments to justify the need to have another investment vehicle for foreign reserves other than the existing SAFE under the People's Bank of China. In addition, further capital injections into CIC will depend on its performance as it competes with other state-owned investment agencies for funding. These factors will lead CIC to make higher risk investments despite its losses in 2008.

Table 4.3: CIC's Major Investments

INVESTMENTS	DATE	STAKE	COST
Blackstone Group	May 2007	9.9%	$3bn+
Morgan Stanley	December 2007	9.9%	$5bn+
Visa			$100m
Nobel Oil Group	October 2009	45%	$300m
Teck Resources Ltd		17.2%	C$1.74 bn+
KazMunaiGas Exploration Production	September 2009	11%	$939 million+
JC Flower Private Equity Fund			$4 bn+
China Railway Group	November 2007		$100m
Agriculture Bank of China (acquired by Central Huijin)	2004	50.0%*	$40-50bn est
Bank of China (acquired by Central Huijin)	2004	67.5%*	$22.5bn
China Development Bank		48.7%*	$20 bn

INVESTMENTS	DATE	STAKE	COST
China Everbright Bank (acquired by Central Huijin)		70.92%	$2.7 bn
China Construction Bank (acquired by Central Huijin)		48.2%*	
Industrial and Commercial Bank of China (acquired by Central Huijin)		35.4%*	$15 bn
China International Capital Corporation		43.35%	
China Reinsurance (acquired by Central Huijin)	2004	85.5%	$4 bn

Source: * CIC Annual Report 2008, p.35, + Sovereign Wealth Fund Institute 18 October 2009 and updated by author from various news articles.

4.3 Temasek Holdings

Temasek is the first non-commodity SWF with a history of more than 30 years. Unlike publicity shy ADIA, it has received a great deal of attention, both positive and negative, on its investments particularly from the domestic market. It is now viewed as a role model for other SWFs. Temasek's investment policy is a mixture of return and strategic motivation and it is known for its holding of stakes in Singaporean companies such as Singapore Airlines, Singapore Telecom and the Development Bank of Singapore etc. While its Asian investments have attracted much scrutiny in the region and on many occasions its overseas investments are criticised by regional governments and press, its domestic investments have drawn scepticism from its own people. Compared with other SWFs, Temasek holds major stakes in Singapore companies and they are also proactive shareholders. Those companies with Temasek as a direct shareholder holding a stake of at least 20% are normally referred to as Temasek-Linked Companies (TLCs).[57] It exercises active control over these companies including the appointment of chairmen, directors and senior management personnel. Basically Temasek focussed more on domestic and regional markets. But since Ho Ching became CEO of the Fund in 2002, it has made more direct investments in the region and in other continents.

---
57 "Temasek companies vs GLCs: There's a difference," Singapore Business Times, 25 June 1999.

To understand Temasek's investment policy and strategy, its investments in the domestic market are first examined, followed by its overseas investments and finally the overall investment portfolio.

4.3.1 Temasek's Investments in Domestic Market

Temasek was set up in 1974 with surpluses from the Ministry of Finance. The investment policy in the early days aimed at transforming the country's economy. Temasek was set up to take over state-owned enterprises and develop key industries, while the government focussed on policy-making and administration. Although the policy to develop key industries is still upheld, this policy is no longer the top priority judging from the Fund's diversification into the region and other markets. The strong presence of Temasek in Singapore's economy has drawn many criticisms both within and outside the country. Temasek was set up at a time when the government policy was to create key industries and provide more jobs for the citizens. Its portfolio includes airlines, financial institutions, property, shipping and telecommunication.

In the early days of Temasek's operation, the focus was to develop key industries in Singapore to reinvent the government-linked corporations (those initially held by the government such as Singapore Airlines, Singapore Telecom, Neptune Orient Lines, etc). In the 1980s it began to sell non-strategic companies and divested the government-linked corporations. In 1985 Singapore Airlines was listed and Singapore Mass Rapid Transit was incorporated.

One investment policy of Temasek is to advance Singapore's economic interests, for example, building up the biomedical industry. Temasek, together with the Economic Development Board and Novartis Bioventures, jointly invested $13.5 million in MerLion Pharmaceuticals to fund the privatised centre for pre-clinical trials of some early stage drugs in 2002.[58] Such a move to fund a start-up industry with long-term investment horizon is not uncommon in the USA. Wisconsin and Pennsylvania state governments have made similar investments to provide seed money for biomedical entrepreneurs. Chartered Semiconductor Manufacturing, a TLC, had been making losses for years and only returned to profitability in 2006. According to Singapore's media in 2004, Temasek held onto the loss-making firm for years because the chip industry

---

58 Andy Ho, "Government should lead the way in funding bio start-ups," *Singapore Straits Times*, 2 November 2002.

contributes significantly to the economy and provides jobs for more than 280,000 people in the country.[59]

Temasek Chairman S Dhanabalan told reporters in an interview in 1999 that the target for TLC's performance is positive shareholder value-added (SVA)[60] with a three-year time frame and monitoring of the firms' performance with an industry benchmark.[61] However, no detail of the benchmark was given. Although Temasek is proactive in the appointment of key personnel, the day-to-day operation was left to the appointed management team. Temasek announced a plan to cut the Fund's influence in the domestic economy in 2002 and outlined a series of overseas investment plans. The reduction in its stake in some of the TLCs was part of Temasek's move to diversify into regional and international markets, although there was speculation that the diversification was driven by the Free Trade Agreement with the US. The diversification is unlikely to be politically motivated because Temasek still has a strong hold on key industries such as logistics, energy, property and telecommunication although it now has a reduced stake in TLCs such as Singapore Telecommunication and sold off its investment in Natsteel. In 2004, Ho Ching from Temasek said the Fund's plan was to invest one-third of its funds in the domestic market, one-third in Asia and another third in other markets.[62] This type of geographical diversification would allow the Fund to gain a presence in regions of high growth and avoid the pitfalls of regional crises. According to the 2009 Annual Report, investments in Singapore went down from 33% to 31%.

4.3.2 Temasek's Regional Investments

In 1989, the Fund started its globalisation and regionalisation drive in America and Europe, with investments that included Thistle Hotels. However, the overseas investment emphasis shifted to Asia-Pacific in 1994 and the Fund concentrated on China, Thailand and Vietnam. Investing in the region allows Temasek to tap into the benefits from regional growth and also enables the Fund to diversify out of the small market in Singapore. Temasek investments in the region can be best summed up as a mixture of direct investments with others in the form of venture capitalisation providing seed money. Some of Temasek's direct investments in the region have met with some political

---

59 Bryan Lee, "What's so strategic about owning a bleeding company?" *Singapore Straits Times*, 16 December 2004.
60 Shareholder value added (SVA) is also known as Economic value added (EVA).
61 "Target: Postive SVA in three years," *Singapore Business Times*, 25 June 1999.
62 "Temasek wants to partner promising Asian firms," *Singapore Straits Times*, 18 August 2004.

backlash from regional governments. It expansion in the region has been perceived as economic imperialism by Singapore.[63]

Between 1994-1996, at least three investment funds were jointly set up by Temasek and other institutional investors to invest in new regional companies. This approach serves Temasek well because teaming up with other institutional investors allows Temasek to tap into the expertise of these investors and at the same time avoid politically sensitive issues when investing in the region. The AIG Asian Infrastructure, which was targeted to reach $1 billion, was jointly set up by American International Group, Temasek, GIC and Emerging Market Partnership in 1994.[64] Temasek and GIC jointly invested $250 million and other investors included institutional investors from China and the US. With investment interest in East Asia, one-third to a half of the Fund was invested in projects in China while the rest moved to Indonesia, Malaysia, the Philippines, Taiwan and Thailand. In the following year, Temasek teamed up with Lazard Asia Investment and the Exor Group (Agnelli family) to set up a $250 million fund to invest mainly in manufacturing and services in China, Indochina and other Asean nations. Temasek provided 20% of the fund. Yet another investment fund was set up with Mitsubishi Corporation and Bangkok Bank to invest in promising new companies in the region. It had an initial capitalisation of $100 million and Temasek contributed 30% towards this.[65] There is hardly any information on the activities of these funds except for their initial launch.

Temasek also takes direct stakes in regional companies. It holds such stakes in banks in China, Indonesia, India, Pakistan and South Korea. There were speculations that Temasek was acquiring regional banks to build a banking network to compete with other Singaporean banks because Temasek is the major shareholder of Development Bank of Singapore (DBS). However, looking at the regional banks that Temasek has invested in, it does not seem that these banks have been acquired to compete with other Singaporean banks. The fund's investment in Indonesian banks could be seen as value-for-money investments. The two banks concerned have well-established branch networks in Indonesia and they are banks which were set up under the Indonesian government's restructuring effort in the country's banking sector after the 1998 financial crisis. Bank Danamon has an extensive branch

---

[63] INVESTMENT- Tough time for Temasek. 10 April 2006, Asiamoney.com, Euromoney Institutional Investor plc.
[64] "S'pore Govt, US firm in mega investment fund," Singapore Straits Times, 22 February 1994.
[65] Conrad Raj, "Temasek teams up with 2 Asian corporate giants," Singapore Business Times, 15 January 1996.

network in Indonesia and has a successful microfinance model in Indonesia. Using a similar microfinance model to Bank Danamon's, Temasek launched microfinance banking in India[66] in 2006 and in China[67] in early 2009 under Fullerton Financial Holding Pte Ltd. Microfinance is potentially a big market in India and China given the large number of small enterprises that lack access to bank loans in these countries. The acquisition of Bank Danamon is part of Temasek's strategic plan to use the bank's microfinance model to build a microfinance market in China and India. Investments in Korean banks and Pakistani financial institutions also form part of Temasek's plan to venture into countries where Singaporean banks do not have a strong presence. Again acquiring banks in China and India forms part of Temasek's strategy to tap into these countries finance industry, which complements the fund's operation in the microfinance industry. However, Temasek was forced to sell off its 56% stake in Bank International Indonesia to Maybank in 2008 due to its failure to merge the two Indonesian banks in its portfolio. Under Indonesia's single-presence policy, investors are prohibited from controlling more than one local bank.

Temasek makes substantial investments in real estate in the region through its subsidiaries Mapletree Investments and Capital Land. Its portfolio includes commercial buildings, office buildings and property developments in countries such as China and India. These investments are acquired through direct investments and fund investments such as Mapletree India-China Fund. It has also bought a 42% stake in Shin Corporpration, Thailand's largest telecommunication company. Most of its regional investments in logistics industries have been invested through its wholly-owned subsidiary, PSA International.

4.3.3 Temasek's International Investments

The investments in Merrill and Barclays indicate a shift of Temasek's investments from Asia to other developed markets. However, this move into the international market has come at the wrong time with the uncertainties after the subprime crisis. Despite making a paper loss on its $4.4 billion investment, Temasek raised its stake in Merrill Lynch to 9.46% in March 2008.[68] When Merrill was taken over by Bank of America in early 2009, Temasek held

---

66 *Official website of Fullerton India Credit Company Ltd, http://www.fullertonindia.com/*
67 *Zhao Hongmei, Sohu Finance, 2 May 2009. http://business.sohu.com/20090502/n263733781.shtml*
68 *John Burton, "Temasek adds to Merrill stake," Financial Times, 16 April 2008. http://www.ft.com/ cms/s/0/e03cb476-0b4b-11dd-8ccf-0000779fd2ac.html*

an approximate 3.8% stake in Bank of America after conversion. However, the entire stake was sold not long after the conversion and the speculated loss was estimated to be around $2 billion.[69] When Temasek sold off its stake in Barclays in 2009, it made a loss of $815 million. Temasek did not buy into Barclays because of the subprime crisis but because of Barclays' attempt to raise funds to buy ABN Amro.[70] Because of these investments in western financial institutions Temasek suffered huge losses.

Temasek also holds stakes in drug development companies in Austria (i.e. Intercell AG) and the US (i.e. Vical Inc). The Fund invested in the biomedical industry as early as 2002 to provide seed money to the local industry. All these investments complemented the Singaporean government's industrial policy to build a biomedical industry in Singapore and to reap the profits from the world's ageing population. Given Temasek's lack of expertise in this sector, they are unlikely to hold significant direct stakes but will make investments through funds.

In view of the potential growth in emerging economies such as Latin America, Temasek has set up an office in Brazil and Mexico. According to Alan Thompson, Managing Director of the Brazil office, there are long-term, attractive investments to be made in Latin America.[71] Prior to setting up the Brazil office, Temasek had already invested in a Brazilian private equity company, GP Partners Capital IV. A Moscow-based investment bank told the media in March 2007 that Temasek is doubling its investment in Russia to $300 million. The investments will be made through the Russia New Growth Fund which targets investments in retail, entertainment and financial businesses.[72] Given Temasek's experience in investing in financial institutions, ports and real estate in Asian emerging markets, it would not be surprise to see Temasek making such investments in Latin America and Russia.

4.3.4 Summary of Temasek's Investments

As a proactive shareholder, Temasek has a strong hold on key industries in Singapore. Many have questioned why the Singaporean government has

---

[69] John Burton, "Temask sells entire stake in BofA," Financial Times, 15 May 2009. http://www.ft.com/cms/s/0/e8496f42-4100-11de-8f18-00144feabdc0.html

[70] Jane Croft and John Burton, "Temasek loses £500m on Barclays sell-off," Financial Times, 4 June 2009. http://www.ft.com/cms/s/0/eab5c5a6-509f-11de-9530-00144feabdc0.html

[71] "Temasek taps Brazil as window to Latin America," Singapore Business Times, 7 January 2009.

[72] Netty Ismail, "Temasek will double Russia fund investment," International Herald Tribune, 6 March 2007.

played such a big role in the private sector, an issue being actively debated not only inside but also outside the country. There is no doubt that Temasek has played a significant role in building key industries in Singapore and indeed in building their (Temasek Linked Companies) TLCs into global brands. As an investment fund without any political consideration, it does make sense for Temasek to hold on to these companies as long as they are generating positive economic added-value (EVA). Temasek has over time reduced its investments in Singapore and currently only one-third of its investments are in the country. Overall, in 2009 Temasek increased its investment in North Asia by 5% but reduced its Asean investment from 12% to 9%. The investment in Singapore was reduced from 33% to 31% (see Figure 4.1).

Figure 4.1: Temasek's Portfolio by Geographic Location in 2008 and 2009

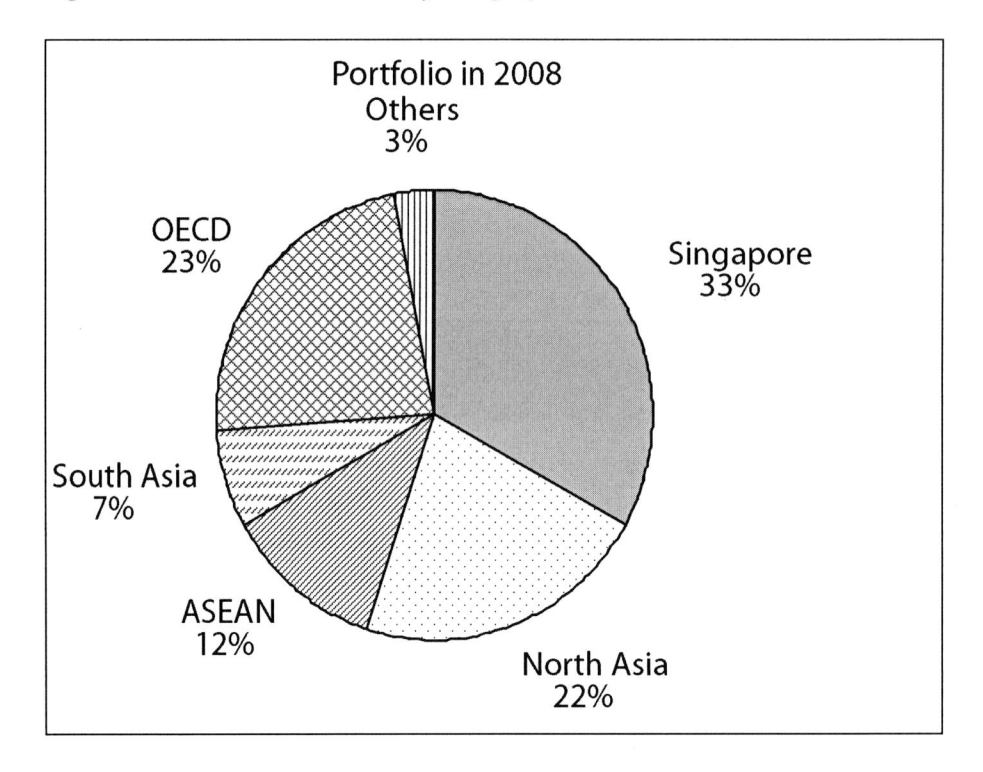

Portfolio in 2008
- Others 3%
- OECD 23%
- Singapore 33%
- South Asia 7%
- ASEAN 12%
- North Asia 22%

CASE STUDIES

Portfolio in 2009

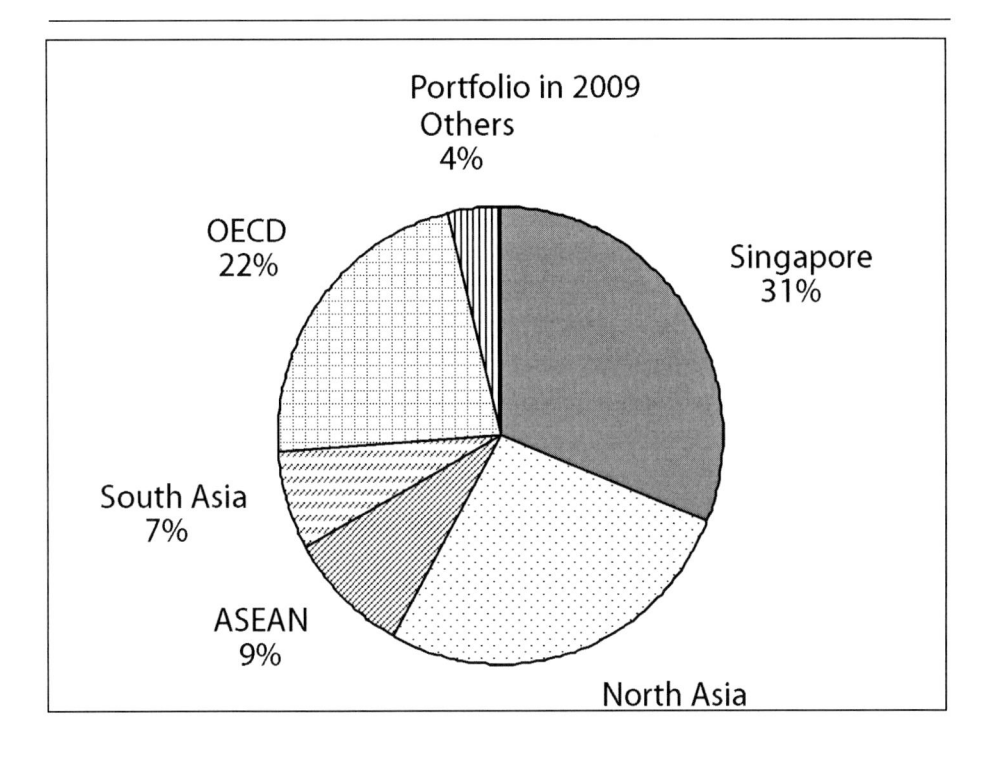

- Others 4%
- OECD 22%
- Singapore 31%
- South Asia 7%
- ASEAN 9%
- North Asia

Source: Temasek Review 2008, 2009.

Note: North Asia includes China, Taiwan and Korea; ASEAN excludes Singapore; South Asia refers to India and Pakistan; OECD excludes Korea. Mexico was classified as OECD in 2004 and reclassified as Latin America and others in 2009.

Temasek has been investing in emerging economies in Asia for many years and given its knowledge of business in the region, the Fund has been aggressively expanding its investments. They are also keen to tap into countries such as Brazil, Russia, India and China (BRIC) where there is high growth potential. Its investments in banks in China, India, Pakistan and South Korea suggest that Temasek will continue to grow its share in the financial services sector in the region and perhaps also in the emerging markets of Latin America and Russia. The Singaporean government is keen to build the country into a key international financial sector and Temasek itself into a global banking network through its direct stakes in foreign banks. The Temasek investment in regional banks is rooted in the belief that the demand for banking services will increase due to the increase of the middle class population in the region.[73]

[73] John Burton, "Temasek develops regional strategy," *Financial Times*, 23 July 2007. http://www.ft.com/cms/s/0/0df7ea98-395b-11dc-ab48-0000779fd2ac.html

Examining Temasek's portfolio in different sectors, we can see that the Fund has continued to concentrate on familiar sectors which have a strong presence in its domestic market. Temasek is keen to make investments in companies they are familiar with. In 2008, 40% of Temasek's investments were in the financial services, 24% in telecommunications and 10% in transportation and logistics. Compared to its sister fund GIC, Temasek is much less aggressive in real estate acquisition. This strategy makes sense because GIC has positioned itself as a big player in global real estate investment whereas Temasek, which concentrates on financial services, telecommunication and transportation and logistics, has aimed to be a big player in its own domestic markets. Termasek's portfolio in different sectors is fairly consistent except for the financial services which had a 5% increase from 2006 to 2008. However, the investment was reduced to 33% as a result of the loss incurred in investing in Merrill and Barclays. As indicated in Figure 4.2, while investments in "Telecommunication and Media", "Real Estate" and "Others" grew in 2009, investment in "Technology" fell from 2% to 1%. It was also reported in the 2009 Annual Report that the Fund held 72% of liquid assets, which implies that most of its investments are in listed companies (see Figure 4.2 on Temasek's portfolio in different sectors).

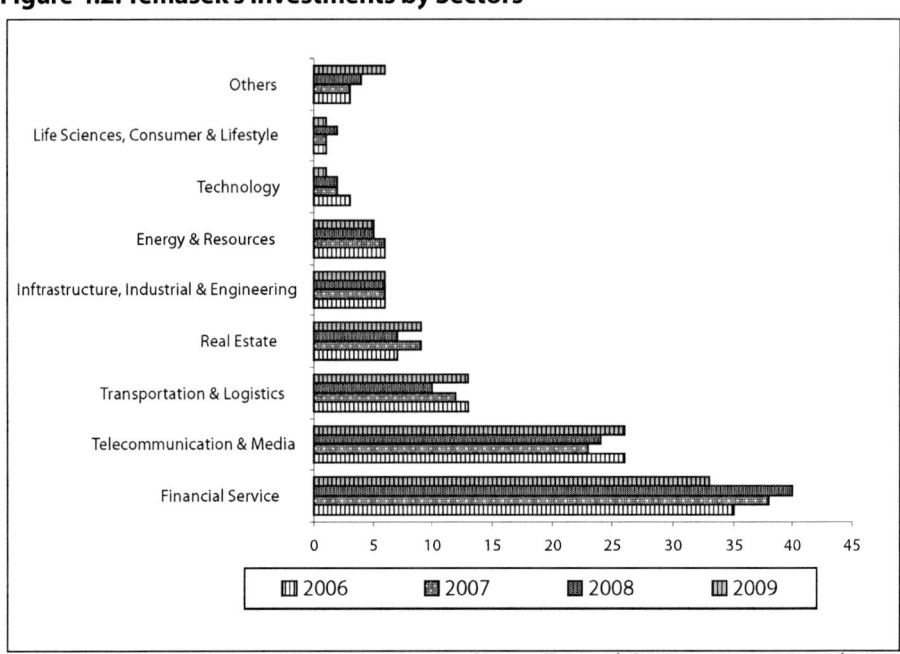

Figure 4.2: Temasek's Investments by Sectors

Source: Temasek Review 2007, 2008 and 2009.

Temasek has been less successful in its investments in western financial institutions and is criticised by Singaporeans for its investment strategies. There was even speculation that Ho Ching's resignation from Temasek was due to the huge losses in Merrill and Barclays. After selling off stakes in these two banks, Temasek has mainly reverted to investments in the emerging economies they are more familiar with. They have also moved into Latin America and Russia and are looking for opportunities in these countries. With its past and continuing successes in emerging economies in Asia, Temasek's interest in Latin America and Russia is a strategic move to tap their expertise in these emerging economies and its own pool of talent.

As reported in its 2008 Annual Report, Temasek is valued at S$185 billion and its total shareholder return is 18% compounded annually by market value. Its one-year total share return (TSR) by shareholder funds is 17%. The value of the Fund in 2008 was S$21 billion more than it was in 2007. The increase in value was partly contributed to by the profits made from selling the Tuas power plant, Bank International Indonesia and a small stake in Telekom Malaysia. In addition, the Ministry of Finance injected a S$10 billion cashflow into Temasek to help boost its portfolio to S$185 billion as of 31 March 2008.[74] Figure 4.3 shows consistent growth for the Fund from 2004 to 2008 but its value fell significantly in 2009 because investments in Merrill and Barclays made huge losses. In February 2009, Temask revealed that it had made a paper loss of S$58 billion in eight months.[75] Hence, the fund value fell to S$130 billion in 2009. Temasek's total shareholder return since its inception fell to 16% compound annually and its one-year TSR by shareholder fund is now -18%.[76] The Fund also made a net divestment of 7% from 1 April 2008 to 31 March 2009.

---

74 *"$10b boost from the Finance Ministry," Singapore Straits Times, 27 August 2008.*
75 *Emilyn Yap, "2 years of Temasek growth wiped out in months," Singapore Business Times, 11 February 2009.*
76 *Temasek Review 2009, p6.*

Figure 4.3: Temasek's Portfolio Value in Singapore Dollars (Billions) as at 31 March

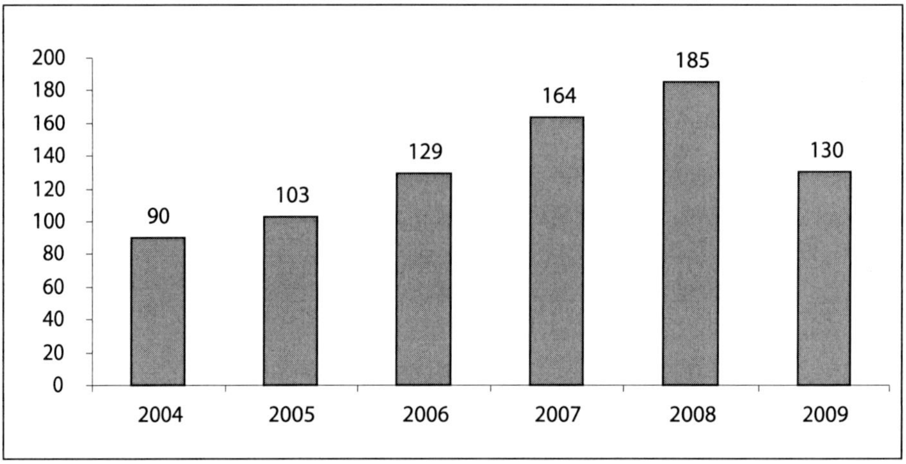

Year	Value
2004	90
2005	103
2006	129
2007	164
2008	185
2009	130

Source: Temasek Review 2008 and 2009

Table 4.4 shows the list of companies in which Temasek has made significant stakes. Unlike other SWFs, Temasek does not shy away from holding large stakes in foreign companies, and in particular banks. But it is also noticeable that, except for Standard Chartered, most of these major stakes are in emerging economies. And it is worth noting that most of the business of Standard Chartered is in Asia. Except for banks, Temasek's investments outside the domestic market are mainly made through its wholly-owned subsidiaries or by funds set up for specific investments. For investments with large stakes, Temasek has a long-term investment horizon and adopts an active management approach. They have taken large stakes in some companies with the view of expanding them.

Table 4.4: Temasek's Major Investments (Percentage of Core Interest as at 31 March)

COMPANIES	DATE	COUNTRY	2008	2009
NIB	2005	Pakistan	63	74
PT Bank Danamon Indonesia	2003	Indonesia	58	68
PT Bank Internasional Indonesia	2003	Indonesia	48	0
DBS Group Holdings	1975	Singapore	28	28
Standard Chartered	2006	UK	19	19
Hana Financial Group	2004	South Korea	10	10

CASE STUDIES

COMPANIES	DATE	COUNTRY	2008	2009
Merrill Bank	2007	US	9	0
ICICI Bank	2003	India	8	8
China Construction Bank	2005	China	6	6
Bank of China	2005	China	4	4
Barclays	2007	UK	2	0
MediaCorp	1992	Singapore	100	100
Singapore Technologies Telemedia	1995	Singapore	100	100
Singapore Telecommunications	1993	Singapore	55	54
Shin Corporation	2006	Thailand	42	42
Bharti Airtel	2007	India	5	5
PSA International	1997	Singapore	100	100
Neptune Orient Lines	1975	Singapore	66	66
Singapore Airlines	1975	Singapore	54	55
SMRT Corporation	1987	Singapore	54	54
Mapletree Investment	2001	Singapore	100	100
Capital Land	2000	Singapore	40	40
Singapore Technologies Engineering	1997	Singapore	50	50
Sembcorp Industries	1983	Singapore	49	49
Keppel Corporation	1975	Singapore	21	21
PowerSeraya	1995	Singapore	100	0
Senoko Power	1995	Singapore	100	0
Singapore Power	1995	Singapore	100	100
STATS ChipPAC	1995	Singapore	83	84
Chartered Semiconductor Manufacturing	1987	Singapore	59	59
Wildlife Reserves Singapore	1975	Singapore	88	88
Li & Fung	2008	Hong Kong	0	5
Fraser and Neave	2007	Singapore	15	15

Source: Temasek Review 2008 and 2009

4.4 Government of Singapore Investment Corporation (GIC)

Unlike Temasek, GIC's funds come from Singapore's central bank, the Monetary Authority of Singapore. With investments in more than 40 countries, GIC is one of the most active SWFs in the international market and has offices in London, New York, Frankfurt, Tokyo and Shanghai. Even though the fund involved is larger, it is less transparent in its investments than Temasek. Reports on the Fund are less detailed although its investments generally generate headlines in domestic and overseas media. GIC does not invest in local stock markets but concentrates most of its investments in developed markets. In particular, GIC is a big player in the real estate sector in such developed countries as Australia and Japan, and in Europe.

To understand more about the investment strategy of GIC, the following section examines its investments in terms of geographical distribution and investment portfolio.

4.4.1 GIC Investments by Geographical Distribution

As can be seen from Table 4.5, investments in America have increased from 40% to 45% in 2009 but there is a 4% increase in investments in the United States. Almost all the investments are based in developed markets except for China (which is classified under "North Asia") and emerging economies such as Russia (classified under "Others"). The subprime crisis and recession in developed economies drove the Fund to increase their investments in Asia and other emerging economies although they are still interested in investing in distressed western financial institutions.[77] The Fund is likely to rebalance its current geographical composition to include more investment in Asia and other emerging economies.

Apart from its real estate investments in China, one of GIC's early ventures into China was a 7.5% stake in the Chinese investment bank CICC. The Fund is likely to increase its investments in China after setting up an office in Shanghai in 2007. Like other SWFs such as ADIA and Temasek, GIC is also actively looking for investments in emerging economy such as BRIC. One interesting point to note is that the percentage of investments in the US, UK and Japan is high

---

77 John Burton, "GIC switches focus to Asian assets," *Financial Times*, 23 September 2008. http://www.ft.com/cms/s/0/87644716-8953-11dd-8371-0000779fd18c.html

and these countries, on the whole, have the most liquid stock markets. In investing almost one-third of its Fund in the USA, GIC apparently adopts a strategy very similar to that of ADIA. However, GIC adopts a direct investment approach in countries where the capital markets are underdeveloped and offer little room for portfolio investments. For example, GIC tied up with a Taiwanese food and animal feed company to develop the feed and poultry market in China's northeast in 1997.[78]

GIC's investments in Taiwan are diverse and consist mainly of publicly listed shares. In 1995 the Fund was allowed to invest up to $300 million in the Taiwan stock market after a good two-year track record. The Taiwan stock market has a ceiling of $200 million to avoid manipulative and speculative activities.[79] As far as GIC's investments in Australia are concerned, real estate investments make up the major component. Their portfolio includes Shangri-La Hotels at The Rocks in Sydney and the Park Hyatt in Melbourne.

Table 4.5: Portfolio by Geographical Distribution as of 31 March (in Percentages)

		2008	2009
America	United States	34	38
	Others	6	7
Europe	United Kingdom	8	6
	France	5	5
	Germany	3	4
	Italy	3	3
	Others	16	11
Asia	Japan	11	11
	North Asia	8	10
	Others	4	3
Australasia	Australia	2	2
Total		100	100

Source: GIC Report on the Management of the Government's Portfolio for Year 2007/08 and 2008/2009 GIC

---

78 Lu Ning, "GIC in US$24m China feed venture: report," Singapore Business Times, 18 February 1997.
79 "Taiwan ups stock investment limit for GIC," Singapore Straits Times, 24 June 1995.

4.4.2 GIC's Investment Portfolio by Asset Class

Table 4.6 shows that GIC had invested 38% of its Fund in equity markets, with 28% in developed markets as at 31 March 2009. The investments in equities in developed markets dropped from 34% to 28% between 2008 and 2009. They invested 24% in fixed income and 30% in alternatives (real estate, private equity, venture capital, infrastructure, absolute return strategies and natural resources). The increase was due to the Fund's increased exposure in real estate, private equity, venture capital, infrastructure and natural resources.

Table 4.6: Portfolio by Asset Distribution as of 31 March (in percentage)

		2008	2009
Public Equities	Developed Markets	34	28
	Emerging Markets	10	10
Fixed Income	Nominal Bonds	20	19
	Inflation-Linked Bonds	6	5
Alternatives	Real Estates	10	12
	Private Equity, Venture Capital & Infrastructure	8	11
	Absolute Return Strategies	3	3
	Natural Resources	2	4
Cash & Others		7	8
Total		100	100

Source: GIC Report on the Management of the Government's Portfolio for Years 2007/08 and 2008/2009

Due to the volatility in the financial market after the subprime crisis, the Fund has reduced its exposure in the equities market, an unusual move for GIC who have usually been active investors. As indicated in Table 4.5, GIC increased its investment in the USA in 2009 which suggests that it is making more direct investments there. In May 2008, the Fund invested $400 million (11% stake) in a US-based energy infrastructure company, AEI.[80] In 2009 GIC held 8% of its fund in cash and other investments in anticipation of opportunities arising from the subprime crisis. This is in line with one of their investment policies – to invest in distressed companies. With this amount of cash in hand, they were able to buy stakes in UBS and Citigroup which were in need of

---
80 "GIC gets energy boost with AEI stake," Singapore Business Times, 14 May 2008.

liquidity due to their huge losses in subprime investments. GIC's investments in distressed companies are made with a long-term view to avoid loss. GIC was reported to have made a profit of $1.6 billion after selling off half of its stake in Citigroup in September 2009.[81] In total GIC has made a profit of $3.2 billion on its investment in Citigroup, including a $1.6 billion unrealised profit.

In 2001 GIC revealed its approach to investment in equity markets. The Fund picks its stocks based on sector rather than country or region. The six global sectors that the Fund has invested in are technology, financial services, consumer cyclicals, consumer non-cyclicals (companies such as food and pharmaceuticals which are not affected by demand volatility), telecommunications and commodities (mainly the major oil companies). It also has a "research portfolio" on investments managed by research analysts and portfolio managers. The research analysts are obliged to express their views and strategies for their portfolios and be accountable for the stocks they have picked.[82]

Table 4.6 shows that GIC holds 12% of its investment in real estate as at 31 March 2009. However, it is difficult to assess the exact value of investments in this sector because it holds these real estate investments in different forms. Prior to its diversifying into other sectors, real estate investments had been its core business since its inception. GIC Real Estate is reported to be among the world's top property investors and the real estate investments have regularly contributed to the Fund's huge gains for almost 20 years. GIC has chosen to invest in real estate because it is less dependent on global financial market movements, and therefore, less risky. Nevertheless, its long-term return is higher than bonds but more stable than equities.

The Real Estate Division of GIC has helped to manage its investments in real estate since 1999. The Fund is invested directly in properties, real estate investment trusts, property companies and real estate debts. Some of these investments are made using subsidiaries such as South East Asia Property Company which was incorporated in Bermuda deliberately to invest in properties in the South East Asia region in 1995. It was reported that GIC will also act through its affiliate Seaprime Investments.[83] GIC also uses wholly-own subsidiary Reco Landmark Tianjin Pte Ltd to invest in real estate in China. It was also reported in 2008 that GIC had invested $300 million

---
81 Kevin Brown and Sundeep Tucker, "GIC makes $1.6bn from Citi stake sale," *Financial Times*, 22 September 2009. http://www.ft.com/cms/s/0/b8479e9a-a75d-11de-9467-00144feabdc0.html
82 Conrad Raj, "GIC research teams to put their money where their mouths are," *Singapore Business Times*, 23 May 2001.
83 Lilian Ang, "GIC joins US$300m fund to invest in South-east Asian property," *Singapore Business Times*, 15 February 1995.

in a US-based property hedge fund.[84] The president of GIC Real Estate said that the Fund is actively looking for investments in emerging economies such as India, Brazil and Russia. In early 2008, GIC Real Estate announced that, in cooperation with the Russian company PIK, the Fund is putting $233 million into Russia to develop a town northeast of Moscow. GIC holds a 25% stake in the venture while PIK holds the rest.[85] GIC's investments in overseas real estate have been fairly successful. It started in Japan and Korea earlier than most international investors. This has shown that fund investments in real estate are for the long term and they do not shy away from nascent markets. In addition, GIC Real Estate invests in European shopping malls such as Southampton West Quay Shopping Centre, Bluewater and Metrocentre in the UK. They also hold a 3% stake in British Land, a real estate investment trust.[86] Its UK portfolio consists of hotels, offices, shopping malls, residential buildings and student accommodation. In other parts of Europe, the Fund bought the Intercontinental Hotel Paris, shopping centres in Rome and in Helsinki and prime office buildings in Munich.

4.4.3 Summary of GIC Investments

GIC benefits from long-term investments in the equity and bond markets and has achieved a real rate of return of 4.5% on its portfolio over the last 20 years. It has attributed the consistent return to its progressive shift from fixed income instruments to equity instruments and alternative investments in private equity and real estate. It has also implemented active management within the asset classes to enable performances above benchmark. However, GIC was reported to have lost 20% of its value due to the subprime crisis and its real rate of return fell to 2.6% in the 2008/2009 financial year. Despite this, GIC was reported to be investing aggressively in Europe in 2008, as it could take advantage of the fall in the Euro and of property prices generally in Europe.

GIC has complicated investment channels which include direct and indirect investments. Indirect investments are made through fund managers and investment fund partnership with other institutional investors through

---

84 "Singapore GIC invests US$300 million in US Hedge Fund," Singapore Straits Times, 16 January 2008. http://www.asiaone.com/News/Latest%2BNews/Business/Story/A1Story20080116-45266.html
85 "Singapore GIC invests US$300 million in US Hedge Fund," Singapore Straits Times, 16 January 2008. http://www.asiaone.com/News/Latest%2BNews/Business/Story/A1Story20080116-45266.html
86 Daniel Thomas and Neil Hume, "Singapore GIC builds stake in British Land," Financial Times, 10 January 2008. http://www.ft.com/cms/s/0/ff10c0c6-bf3e-11dc-8052-0000779fd2ac.html

subsidiaries. Some of these investments are made through affiliates which in turn partner with other institutional investors to set up new funds which are specific to the investment projects. This has made it difficult to estimate or trace the Fund's investments. GIC also partners with Temasek to invest overseas and their joint investments include Mount Charlotte Investments which operates hotels in the UK. GIC teams up with domestic bank OCBC and Thai firms to set up joint venture companies to invest in unlisted companies and new projects in Thailand. Likewise, it teams up with Hong Leong, a Singapore listed company, to purchase stakes in hotels in Hong Kong.

GIC's investment portfolio is mainly in equities and real estate in developed markets. Singapore's industrial policy does not seem to affect GIC's choice of investments except for investments in the financial sector. GIC's investments are in financial institutions, private equities and venture capital. The government of Singapore is actively developing the country into an international financial centre so GIC's investments in financial firms can help. As early as 1994, GIC aimed to develop the domestic fund management industry and placed part of the Fund with local and foreign fund managers based in Singapore. However, the amount of the fund being managed by external fund managers was never disclosed. In an interview in 2001 Ng Kok Song, GIC's Managing Director for public markets, revealed that S$30 billion was in the care of foreign fund managers to allow GIC to gain insights on how foreign fund managers work.[87] GIC's investment strategy is shrewd and they can make good judgement on valuing investment. Occasionally they behave opportunistically and invest in distressed companies. In terms of investment in the real estate sector, the Fund has an eye for value and normally enters the markets ahead of other investors. In the 1990s, they were busy investing in real estate in Asia and started investing in real estate in Europe in 2002. However not all GIC investments in GIC are profitable. In January 2010, GIC was said to have booked losses of $675 million invested in Stuyvesant Town, a apartment complex in New York.[88] GIC Real Estate President, Seet Ngee Huat, expressed in an interview in 2001 that given their limited manpower resources, they chose to work with local partners and product specialists. They have forged joint ventures with key players in the region. For product-based investment such as investing in the hotel industry, they choose to work with established

---

[87] "$30b in the care of foreign managers," Singapore Strait Times, 23 May 2001.
[88] "GIC says booked loss from $675mln in Stuyvesant investment," reported by Kevin Lim, edited by a Neil Chatterjee, Reuters, 10 January 2010. http://www.reuters.com/article/idUSSGE60-A0EF20100111

professionals in the industry.[89] It is difficult to assess GIC's investments in other sectors which are not reported in the media or included in its annual report. GIC is known to have been among the earliest institutional investors in venture capital funds in Silicon Valley, and it has invested in Sequoia Capital, Matrix Partners, Summit Ventures and TA Associates.

4.5 Government Pension Fund – Global (GPFG)

GPFG is the second largest SWF and the management of GPFG is often cited as an example to follow. The good practices of the Fund include ahigh degree of transparency on all aspect of its operations, non-controlling stakes, non-strategic holdings, a clear line of responsibility between government and operational management. GPFG was established to manage Norway's revenue from petroleum and it serves as a stabilisation fund and saving fund. As a stabilisation fund, GPFG is deployed to shield the Norwegian economy from fluctuations in oil prices while as a saving fund it has to meet the pension obligations of the future. With these two purposes, GPFG invests outside of the Norwegian economy. In addition, the accumulation of foreign currency through the Fund's investments counteracts any appreciation of the Norwegian krone. The Fund is fully integrated into the state budget and the Ministry of Finance is responsible for defining the investment strategy. The Fund's strategy is to achieve high financial returns subject to moderate risk. In particular, the Fund investment principles are based on good and sustainable global development; economically, environmentally and socially; to achieve a solid return over time.

Unlike the SWFs in Asia and Middle East, GPFG has publicly announced its investment strategy and any significant changes to its investment activities is available on its official website. This high level of disclosure on investment strategy helps to eliminate market speculation and fear of SWF's investment motives. The following section examines GPFG investment strategies, followed by GPFG's investment activities in 2008 and finally a summary of GPFG's investments strategies. In particular, GPFG's active management of portfolios and consideration of ethnical issues in its investments will be discussed.

---

89 "Singapore owns choice real estate in world capitals," Singapore Business Times, 23 May 2001.

4.5.1 Investment Strategy

'What constitutes a good investment strategy for the Government Pension Fund is determined by the characteristics of the Fund, the purpose of the investments, the owners (the people of Norway, represented by the political authorities), tolerance of risk, and assumptions about how the financial markets work.'[90] GPFG is a financial investor and has set out very clear investment policies on their investment policies and strategies. The investment strategy of GPFG evolved over time; investment in equities was introduced into the benchmark portfolio in 1998; five emerging market countries was added to the equity benchmark portfolio in 2000; non-government bonds were added to the fixed income benchmark portfolio in 2002. GPFG considered investments in higher risk assets to increase long-term returns in 2006. A small-cap segment was included in the benchmark portfolio and the equity portion was increased from 40% to 60% in 2007. The Norwegian government decided that the Fund would start to build up a portfolio of real estate investments and also increase its exposure to emerging stock markets in 2008. The Ministry of Finance has included 19 new emerging equity markets in the equity benchmark portfolio. This change allows GPFG to better diversify its portfolio and tap into higher returns in the emerging market. There are also plans to include assets such as commodities and infrastructure.[91] The limit on ownership stakes for equity investments in individual companies was raised from 5% to 10%. The Fund takes larger and more concentrated positions in particular companies and market segments where the trade-off between risk and return is attractive in the longer term.

The GPFG has a long-term investment strategy where the capital is invested in a broad-based portfolio which is comprised of securities from many countries and industries. Its long-term investment allocation is 60% in equities and 40% in fixed income. Out of the 60% capital allocated to equities, 35% is invested in US and Africa, 50% in Europe and the remaining 15% in Asia and Oceania. The benchmark index for equities comprises almost 7,700 companies across 46 countries. While 40% of the capital is allocated to fixed income, 35% will be invested in US and Africa, 60% in Europe and 5% in Asia and Oceania. The benchmark index for fixed income comprises more

---
90 Ministry of Finance, Norway, Report No. 20 to the Storting (2008-2009) On the Management of the Government Pension Fund in 2008, p.12. http://www.regjeringen.no/pages/2185603/PDFS/ST-M200820090020000EN_PDFS.pdf
91 Caroline Liinaki, "Norway's pension fund to diversify," Financial Times, 20 April 2008. http://www.ft.com/cms/s/0/599d75b6-0d6e-11dd-b90a-0000779fd2ac.html

than 10,000 individual securities across approximate 1,600 issuers in the 21 currencies. See Figure 4.4 for GPFG's benchmark portfolio. The current asset allocation will be changed to 35% in fixed income and 5% in real estate once the Fund starts investing in real estate. This prudent strategy is reflected in the benchmark portfolio that forms the basis for Norges Bank's management of the Fund. Norges Bank seeks to achieve the highest possible return compared with this benchmark portfolio by selecting an actual portfolio which differs from the benchmark portfolio and manages the actual portfolio through active management. The Ministry of Finance has stipulated limits as to how large this difference between the benchmark portfolio and the actual portfolio may be. The limits that apply to the maximum deviation between the actual portfolio and the benchmark portfolio are: asset class (2.5%), geographical (5%), sector deviation (5%), government bonds (no restriction) and other sectors in the fixed income portfolio (10%).[92] The benchmark portfolio is also used as a tool to manage market risk. The expected return from investments may deviate from the expected return from the benchmark portfolio by 1.5%.

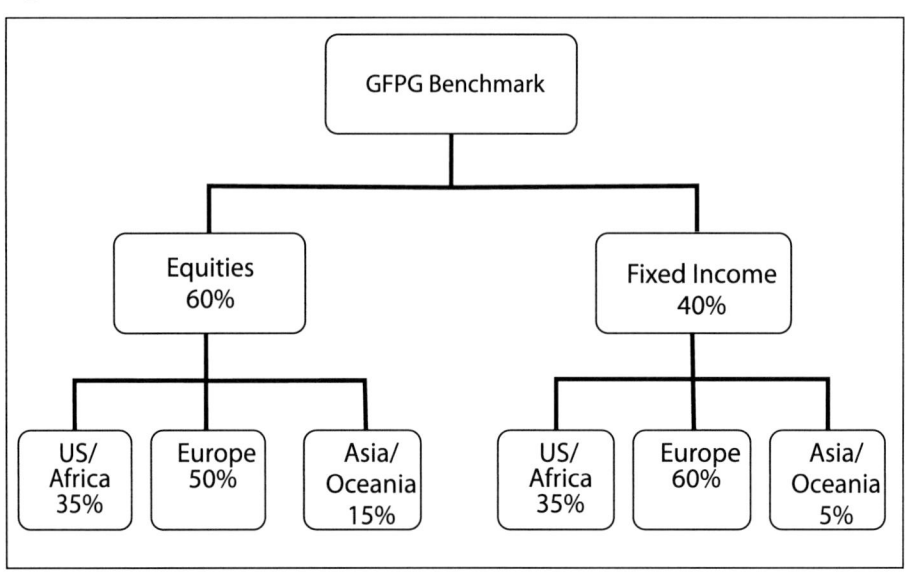

Figure 4.4: GPFG Benchmark Portfolio

```
                         GFPG Benchmark
                        /              \
                 Equities              Fixed Income
                   60%                      40%
              /     |     \            /     |     \
           US/   Europe  Asia/       US/   Europe  Asia/
          Africa  50%   Oceania     Africa  60%   Oceania
           35%           15%         35%            5%
```

Source: Source: Ministry of Finance, Norway, Report No. 20 to the Storting (2008-2009) On the Management of the Government Pension Fund in 2008.

---

[92] Investment Mandate issued to Executive Director of NBIM. http://www.norges-bank.no/upload/77273/4_mandate.pdf

GPFG uses active management to turn its long-term investement horizon and its substantial size to its advantage. This strategy improves the trade-off between risk and return of the portfolio. GPFG's active management strategy is predicted on the time-varying investment opportunities in the market. The strategy is implemented through three processes: (1) The management of market porfolio where the Fund takes active decisions to ensure cost-effective management of equities and fixed income instruments, (2) The management of risk in individual companies based on analysis of securities issued by the companies as part of their equity financing and (3) The management of systematics is taken with a view to increase returns and improve the long-term trade-off between expected return and risk.[93] When GPFG posted a 23.3% loss in 2008, there was called for the Fund to change its active management to passive management.[94] The loss has also led to the Ministry of Finance to commission three finance professors to evaluate the Fund's active managmnet strategy. The report indicated that the loss suffered the active management in 2008 and early 2009 was due to systematic risk factors. The professors recommended that GPFG create a custom, completely liquid benchmark which captured exposure to an arrays of systematic risk factors, such as liquidity risk and volatility risk.[95]

GPFG is the only SWF which has incorporated ethical considerations into its investment strategies. The Fund takes ethical issues and corporate governance of the companies they have invested in very seriously. The Ethical Guidelines for the GPFG stipulate that the financial wealth must be managed to generate a sound return in the long-term which is contingent on sustainable development in the economic, environmental and social sense. The Fund should not make investments which constitute an unacceptable risk that the Fund may contribute to unethical acts or omissions, such as violations of fundamental humanitarian principles, serious violations of human rights, gross corruption or severe environmental damages.[96] This is achieved through <u>active ownership</u> right, negative screening of companies and exclusion of

---

[93] Norges Bank assessment of theoretical and empirical basis for active management and our strategy for the management of the Government Pension Fund Global. http://www.norges-bank.no/upload/77928/active_management_enclosure.pdf

[94] "Calls for Norway to go passive," Financial Times, 17 January 2009. http://www.ft.com/cms/s/0/db242cda-0202-11df-8b56-00144feabdc0.html

[95] Ang, A., Goetzmann, W.N., Schaefer, S.M. (2009) Evaluation of Active Management of Norwegian Government Pension Fund – Global. http://www.regjeringen.no/upload/FIN/Statens%20pensjonsfond/rapporter/AGS%20Report.pdf

[96] Ethnical Guidelines for the Government Pension Fund – Global. Issued 22 December 2005 pursuant to regulation on the management of the Government Pension Fund – Global. http://www.regjeringen.no/en/dep/fin/Selected-topics/the-government-pension-fund/ethical-guidelines-for-the-government-pe/the-ethical-guidelines.html?id=434894

companies from its portfolio. In late 2009, the NBIM called for shareholders to vote on separating the role of chairman from chief executive at four US companies.[97] The Fund announced that 17 tobacco-producing companies would be excluded from its portfolio in 2010. The Ministry of Finance is also considering excluding companies which violate carbon emission levels from GPFG's portfolio.[98] The Fund has also publicly announced a list of companies in which they will not invest for ethical reasons. In particular, GPFG screens its investments in emerging market for ethical, environment and human right infringement. One such example is Dongfeng Motor, a Chinese firm. This company was excluded from GPFG's investments because it had sold military trucks to Burma.[99]

GPFG uses the model-based risk systems coupled with other supplementary risk management methods to manage the Fund's risk. The statistical models are based on historical pricing where estimates of risk are made on the basis of historical relationships. However, the models underestimated the expected relative risk and the correlation between different active positions during the subprime crisis as the models are based on historical events. To supplement the statistical models risk in three main areas are now also managed. The three areas are concentration analysis, factor exposures and liquidity exposure.[100]

4.5.2 Investment Activities

According to its 2008 Annual Report, GPFG holds shares in 7,900 companies and owns approximately 0.77% of the global equity market. The majority of these holdings are below 1% of the equity.[101] During 2008, the NOK384 billion capital inflow was entirely invested in global equity markets. The Fund adopted an aggressive approach during the subprime crisis to increase its holding of global equity ownership particularly in Europe. As at 31 December 2008, the ownership of European companies was 1.33% of the total market

---

97 Kate Burgess, "Norges seeks reforms at US governance," Financial Times, 7 October 2009. http://www.ft.com/cms/s/0/a332c1e0-b38f-11de-ae8d-00144feab49a.html
98 Valeria Criscione, "Pension fund treads a thorny path," Financial Times, 16 March 2009. http://www.ft.com/cms/s/0/5fe99214-11c9-11de-87b1-0000779fd2ac.html
99 Marianne Stigset, "Norway bans Dongfeng fromoil fund," Bloomberg, 13 March 2009. http://www.bloomberg.com/apps/news?pid=20601100&sid=aRPV78f6WxRo&refer=germany
100 See Norges Bank website for detail on risk management of GPFG. http://www.norges-bank.no/templates/article____73791.aspx
101 Government Pension Fund - Global Annual Report 2008, Norges Bank. http//www.norges-bank.no/upload/73979/nbim_annualreport08_rev.pdf

value of the companies included in the benchmark portfolio. The equity portfolio by region was 48.6% in Europe, 35.2% in Americas and 16.2% in Asia and Oceania. While the fixed income portfolio by region was 59.9% in Europe, 34.3% in Americas and 5.8% in Asia and Oceania (See Figure 4.5). Comparing the asset allocation, GPFG investments in Asia and Oceania were dominated by equities while investments in Europe were dominated by fixed income. The investments in Asia and Oceania were concentrated on equities due to higher returns in the Asia emerging markets and the lack of investment grade fixed income in the region. In addition, the Asian equities market is more liquid than the bond market.

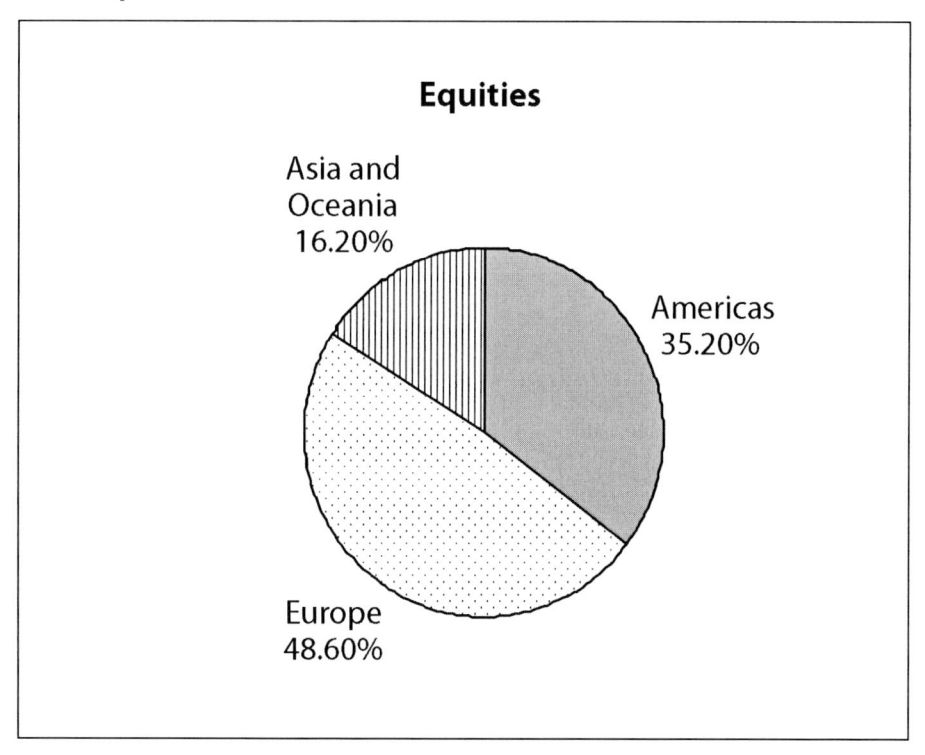

Figure 4.5a: GPFG's Investments by Geographic Location as at 31 December 2008 – Equities

Equities

- Asia and Oceania 16.20%
- Americas 35.20%
- Europe 48.60%

Figure 4.5b: GPFG's Investments by Geographical Location as at 31 December 2008 – Fixed Income

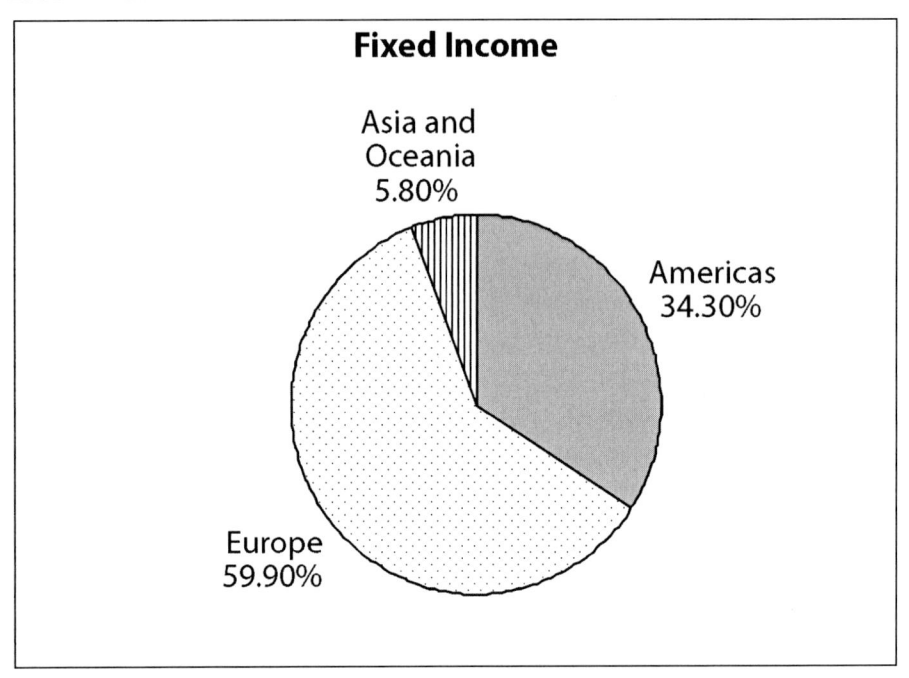

Fixed Income

- Asia and Oceania 5.80%
- Americas 34.30%
- Europe 59.90%

Source: Government Pension Fund – Global Annual Report 2008

The year 2008 was GPFG worst performance since the Fund inception. The Fund made a negative return of 23.3% in international currency[102] which is equivalent to $92 billion.[103] This return was 3.4% lower than that on the benchmark portfolio against which the GPFG was measured. The poor performance was due to less well-diversified fixed income portfolio, having investments exposed to changes in the price of liquidity and fall in stock markets. However, GPFG recouped its loss in 2009 and its return in international currency basket in the third quarter of 2009 was 13.5%. The overall return in the first nine months of 2009 was 21.8% (NOK 529 billion). The high return was attributed to a 17.7% return in equity portfolio. GPFG's aggressive accumulation of global equities in 2008 has paid off and the Fund revealed that it has enjoyed the biggest gain in 13 years in its third quarter of 2009 report. It was also reported that GPFG owns 1% of all world stocks.[104]

---

102 The fund's currency basket which reflect Norway's international purchasing power. For more detail refer Norges Bank official website. http://www.norges-bank.no/default____106.aspx
103 "Norway pension fund loses $92bn," BBC News, 11 March 2009. http://news.bbc.co.uk/1/hi/business/7937360.stm
104 Andrew Ward, "Norway enjoys biggest gain in 13 years," Financial Times, 15 November 2009. http://www.ft.com/cms/s/0/b684798a-d083-11de-af9c-00144feabdc0.html

CASE STUDIES

Figure 4.6 shows the consistent growth of the Fund from 2004 to 2008. However, this growth in the Fund's value was due to the largest inflow in the Fund's history. New capital of NOK 384 billion was transferred to the Fund during 2008. The huge loss incurred by GPFG in 2008 resulted in the Fund's value being reduced by NOK 633 billion while a weaker krone in relation to the currencies in which the fund is invested increased its value in NOK terms by NOK 506 billion.[105] GPFG's value as at 31 December 2008 was NOK 2,275 billion, slightly below the forecasted size. (NOK 2,300 billion at beginning 1 January 2009).[106]

Figure 4.6: Government Pensions Fund – Global's Portfolio Value in NOK (Billion) as at 31 December

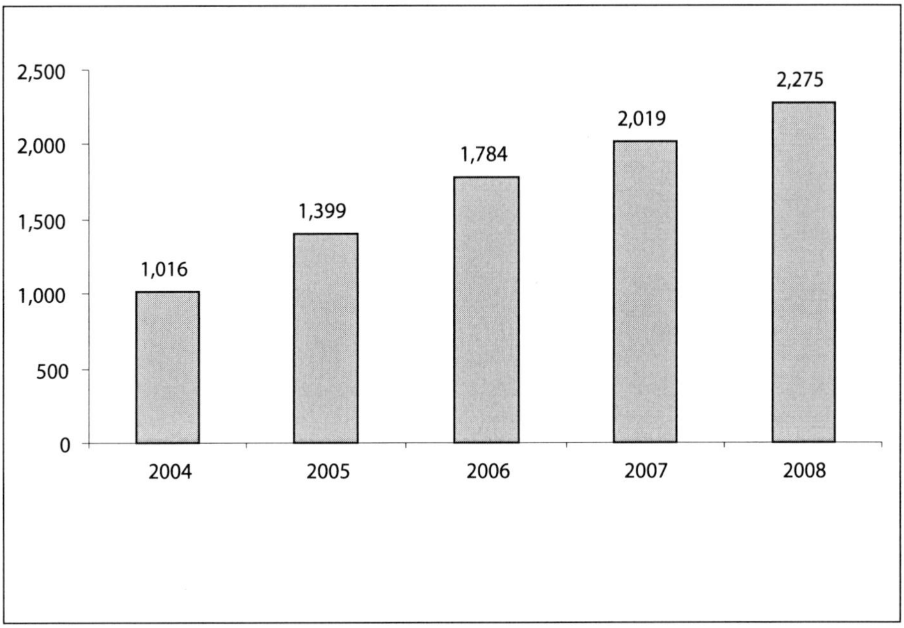

Year	Value
2004	1,016
2005	1,399
2006	1,784
2007	2,019
2008	2,275

Source: Norges Bank, The Government Petroleum Fund Key Figure 2008

GPFG invests in wide range of companies in many different countries. Most of the Fund's largest holdings were in Europe and four out of the ten largest equity holdings were in oil companies. Given that GPFG is a commodity-based SWF, ideally the Fund should invest to hedge against fluctuations in oil prices. However, given that GPFG invests to get higher long-term returns,

---
105 Government Pension Fund – Global Annual Report 2008, p. 22.
106 Forecast for the Size of the Government Pension Fund, Norges Bank.
http://www.norges-bank.no/templates/article____42083.aspx

including oil companies would raise its future return with the higher demand for commodities from developing countries. See Table 4.7 on GPFG's largest equity holding.

Table 4.7: Largest Equity Holdings on 31 December 2008

COMPANY	COUNTRY	HOLDING IN MILLIONS OF NOK
Royal Dutch Shell	UK	15,263
Nestle SA	Switzerland	14,901
BP plc	UK	13,151
Exxon Mobil Corporation	US	12,217
Total SA	France	11,314
HSBC Holdings plc	UK	10,562
Vodafone Group plc	UK	10,354
Novartis AG	Switzerland	10,350
Roche Holding AG	Switzerland	9,997
E.ON AG	Germany	9,090

Source: Government Pension Fund – Global Annual Report 2008

The return in international currency on the equity portfolio was – 40.7% in 2008. The four types of strategies employed by the Fund to beat its benchmark are enhanced indexing, capital raising, internal sector mandates and external mandates. However, the Fund's equity portfolio under-performed its benchmark by 1.15% in 2008.

In term of bond holdings, the Fund has large holding of government debt and debts issued by quasi-government institutions. The three largest bond holdings were German government bonds, followed by UK government bonds and Italian government bonds. See Table 4.8 on largest bond holdings on 31 December 2008.

Table 4.8: Largest bond holdings on 31 December 2008

ISSUER	COUNTRY	HOLDING IN MILLIONS OF NOK
Federal Republic of Germany	Germany	94,976
UK Government	UK	85,500
Italian Republic	Italy	81,781
Fannie Mae	US	68,339
United States of America	US	65,896
Japanese Government	Japan	55,721
European Investment Bank	Supranational	49,009
French Republic	France	46,656
Kreditanstalt für Wiederaufbau	Germany	37,374
Freddie Mac	US	32,625

Source: Government Pension Fund – Global Annual Report 2008

GPFG held large positions in several parts of the fixed income market which were hit by credit premiums and falling liquidity anda this resulted in a –0.52% return measured in the Fund's currency basket. The US securitised debts were managed by external managers and the total exposure to securitised debts was far higher than allocated capital. The actual fixed income portfolio consisted of NOK 54 billion non-agency Mortgage Backed Securities (MBS) while agency MBS made up the bulk of the benchmark portfolio. The proportion of non-agency MBS was higher than the proportion of agency MBS which made the risk of actual fixed income portfolio higher than that stipulated by the benchmark portfolio. Following its losses, the Fund's fixed income management was re-organised and two main areas on fixed income management were created. One portfolio is for indexing and re-balancing and will be responsible for cost-effective implementation of the strategic objectives for the fixed income portfolio. Another portfolio contains large and illiquid fixed income where the investments will be held till maturity to limit realised losses. In addition, NBIM is likely to establish its own expertise in securitised debt in future to assume management of the sector and make adjustments to the portfolio when needed. GPFG is not new to managing fixed income in a market in turmoil. It was reported that GPFG was one of the biggest investors to profit from the turmoil in the Icelandic bond markets in 2006.[107]

---

[107] Ivar Simensen, "Norway profits from Iceland," *Financial Times*, 11 April 2006. http://www.ft.com/

GPFG is also actively building up its portfolio in sectors concerned with sustainable development. The Fund has directed 1% of its investments into "green shares" targeting investments in developing countries. As part of this initiative, GPFG has invested in 232 Indian companies that supported environmental sustainability and clean energy.[108] In addition, the Fund has added sustainable water management to its range of shareholder activism and will aim at companies with operations in sectors and regions that are exposed to water scarcity, water pollution and water related risk.[109]

4.5.3 Summary of GPFG's Investment Activities and Strategies

GPFG is an integrated part of Norway's state budget and the Fund has to be managed prudently to meet the country's public finance needs. The Fund has a very diversified portfolio in a range of companies with most stakes lower than 1%. Overall, GPFG is managed prudently and the losses during the subprime crisis should not be seen as a change in the Fund's investment approach. Unlike the Asian and Middle Eastern SWFs which bought stakes in investment banks during the subprime crisis, GPFG increased its investment in global equities and the loss was as a result of systematic risk which was high during the crisis. However, the Fund recouped its loss and made a profit in 2009. GPFG strategy of increasing equity holding in 2008 has worked to the fund's advantage because of its long-term investment horizon.

GPFG active management of its capital against the benchmark portfolio set by the Ministry of Finance suits the Fund's long-term investment horizon and substantial size. However, with the addition of real estate and the expansion of investments in emerging markets in its portfolio, the Fund may not be able to rely entirely on the current approach which caters to financial investors. Investments in real estate and emerging markets would eventually lead to GPFG holding direct investments because they both offer limited opportunity for financial investments. Thus the need for different approaches to manage these types of investments. The lessons from the subprime crisis may also result in GPFG managing their portfolio's systematic risk more actively and relying less on external fund managers. The combined value of

---

cms/s/0/56c7bafc-c8f8-11da-b642-0000779e2340.html
108 James Lamont, "Norway fund in green push," Financial Times, 1 September 2009. http://www.ft.com/cms/s/0/c77ffe8a-9690-11de-84d1-00144feabdc0.html
109 Valeria Criscione, "Norway's state pension fund wise to risk water," Financial Times, 23 August 2009. http://www.ft.com/cms/s/0/8e27c7fc-8fd9-11de-bc59-00144feabdc0.html

externally managed portfolios was NOK 300 billion at the end of the year. This amount is relatively small compared to the Fund's value at NOK 2,275 billion. Given that the Fund adopts an active management approach, having most of its assets under internal management enables it to make timely adjustments, the amount of fund managed by external fund managers may fall except for sectors and markets which are unfamiliar to the Fund.

Previously, GPFG invested in listed equities and fixed income only. The Fund expanded the asset class to include real estate and such investments suit the Fund's long-term investment horizon and at the same time limit the risk of inflation. The Fund has also planned to invest in other assets such as commodities, infrastructure and pre-IPOs which would increase the overall risk of the portfolio. However, diversifying into a bigger range of asset classes would allow GPFG to better diversify its portfolio risk and bring its investment portfolio more in line with the Fund international counterparts. Examining GPFG's investment activities, one can see that the Fund introduced riskier assets into its portfolio gradually. Such a cautious approach is a good practice that other newer SWFs should follow.

4.6 Summary of Investment Activities and Strategies of Five SWfs

These five SWFs have experienced a rollercoaster ride in 2008 and all have suffered huge losses. However, they have a long-term investment horizon and are able to withstand the short-term volatility in the market. Most of them recouped their losses and were able to make higher profits after the subprime crisis. Despite these SWFs having a common investment horizon – a long-term investment horizon – they are managed differently due to differences in objectives and their assets classes.

In comparing the five SWFs, we find that CIC adopts an investment strategy similar to that of Temasek whereas ADIA and GIC are more similar to one another. CIC and Temasek both hold direct and indirect investments and some investment activities are in line with their country's industrial policies. These SWFs do not appear to base their investments on the Asset Liability Management (ALM) model which is applicable to most pension funds, endowment funds and insurance funds where a constant outflow of funds is needed. Instead their investment model is a mixture of capital growth and benchmarking against certain indices. This benchmark approach is common among endowment funds. ADIA and GIC behave more like an investment house that invests in developed markets. ADIA and GIC are less strategic in their investments because Abu Dhabi and Singapore each already have another SWF which invests strategically for domestic industrial policy. Mabuldala Investment Company invests strategically for the UAE and Temasek invests strategically for Singapore. While China already has various state-owned enterprises and agencies, they lessen the burden on CIC of helping to develop the country's industrial policy. GPFG's investment strategy is different from the other four SWFs. The Fund's investment strategy is similar to pension fund and endowment fund where the Fund is a financial investor. However, with the inclusion of real estate in its portfolio, the Fund is likely to hold direct investment in real estate in future. GPFG's investments are not related to the country industrial policy, the Fund invests purely to obtain a higher return from its petroleum revenue. GPFG appears to manage its assets base on an ALM approach where its return is aligned with the outflow of fund which try to match the state budget. In particular, it GPFG tried to keep its outflow of fund at 4% which is the targeted real return of the Fund.[110]

In general, these five SWFs invest in domestic, emerging and developed markets, except GPFG which does not invest in its domestic economy as Norway already has another fund which does this. However, after the subprime crisis, these funds have shied away from US markets and concentrated instead in their regional markets and emerging economies like Brazil and Russia. While the UK is the popular choice for their investments in Europe, most of these SWFs hold financial and direct investments in UK. These funds are also increasing their investments in real estate, natural resources and infrastructure after the subprime crisis. Another trend is that they are increasing investments in the countries of other SWFs. For example, ADIA invests in China, China invests in the Middle East, and GIC and Temasek in China and the Middle East. ADIA, GIC and Temask are capitalising on China's economic growth while China is making investments to ensure the country's access to commodities for its economic growth. In the future, SWFs are likely to have increased collaboration, like GIC and Temasek who already have joint venture in their overseas investments as do CIC and GIC in China's CICC. GPFG is likely to increase investment in Asia with an office being set up in Shanghai in 2007. There could also be collaboration among these SWFs in investments in clean

---

[110] "The long-term strategy of Norwegian Petroleum Fund," address by Governor Svein Gjedrem at the Argentum Conference, Norges Bank, 30 September 2004. http://www.norges-bank.no/templates/article____17924.aspx

energy, with ADIA, GPFG and the Chinese government indicating interest in the industry.

The investments of these funds in financial institutions may not be purely economically motivated. In fact, having financial institutions in their portfolios allows them to tap into the financial expertise of these institutions. The professionals in the financial markets have described ADIA and GIC managements' keen interest to know details of deals as an indication that acquiring the financial expertises of financial institutions that they invest in is a primary motive for the deal. Although many critics have commented that these SWFs ventured into western financial institutions at the wrong time, no one including policymakers would have anticipated that the market would dive even further at the time of purchase. It is sensible for them to invest in financial institutions since they can recover from economic crisis or recession more quickly than any other industry. Just like private equity firms, these SWFs invested in distressed companies at the time when most of these financial institutions were in need of liquidity.

By holding stakes in private equity firms the four Asian and Middle Eastern SWFs all enjoy three advantages. First, they are keen to develop the financial markets in their home countries and can buy US private equity firms to obtain their financial expertise. The respective governments spearhead the development of a fund management industry, e.g. Abu Dhabi's Abu Dhabi Investment Company, China's CICC and the Singaporean government are all building up their countrys' fund management industries. Secondly, these SWFs can learn how to manage their own funds from private equity firms. Thirdly, private equity firms and hedge funds are immune from public scrutiny and exempted from public accountability, thus reducing their need for disclosure and transparency. Using this loophole, SWFs can avoid disclosing their cross-border transactions by partnering with private equity firms. The secretive nature of private equity firms provides a good shield for those SWFs that are secretive in their investments.

Unlike GPFG and Australian Government Future Fund, the four Asian and Middle Eastern SWFs are similar in that they are both financial investors and direct investors. It is just as likely for them to take direct stakes in their home countries, emerging markets and the real estate industry. Except for CIC and GPFG, the other three SWFs have extensive investments in real estate. CIC has a relatively shorter history and will probably get more involved in the real estate industry in the near future, particularly as other SWFs have indicated plans to increase their investments in real estate. While GPFG has announced plans to include real estate in its benchmark portfolio in 2008. As financial investors, these funds invest in pre-IPO shares, unlisted and listed equities. Among the funds, only Temasek has actively participated in its domestic stock markets and even then most of its activities related to Temasek linked companies. ADIA, GIC and GPFG have made an explicit statement that they will not invest in domestic stock markets because their huge funds would destabilise stock markets that are relatively small. CIC is also unlikely to invest in China's stock market but will follow in the footstep of other SWFs by investing in developed financial markets through external fund managers. CIC, GIC, GPFG and Temasek have part of their portfolios managed by external fund managers. As for ADIA, there is no report that external fund managers are managing its portfolio. However, it would not be unusual for ADIA to have part of its assets managed by external fund managers given the huge amounts of capital and diversified portfolio the Fund has.

ADIA, CIC, GIC and Temasek have also set up wholly-owned subsidiaries in different countries to manage their investments. These subsidiaries either team up with other investors or make sole investments. They make tracking SWF investments a difficult task. In addition, investments funds and wholly owned investments were also established to manage part of their funds. For example ADIA has Tasameem for its real estate investments. CIC has Stable Investment Corporation to invest in short-term financial instruments. GIC has Reco Bay NSW as one of its investment vehicles. Temasek has Fullerton Fund Management which manage mutual funds and funds of funds. Given the extensive companies, sectors and countries they have invested in, it is impossible to know the exact investments of these SWFs which invest through multiple investment channels. The investments channels of ADIA and GIC are particularly complicated and it is even more difficult to track their investments. Furthermore, they avoid holding large stakes in listed companies to avoid disclosure to regulators. As for real estate investments, not all transactions are reported in the media.

Given the success of ADIA, GIC, GPFG and Temasek prior to the subprime crisis, potential SWFs and some of the existing SWFs could follow their path. However, the investment models of these funds are only suitable for SWFs which have built up enough assets to be able to buffer swings in financial markets and when their country has excess liquidity to meet the import and capital outflow. SWFs with the objective of capital preservation should follow the investment strategy of GPFG where the assets are more liquid and less risky but have a higher return than the central bank's investments. GPFG's approach of managing its investments against a benchmark portfolio also suits new SWFs where the cost of managing funds is lower. ADIA also invests about 60% of its assets using the indexing approach. One notable similarity between ADIA and GPFG is that they allow variations in their strategic asset allocation. However, ADIA has allowed higher levels of variation. Flexibility in asset allocation allows the fund to re-balance its portfolio according to market sentiments.

The next chapter will examine the future of SWFs and the effects they have on global markets.

CHAPTER 5
Future Developments

In Chapter Four we discussed five of the largest SWFs from Asia, the Middle East and Scandinavia, their developments and investment allocations. The Asian and Middle Eastern SWFs have been aggressively buying up global companies during the financial crisis and the trend of cross-border investments is likely to continue but at a slower pace. As SWFs are buying up global companies, the speed of their growth is faster than that of any other investment vehicles. Despite the subprime crisis and economic deterioration, according to Maslakovic (2009), the assets under SWF management are estimated to have grown by 18%. While other investment vehicles have shrunk significantly due to the financial crisis, SWFs have defied the economic uncertainty and now have a more prominent presence in the financial sectors. The general market consensus is that the size of SWFs will have sustained growth and the number of new SWFs is likely to increase over the years. According to an estimate by Stephen Jen from Morgan Stanley, SWFs will be worth $12 trillion by 2015 as they are expected to grow rapidly in the immediate term.[1] Deutsche Bank is also bullish on these funds and it has estimated that SWFs would be worth about $10 trillion by 2015. The projected growth estimated by Deutsche Bank (Figure 5.1) shows that SWFs will grow steadily over the years at an average rate of 15% per annum.

---

1 Manoj Pradhan, "The news and the future (s)," Morgan Stanley, Global Economic Forum, 4 May 2007. http://www.morganstanley.com/views/gef/archive/2007/20070504-Fri.html

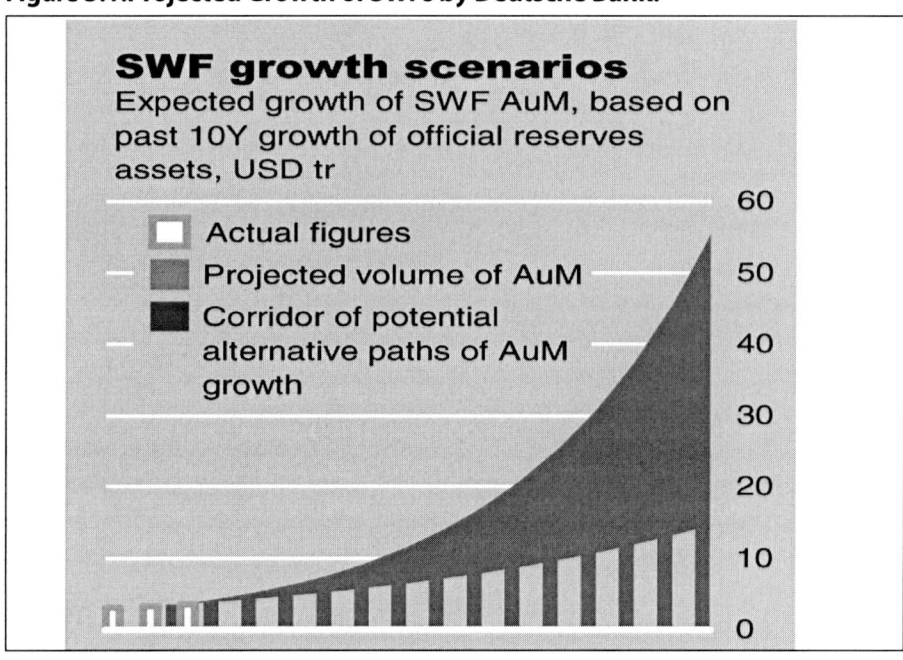

Figure 5.1: Projected Growth of SWFs by Deutsche Bank.

SWF growth scenarios
Expected growth of SWF AuM, based on past 10Y growth of official reserves assets, USD tr

- Actual figures
- Projected volume of AuM
- Corridor of potential alternative paths of AuM growth

Projected volume of SWF AuM based on 15.01% 10Y CAGR[2] of official central bank reserves. Corridor of potential alternative paths of AuM growth based on 21.72% 5Y CAGR of official central bank reserves high-growth scenario and 10.64% 20Y CAGR for low-growth scenario. Actual figures as observed.
Source: DB Research 2008.

If the reserve accumulation grows at a moderate rate, SWF growth will be lower at $7 trillion by 2015. However, if the reserve accumulation continues to grow at a faster rate as it has been doing in recent years, the SWFs will be worth $14 trillion by 2014. Many other industry players, academic researchers and policymakers believe that SWFs will become a dominant force in the global financial markets, helping to shift economic power from the West to the East. The size of SWFs will swell not only as a result of petrodollars and foreign reserves, but also through the gains of their investments. How the vast capital of SWFs is invested will also shape future financial markets. SWFs will continue to play a significant role in global financial markets in the near future. Their growth will have substantial effects on the financial markets and these implications need to be incorporated into governments' future policies with regard to foreign investments either in domestic or overseas markets.

---
2 *CAGR refers to the compound annual growth rate.*

The SWF asset allocations, particularly for large SWFs, will also affect asset prices and the direction of future capital flows substantially.

This chapter aims to examine the growth of SWFs, the implications of their growth on financial markets, companies and the countries they invest in, international guidelines and the development of SWFs and the conflicting roles played by SWFs. The growth of commodity-based and non-commodity SWFs will be discussed. Factors affecting the different sources of funds are examined and how they impact the size of SWFs is analysed. The implications of SWFs growth on the financial markets, the companies and countries they invest in will also be discussed. In addition, we will also investigate how the proposed new guidelines for increased transparency will affect SWF operations. The implications of SWFs on the stability of global financial markets are highlighted. Will their activities destabilise the financial markets or are they actually playing a stabilising role? Lastly, the conflicting role of SWFs will be analysed. They have an awkward role because the state is the shareholder, yet the fund is normally run as a private corporation. The fund is accountable to stakeholders, yet the state is also accountable to its citizens. Is it really possible to separate the state from the SWF?

5.1 Growth of SWFs

There has been a spectacular growth in the size of SWFs since 2005 as a result of the establishment of the first SWF in many countries. Countries like Japan are planning to set up their first SWF.[3] Despite the optimistic view towards the growth, there are uncertainties in their sources of funding in relation to commodity prices, economic growth, monetary policy and political issues which will affect the size of the SWFs. Unlike other types of investment vehicle, SWFs have complications resulting from the state being the shareholder. Furthermore, most SWFs which have suffered huge losses after the global recession will take years to recover. Will these losses dampen the enthusiasm of potential SWFs? The effects of the subprime crisis on SWFs had not been taken into account in the previous forecasts. For example, ADIA, GPFG and Singapore's SWFs have suffered huge losses from the subprime crisis (see Chapter 3 on losses incurred by large SWFs).

---

3 Michiyo Nakamoto, "Call to set up Japan sovereign fund for pensions," *Financial Times*, 4 July 2008. http://www.ft.com/cms/s/0/3bc04f4e-4961-11dd-9a5f-000077b07658.html

5.1.1 Growth of Commodity-based SWFs

Since most SWFs are funded by revenues from commodities, commodity sales and prices will hugely affect their growth. For commodity-funded SWFs such as those based on oil, supply and demand has a big impact on the availability of capital. The sharp rise of the oil price in recent years has enabled oil-rich countries to accumulate large amounts of petrodollars. However, the future demand for oil is uncertain due to the recent subprime crisis and global recession. Yet despite this uncertainty, the oil price stood at $99 per barrel in 2008. The current price at $73 per barrel is still very high as compared to $15.05 per barrel in 1986, and a further big plunge in oil price is less likely to happen. Nevertheless, it is unlikely that we will see a huge surge in oil prices and the demand for oil under the current economic climate (see Figure 5.2 for crude oil prices).

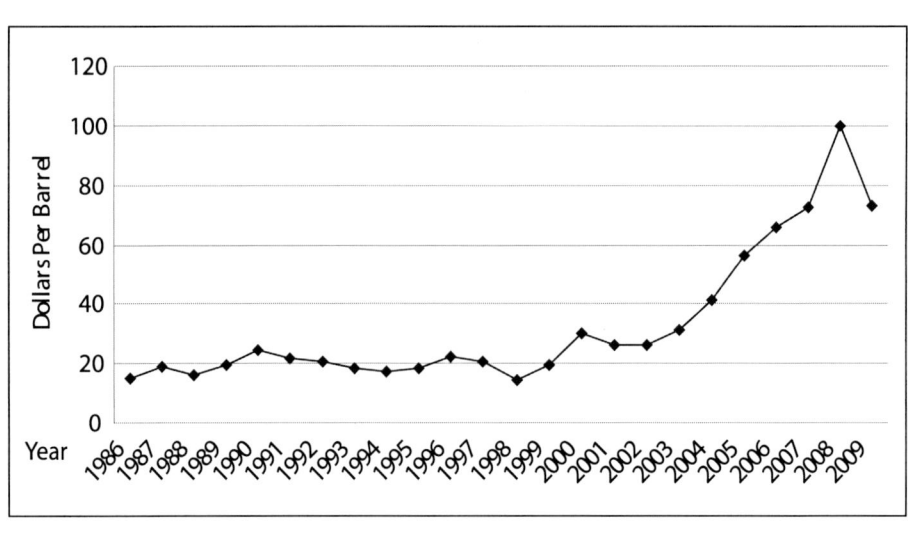

Figure 5.2: Crude Oil Spot Prices (Dollars per Barrel)

Source: US Energy Information Administrator

Setser and Ziemba (2009) modelled the size and the possible growth of Middle Eastern foreign assets under different assumptions about oil prices. Their predictions are based on the level of oil production before the December 2008 round of Organisation of Petroleum Exporting Countries (OPEC) cuts.[4] If

---

4 151st (Extraordinary) Meeting of the OPEC conference, No.17/2008, Oran, Algeria, 17 December 2008. http://www.opec.org/opecna/press%20releases/2008/pr172008.htm

the average oil price is $50 a barrel, the Gulf will need to draw on its interest and dividend to support the current level of imports even if the production level of oil remains uncut. At $75 a barrel, the GCC[5] would have approximately $140 billion to add to the foreign reserves of central banks or SWFs' foreign investments, almost as much as 2005 when the average oil price remained at $53 a barrel. If the oil price is at $100 a barrel, the Gulf will flourish. If the oil price falls to $25 or remains at $50 a barrel, the Gulf governments will need to draw heavily on foreign assets even if ambitious investment projects are cancelled. (See Figure 5.3 on Setser and Ziemba's (2009) estimates of GCC purchase of foreign assets). The figures show that GCC will draw down their foreign assets when oil price falls to $25 and invest in foreign assets if the oil price is $75 a barrel. Their projection shows that the Gulf is likely to reduce its investments in foreign assets and possibly would have to sell off its foreign assets to finance imports if the price of oil were to fall to $50 a barrel. It also shows that whatever the oil price is, these countries will reduce their investments in foreign assets and hold fewer foreign assets as compared to the figures in 2008 when holdings of foreign assets were at their peak.

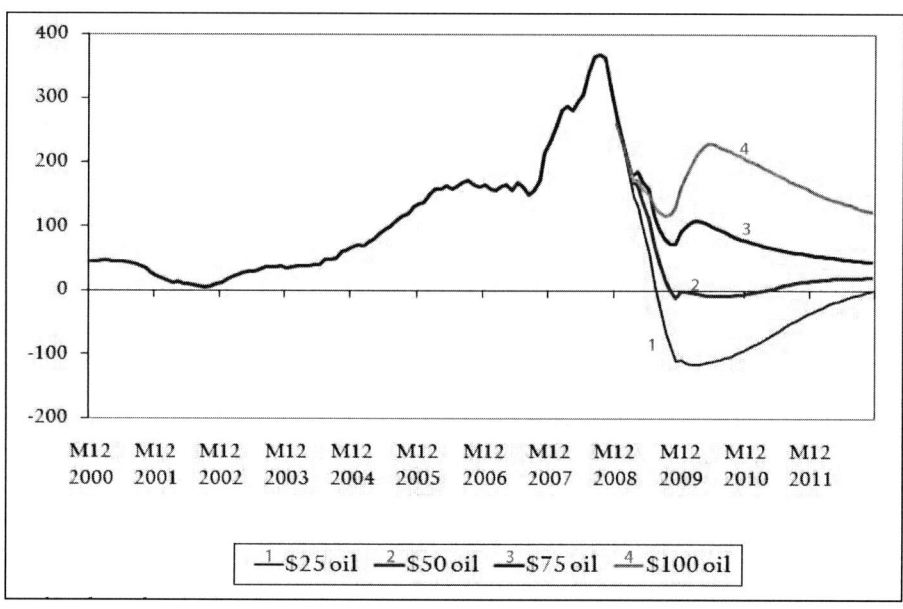

Figure 5.3: Estimate of GCC Purchase of Foreign Assets

Source: Setser and Ziemba (2009)

---

5 Members of GCC include Bahrain, Kuwait, Oman, Qatar, Saudi Arabia, and the United Arab Emirates.

With Dubai's debt crisis, some Middle Eastern governments may have difficulty rolling over their debts and may need to draw down their SWFs for imports and government spending. All these factors have affected the growth of Middle Eastern SWFs.

Despite the pessimistic picture painted above, non-Middle Eastern oil-based SWFs have potential to grow because they did not participate in the period of high SWF growth prior to the subprime crisis. The current high oil prices and the constant demand for oil are sufficient to sustain their growth. Even if oil prices were to fall, oil-rich countries will continue to inject capital into SWFs as long as the investments can provide higher returns compared to central banks' investments. Whatever happens, capital injection should be lower than it used to be.

If the oil price is maintained at the current level, countries such as Kuwait, Saudi Arabia and the UAE which have huge oil reserves will have the capital to inject more capital into their SWFs, while oil-exporting countries with no SWF will establish one to reap higher returns from their oil revenues, thus enabling their funds to grow bigger (Table 5.4). Besides the Middle East, other oil-rich countries such as Russia and Venezuela are likely to inject their capital into SWFs. Commodity-exporting countries like Bolivia, Brazil, Canada and Nigeria are expected to set up their own SWFs.[6]

Table 5.4: SWFs With Reserves

COUNTRY	NAME OF FUND	FOREIGN EXCHANGE RESERVES (IN USD MILLION AS OF 2008	OIL RESERVES (IN BILLION BARRELS
Algeria	Revenue Regulation Fund	145,363	12
Angola	Reserve Fund for Oil	12,290	9.035
Australia	Australian Government Future Fund (AGFF)	37,312	4.158
Azerbaijan	State Oil Fund	9,316	7
Botswana	Pula Fund	10,000	0
Brunei	Brunei Investment Agency (BIA)	Not Available	1.2
Canada	Alberta Heritage Fund (AHF)	42,624	27.644

6 Steffern Kern, "SWFs and foreign investment policies – an update," Deutsche Bank Research, 22 October 2008.

COUNTRY	NAME OF FUND	FOREIGN EXCHANGE RESERVES (IN USD MILLION AS OF 2008	OIL RESERVES (IN BILLION BARRELS
Chile	Economic and Social Stabilization Fund (ESSF), Chile Pension Reserves Fund	23,560	0.15
China	China Investment Company Ltd., Central Hujin Investment Corp.	1,946,000	16
East Timor	Timor-Leste Petroleum Fund	Not Available	0
Hong Kong	Hong Kong Monetary Authority Investment Portfolio	193,410	0
Iran	Foreign Exchange Reserve Fund	81,000	138.4
Ireland	National Pensions Reserve Fund (NPRF)	959	0
Kazakhstan	Kazakhstan National Fund (KNF)	19,479	30
Kiribati	Revenue Equalisation Reserve Fund (RERF)	Not Available	0
Kuwait	Kuwait Investment Authority (KIA)	19,630	101.5
Libya	Reserve Fund	79,000	41.464
Malaysia	Khazanah Nasional BHD (KNB)	87,700	4
Mauritania	National Fund for Hydrocarbon Reserves	Not Available	0.1
New Zeland	New Zealand Superannuation Fund	11,668	0.06
Nigeria	Excess Crude Account	45,000	36.22
Norway	Government Pension Fund - Global (GPFG), Government Petroleum Insurance Fund (GPIF)	47,927	6.68

SOVEREIGN WEALTH FUNDS

COUNTRY	NAME OF FUND	FOREIGN EXCHANGE RESERVES (IN USD MILLION AS OF 2008)	OIL RESERVES (IN BILLION BARRELS)
Oman	State General Stabilisation Fund (SGSF)	7,004	5.5
Papua New Guinea	Mineral Resources Stabilization Fund (MRSF)	2,193	0.088
Qatar	Qatar Investment Authority (QIA)	6,368	15.21
Russia	Stabilization Fund of the Russian Federation (SFRF)	383,905	60
Saudi Arabia	SAMA Foreign Holdings	31,320	266.71
Singapore	Government of Singapore Investment Corporation (GIC), Temasek Holdings	170,101	0
South Korea	Korea Investment Corporation (KIC)	212,478	0
Taiwan	Taiwan National Stabilisation Fund (TNSF)	312,642	0.002
Uganda	Poverty Action Fund	2,800	0
United Arab Emirates	Abu Dhabi Investment Authority (ADIA), Dubai Intern. Financial Centre Investments (DIFC)	29,620	97.8
United States of America	Alaska Permanent Reserve Fund Corperation (APRF), New Mexico State Investment Office Trust Funds, Permanent Wyoming Mineral Trust Fund (PWMTF)	75,877	21
Venezuela	Investment Fund for Macroeconomic Stabilization (FIEM)	42,628	87.035

Sources: SWF Institute, IMF International Financial Statistics, Oil & Gas Journal Dec 24, 2007

5.1.2 Growth of Non-commodity SWFs

As far as SWFs funded by excess reserves are concerned, the amount that these funds can grow in the long run will depend on their net exports and potential to attract foreign direct investments. In the short run, the massive reserves that the Asian central banks have accumulated will enable these countries to increase their capital in the Asian SWFs. Looking at the example of China, with its huge foreign reserves from exports and foreign direct investments, it is clear that CIC has the potential to grow into the biggest SWF. In late 2009, the Chinese media reported that CIC might obtain an additional $200 billion from the government.[7] If this capital injection materialises, CIC will be the second largest SWF after ADIA. However, in the long run it depends very much on whether Chinese exports continue to grow and also on how long China's domestic demand can be kept at a low level to fund its reserves. The exports of China and other Asian countries depend on global demand, and the recent subprime crisis which hit the Asian exporting countries hard has led to a plunge in their export earnings. Even with the end of the recession, the economic recovery is slow. Will Asian exporting countries continue to export large amounts of goods to build up their foreign reserves? Will the high balance of payment deficits in developed countries, ,particularly in the US, continue? China is undergoing changes to its economic structure so that it relies less and less on exports but more and more on increased domestic demand for growth.

The exchange rate policy of those countries with SWFs also affects the future size of SWFs. If these countries move towards a more flexible exchange rate system, they do not have to accumulate huge foreign reserves to defend their currency. In particular, China receives constant pressure from the West to allow its currency to appreciate against the US dollar and Euro. The West argues that the low exchange rate is the main factor contributing to the success of its cheap exports and hence accumulation of huge foreign reserves. The appreciation of the currency will not only slow down the growth of foreign reserves but also reduce the competitiveness of the country's exports, the major source of the country's foreign reserves. In addition, with the strengthening of the economy, Chinese officials have the ambition for the renminbi to replace the US dollar as the world's reserve currency.[8] China's central bank, the People's

---

[7] Karen Yap and Mao Lijun, "Sovereign wealth fund may get $200 billion cash injection," Chinadaily.com, 22 December 2009. http://www.chinadaily.com.cn/bizchina/2009-12/22/content_9211206.html

[8] Gordon G. Chang, "China's assault on the dollar," Forbes, 26 March 2009. http://www.forbes.

Bank of China, has announced that it will allow the renminbi to be used to settle certain regional transactions. This loosened control over renminbi will reduce China's reliance on the US dollar. All these would affect the growth of CIC in the long run but in the short run, China has a huge pool of foreign reserves available to inject further funds into CIC.

Besides China, other Asian countries such as Malaysia and Singapore use some form of exchange rate management to keep their currency from appreciating against the US dollar. If these countries were to move to a more flexible exchange rate system, the accumulation of foreign reserves would slow down, thus reducing the amount of capital available to the SWFs. The economic growth of these Asian countries is highly dependent on exports and foreign direct investments which will in turn affect their foreign reserves. Table 5.4 shows that China, Taiwan and Russia still have ample foreign reserves to increase capital in their SWFs. In addition, countries moving towards a more flexible exchange rate system can afford to transfer significant amounts of reserves to SWFs and still have sufficient foreign reserves to meet short-term needs such as funding imports.

Despite the uncertainties in the Asian export sector and its foreign reserve accumulation, the policy of Asian central banks gradually reducing holdings of US treasuries will result in more funds being transferred into SWFs in the short and medium run. Japan, as one of the biggest investors in US treasuries, is planning to set up its first SWF and model it on Singapore's Temasek to sustain pension commitments for its ageing population.[9] With Japan seeking a higher return on its foreign reserves, it is likely that the government will transfer part of its foreign reserves from central banks to an investment vehicle such as a SWF. The recent volatility of the US dollar has led central banks in India and Sri Lanka (see Chapter 1) to buy gold instead of holding US dollars. These countries may consider setting up an SWF to hold their foreign reserves in more diversified assets. In the short run, the growth potential of SWFs in Asia is optimistic.

---

com/2009/03/26/zhou-xiaochuan-geithner-renminbi-currency-opinions-columnists-dollar.html

9 S. Venkitaramanan, "Japan experiments with Singapore sling!" *The Hindu Business Line*, 11 June 2007. http://www.hindubusinessline.com/2007/06/11/studies/20070601100040900.htm

5.1.3 Summary of the Growth of SWFs

The above discussion suggests that despite the uncertainties in funding sources, forecasts for the growth of SWFs are optimistic. If the growth in petrodollars and foreign reserves is slow due to a fall in oil prices and exports, there is a greater need for governments of SWF countries to invest in assets with higher returns to ensure that the national wealth (or the country's income) is kept at an optimal level to meet the countries' future expenditure. If these higher returns materialise, these countries will increase the size of their SWFs even more than previously predicted.

The growth of existing SWFs is affected by many factors that are beyond the control of the shareholders (or the sovereigns) but, in the short to medium term, we would anticipate an increase in their size due to existing funds plumping up their capital and new funds being set up. Encouraged by the success of the existing SWFs, many countries are considering setting up their own SWFs in the coming years.

5.2 Implications of SWFs Growth On The Financial Markets

With the growth of SWFs, the demand for US dollars and US treasuries will fall as SWFs invest in more diversified asset classes compared to the central banks. The emergence of SWFs will witness a shift of investments from US treasuries to other assets such as listed and unlisted equities, real estate and direct investments in private companies. This would put an end to the accumulation of US treasuries in Asian countries and thus an end to the severe mispricing of US treasuries. This might lead to a fall in capital inflows into the US and eventual depreciation of US dollar. However, the shift from US treasuries to other assets by SWF governments would lead to higher returns on US assets and eventually an adjustment of part of the global imbalances. The change in asset returns might also reduce the difference between US earnings from foreign assets and payments for foreign liabilities. A similar trend is observed when central banks reduce holdings of government bonds in developed countries. The re-balancing of the public sector's investments is good for the global financial market as a whole because diversification by the public sector helps to avoid concentration of demand in only one asset class, e.g. gold. In order to hedge against the volatility of the US dollar, central banks usually buy gold when there are large swings in US dollar thus leading to surges in the price of gold. If governments are able to use SWFs to invest in a range of assets denominated in other currencies (particularly in the currencies of trading partners), this will avoid a large swing in asset prices because central banks would no longer have to hedge against the volatility of the US dollar.

To quantify the effects of SWF investments on the global markets, the IMF (2008) used the IMF's Global Integrated Monetary Fiscal Model to indicate how the shift of investments from US treasuries to a diversified portfolio via SWF would affect the USA. Using two hypothetical portfolios to mimic the asset allocations of two existing SWFs, two scenarios were compared where assets are kept as central banks reserves and where assets are invested via SWFs. The result suggests that the US real interest rate will increase by 10 to 20 basis points and the US dollar will depreciate from 2 to 5 %, and the US current account deficit would improve from 0.25 to 0.5% of GDP. Higher capital inflows will lead to a lower real interest rate for the rest of the world and more currency appreciation in real effective terms. However, if Asia continues to peg its currency to the dollar, inflation in Asia will rise. Overall, the diversification of foreign reserves into a wider range of assets allows prices of government debts from developed countries to adjust to better reflect the economic situation of these countries.

In addition, the growth of SWFs will increase the demand for financial expertise in the fund management industry and change the way some financial industries work. This will also create job opportunities in the financial sector, and financial institutions and their advisors can profit from SWFs by providing consulting and asset management services.[10] This will also increase the demand for research and analytical support services and joint ventures for deals. Currently State Street Global Advisors manage assets for government clients through the Official Institutions Group and the term *Sovereign Wealth Fund* was coined by the company. Other financial advisory firms will increasingly capitalise on the growth of SWFs and work closely with private equity firms in management buyouts and with venture capitalists to provide seed money for start-up companies. Stephen Barrette, International Chairman of Corporate Finance at KPMG, anticipates that SWFs will evolve towards a similar operation pattern as private equity firms and eventually become stiff competitors to private equity firms.[11] Similarly, Epstein and Rose

10 Chris Larson, "Managers eye SWF billions," Financial Times, 3 August 2008. http://www.ft.com/cms/s/0/9f9f1256-601e-11dd-805e-000077b07658.html
11 "Rosy picture predicted for sovereign wealth funds," KPMG, 29 January 2008. http://www.kpmg.

(forthcoming) claim that the future of private equity firms and the future of SWFs are inescapably intertwined. David Rubenstein, founder of the Carlyle Group, suggests that SWFs and private equity firms could form a "positive partnership".[12] This trend is observed in large SWFs such as ADIA and GIC (see ADIA and GIC joint ventures with private equity firms in Chapter 4). The recent financial crisis has put the squeeze on the cash flows of investment banks which has enabled SWFs to fill in the gap and provide funding to private equity firms. Moving forward, more SWFs will form partnership with private equity firms to invest in riskier assets.

Although there are calls for SWFs to outsource the management of fund investments to external fund managers to avoid direct government intervention, this is unlikely to happen. SWFs will outsource part of their funds but retain active management of most of them (see Chapter 4 for examples). As most governments are criticised for lacking the expertise to manage investments, SWFs have sought either partnerships or advice from financial experts while building up their own investment expertise. Some SWFs have been forming and training their own in-house team of fund managers and dealmakers so that they will be less dependent on external experts in the future. For example, ADIA has employed some veterans from the investment industry to head up its investment division. For new SWFs, it will take time to establish their own team of investment experts, whereas for small SWFs, outsourcing their asset management functions is more cost effective than building up their own team of experts. The increasing demand for investment management by the SWFs could create a distinct breed of fund managers. Roger Jerkins, a top dealmaker of Barclays involved in Qatar Investment Authority after the subprime crisis, announced his plan to leave and set up his own advisory business for sovereign investors in August 2009.[13] According to a survey by Clarke and Monk (2009), most fund managers are positive about the demand for professional services by SWFs which tend to use asset managers for private equity and infrastructure deals. The survey has also shown that asset managers from private equity are the largest beneficiaries of SWF investments. Unlike other state-owned enterprises or government agencies, these funds are keen to be seen as a sophisticated investment house rather than having a political image attached to them. Judging from the reaction

com/Global/IssuesAndInsights/ArticlesAndPublications/Pages/Sovereign_Wealth_Funds.aspx
12 Martin Arnold, "Private equity turns to sovereign wealth funds," Financial Times, 27 February 2008. http://www.ft.com/cms/s/0/2057fc20-e566-11dc-9334-0000799fd2ac.html
13 "Barclay's Jenkin exits to set up advisory firm," reported by Steve Slater and edited by Simone Jessop, Reuters, 14 August 2009. http://www.reuters.com/article/rbssFinancialServicesAndRealEstateNews/idUSLE40321620090814

of the financial industry to the growth of SWFs, these funds are viewed as genuine investors rather than a political tool of their governments.

The increasing demand for financial services by SWFs is beneficial in that it absorbs excess financial expertise from investment banking resulting from the downsizing of the investment banking sector. Financial institutions have also been hiring and training financial experts to deal with SWFs. As SWFs grow in size and complexity, there is a need to train experts in this area. Unlike other types of investment vehicle, the nature of SWFs demands a more rigorous corporate governance structure and the need for monitoring their operations would open up a new field of service for financial experts. This is particularly true for SWFs if the policies in their own countries conflict with those of the recipient countries. In addition, SWF is a hybrid of public and private sectors so a new class of financial expertise in risk management is needed to deal with the risks involved (see Chapter 3 on ALM).

5.3 Implications of SWFs' Investments on Companies and Recipient Countries

In general, the private sector has welcomed the entry of SWFs into the global markets. Peter Weinberg, an investment banker, commented that SWFs have the best and brightest people from their own countries and recently SWFs have hired industry veterans to beef up their investment teams. Shareholders will benefit from SWFs sitting on the board of directors because they can bring in their experience and expertise and provide a global perspective to the companies in which they invest.[14] Most policymakers and academics argue that SWFs should refrain from doing so as to avoid involving the political agendas of the SWF shareholders (see Chapter 2 for suggestions on corporate governance to involve no voting right for SWF shareholders). The absence of voting right for some shareholders will potentially increase the agency cost of companies, therefore, proper exercising of voting rights for SWFs is a better solution. Furthermore, no SWF investor will consider taking a large stake of a company if an investment does not come with the right to monitor the company's management. As SWFs grow, there is potential for these funds to hold larger stakes in companies such as clean energy where a greater

---

14 Peter Weinberg, "Sovereign funds offer a wealth of benefits," Financial Times, May 22 2008. http://www.ft.com/cms/s/0/171c7bf0-280e-11dd-8f1e-000077b07658.html

initial outlay is required. SWFs should have the same right to monitor the management of the companies as other types of shareholders. To minimise the risk of SWF shareholders, companies should have a proper procedure to ensure that they can exercise the voting right in a cautious manner and vote in the interests of the company and not those of their sovereign (refer to the Santiago Principles in Chapter 3).

In addition, the chairman and chief executive of Blackstone commented that using SWFs to recycle the large surpluses of central banks in Asia can be beneficial, particularly to the West which needs the capital.[15] The ability of excess capital to flow to other regions and industries would benefit both the SWFs and the recipient countries. In a *Financial Times* special report on SWFs, Nuno Fernandez and Artuno Bris raise the positive impact of SWF investment in a company as this guarantees stable long-term finance and reduces the company's cost of capital.[16] Typically, an SWF has a long-term investment horizon and it is unlikely for it to withdraw the investment in the short run, thus allowing the company to formulate long-term strategies without the fear of sudden funding withdrawal. Other benefits of SWF investments, as noted by Howard Socol, CEO of Barney, include the expansion of the business to foreign markets. For instance, Barney plans to expand to the Middle East since Dubai's Istithmar acquired the company in 2007.[17] All of these point to the benefits of having SWFs as strategic investors and the potential of SWFs to be a major source of funding in the global financial markets.

Besides the positive attitude of the private sector towards SWF investments, research also shows that investors in general react positively to the news of SWF investments. Empirical research by Chhaochharia and Laeven (2008) and Bortolotti et al. (2009) indicate a positive reaction of investors at the announcement of SWF investment. However, Chhaochhria and Laeven (2008) showed a poor long-run performance of the target firm. Bortolotti et al. (2009) also show a deteriorating performance of firms after SWFs' acquisitions and attribute the poor performance to the rise of agency costs.

Rios-Morales and Brennan (2009) examined the potential impact of SWFs on economic growth and likened the role of SWFs to foreign direct investments (FDIs). It is true that SWFs can play an important role in economic growth. For

---

15 Stephen Schwarzman, "Reject sovereign wealth funds at your peril," Financial Times, 19 June 2008.
   http://www.ft.com/cms/s/0/405b8888-3dff-11dd-b16d-0000779fd2ac.html
16 Buno Fernandez and Artuno Bris, "Sovereign wealth revalued," Financial Times, 12 February 2009.
   http://www.ft.com/cms/s/0/2c8e3874-f7d0-11dd-a284-000077607658.html
17 "Istithmar agrees to acquire Barneys New York for USD 825 million," AMEinfo.com, 23 July 2007.
   http://www.ameinfo.com/124329.html

example, ADIA has signed a memorandum of understanding with India to develop the country's highway infrastructure. Moreover, SWF investments can lead to more open and better functioning markets within the investee nation. The recipient countries can ask the investor countries for reciprocal treatment, thus encouraging globalisation. Rose (2008) suggests that the USA's openness to CIC's investment in their enterprises has encouraged Chinese reciprocity and allowed US firms to gain more access to China's markets.

However, critics of SWFs, particularly policymakers from the USA and the EU, point out that having an SWF as an investor would cause harm to a company, especially if the investment is related to sensitive industries that might affect the security of the recipient country. As US Treasury Deputy Secretary Robert Kimmitt (2008:128) commented, 'profit maximisation may not be considered the primary objective' of SWFs.[18] Another problem is the additional regulations and lengthy checks involved to review an SWF investment by some countries. This increases the cost of foreign direct investment. To avoid this additional cost, SWFs should maintain an arms length relationship with the investee companies and not directly involve themselves in the operation of the company. This will avoid political backlash and separate politics from private sector operations.

Countries with excess reserves will be keen to emulate the success of existing SWFs and more state-owned investment vehicles will be set up, either in the form of SWFs or state-owned enterprises. In order to diversify risk, these new funds will need to be diverted to cross-border investments. Therefore, it is likely we will see an increase in competition between SWFs and state-owned enterprises fighting for profitable investments. For example, Cathay Pacific and Singapore Airlines (with its parent company Temasek) competed in a bid to acquire China Eastern Airlines.[19] Some countries set up more than one SWF to spur competition among their own SWFs. Abu Dhabi, Dubai, Singapore and Russia have more than one SWF and China's CIC appears to have been created to compete with SAFE. Abu Dhabi's new SWF, ADIC, was initially thought to have been set up to take over ADIA's domestic investments but instead this new fund is apparently competing with ADIA (refer to ADIA in Chapter 4). However, to date there is no report of SWFs from the same country competing for the same investment and no incidence of any internal competition which has led to a bidding war. This implies that the competition brought about by

---

18 Robert M. Kimmitt "Public footprints in private markets: Sovereign wealth funds and the world economy," Foreign Affairs, 87(1), 19-130, 2008.
19 Irene Shen, "Cathay Pacific falls after droping Eastern bid," Bloomberg, 25 September 2007. http://www.bloomberg.com/apps/news?pid=20601089&sid=ai5O0UNJTCvA&refer=china

the growth of SWFs has been healthy and it is unlikely to create asset bubbles. The huge supply of capital from SWFs could drive up the price of assets and slow down potential returns. It is also argued that SWFs, which have access to more information than the private sector, will have the upper hand in making investments, thus resulting in unfair competition. Nevertheless, the increase in competition will lead to a more diligent search for profitable investments by all investors and it is likely that SWFs will diversify their investment portfolios further into sectors/countries in which they have not previously invested. Unlike SWFs, the Asian central banks invest mainly in US treasuries which only help to lower the interest rates and indirectly cause asset bubbles in the US. Unlike the situation in central banks, the increase in competition among SWFs will not lead to asset price inflation because they will be investing in diversified asset classes.

In examining the arguments for and against the emergence of SWFs, we can see that the private sector is more positive about the emergence of SWFs as a major player in the global market, whereas most policymakers and academics hold a negative view. In addition, the latter group have politicised the existence of SWFs, which have tried hard to avoid being portrayed as having political motives by refraining from sensitive industries and keeping a low profile for their investments. In fact, some SWF deals broke down due to the publicity and media speculation on their investment motives (see CIC's bid for Uncol and the acquisition of P&O by Dubai World Port in Chapter 3). Very often the publicity surrounding the government-related agencies for overseas investments fails to examine why the investments were made or intended in the first place.

The rapid growth of SWFs has caused concerns for policymakers and raised the question of whether these funds will represent a permanent flow of capital from East to West. In addition, these funds are huge and the capability of the SWFs to raise capital from their governments poses the question of whether the massive flow of funds between industries and between countries will destabilise the international financial market. The next section analyses if these possibilities are likely.

5.4 Effects of SWFs on Stability of Global Financial Markets

Given their lack of transparency and the huge volume of capital control by investors, what does the emergence and growth of the SWFs mean for the global financial markets? One of the fears raised is whether a substantial portfolio adjustment would destabilise them. This concern is highlighted by Clay Lowery from the US Department of the Treasury[20] and echoed by many policymakers. Furthermore, would these funds exhibit herding behaviour in times of financial crisis in certain markets when liquidity is needed the most? All these huge flows of funds could jeopardise stability in financial markets and economies. The lack of transparency in these funds' asset allocations makes the situation worse because market players will speculate on SWFs' moves. Judging by their moves in the recent subprime crisis, the SWFs have rather, however, played an important role in stabilising the banking system by providing much needed liquidity. The amount of funds pumped into the financial markets by the SWFs during the financial crisis was second only to the US government's rescue package. In fact, the aggressive investments made by SWFs during and after the subprime crisis made them suffer their biggest losses since their inception. In particular, the fall in the global stock markets bought huge losses to ADIA, CIC, GIC, Temasek and GPFG (refer to Table 3.2 for estimated losses by selected SWFs).

The effect of the subprime crisis has shown that when the global financial markets fall, the SWFs are adversely affected. If financial markets are unstable, more harm than benefit is created, SWF investments will suffer directly and the global economy will be impacted indirectly, adversely affecting those SWF countries which are highly dependent on the developed countries for their own economic growth. The Middle Eastern countries, for instance, would be affected by a fall in oil demand and prices, while the Asian countries would be affected by a fall in demand for their exports and the flow of foreign direct investments into their region. The stability of financial markets and the global economy is therefore more important to these countries than any benefits that might be gained from destabilising the financial markets. In addition, some of the SWFs are run by management bodies separated from the government, or

---

20 "Remarks by Acting Under Secretary for International Affairs Clay Lowery on sovereign wealth funds and the international financial systems," US Department of Treasury, Press Room, 21 June 2007. http://www.ustreas.gov/press/releases/hp471.htlm

by external fund managers whose performances would be affected if markets were destabilised. Similar concerns over the funds' capability to destabilise markets were also raised when hedge funds first emerged in the financial markets, and to date such concerns have not been justified. In relative terms shareholders of SWFs will lose more than the hedge funds or any other institutional investors if the markets are destabilised, resulting in a double whammy with a direct loss in national wealth and an indirect loss due to the poor economic performance of the fund.

As a group, the SWFs are relatively conservative investors who have a long-term investment vision but no external liabilities. Such investors are less affected by short-term volatility and they are more prepared to buy assets when prices are low and hold them for a longer time (refer to real estate purchases by ADIA and GIC as long-term investments in Chapter 4). Unlike other types of investors, the SWFs will not be forced to divest their investments due to capital requirements because as a group they do not have any external liability (only Dubai World and Temasek have announced that they have external debts but it is understood that some of the SWFs' real estate investments are financed by mortgages) nor external obligation such as pension fund obligation except that they have to make allowances to meet their governments' needs for contingent cash flows. This contingent cash-flow need is usually taken into account in the SWFs' portfolios where most SWFs hold a certain percentage of their funds in either government bonds or money market instruments. For some SWFs, this contingent liability is included in the central bank's investments because they are set up using excess liquidity from central banks' balance sheets. The Norwegian and Australian SWFs are saving funds and their pension obligations are in the future. Unlike insurance companies, SWFs are not obliged to make insurance settlements. This buy-and-hold approach prevents asset prices from falling and reduces the danger of market collapse, particularly in times of financial turmoil. For example, the SWFs bought stakes in western financial institutions during the 2007/2008 crisis which prevented a further collapse of banks even though some stakes were sold in 2008 (the sales were carried out when the market was stable). Temesak sold off its stake in Merill Lynch in 2008 at a loss and the Qatar Investment Authority cut its stake in Barclay in 2009. The large SWFs have an interest in adjusting their portfolios gradually to limit adverse effects on their transactions. These transactions are based on the market price and any negative price movement would affect the SWFs' profits. Overall, there is no evidence to suggest that SWFs have destabilised or will destabilise the financial system. In fact, the emergence of SWFs has provided much-needed liquidity in the banking system during the subprime crisis and has helped to stabilise the share prices of banks. Robert Kimmitt of the US Treasury noted that, given the SWFs' position as long-term investors with a strong and positive track record, they will not deviate from their strategic asset allocations in times of short-term volatility, and should therefore be considered a force for financial stability.[21]

Research has also found that SWFs have a positive effect on the stability of the financial markets. Drezner (2008) maintains that SWFs are expected to function in a counter-cyclical manner and they act as stabilisers in times of financial turmoil as observed during the subprime crisis. This implies that SWFs are socially responsible and the SWF governments play a political role in stabilising the financial market. Utilising data from 166 events, Sun and Hesse (2009) show that SWFs have no significant destabilising effects on the equity market. Chen (2008) from CIC concludes that SWFs are helpful for realising the alignment of macroeconomic policy internally, and for stabilising financial markets externally.

As the SWFs grow and become more active players in the global financial market, a destabilised financial system will increase their costs. As public entities, SWFs have a greater interest in ensuring the stability of financial markets, with the understanding that a destabilised financial market would have dire consequences on the global economy and their own economies. Many policymakers fear that those SWFs with less democratic governments will use their funds for political motives, thus destabilising the financial markets. From a geopolitical point of view, Shih (2009) argues that a unified authoritarian regime is more likely to operate an SWF in a manner that maximises profit. The governments of such regimes have a higher incentive to conduct economic policies in such a way that ensures long-term growth. [22]

Even though SWFs may not destabilise the financial system directly, they may do so indirectly. Their low level of transparency would lead to other investors misreading SWF motives and lead to herding effects in the financial markets. SWFs making large divestments in a certain market could be misread by other investors as an exit from the industry and could lead to a rush to sell stakes in the market. This might create speculative herding behaviour, resulting in volatility in the financial markets generally. A higher level of transparency

---
21 See Note 18.
22 Mancur Olson, "Dictatorship, democracy, and development," *American Political Science Review*, 87(3), p10, 1993.

on their asset allocations and a broader spectrum of asset allocations and risk preference would help to avoid large price fluctuations and the markets would then be able to anticipate and absorb the large flow of funds. In addition, increased transparency would also reduce market speculation that could lead to the mispricing of assets. On the other hand, SWFs' investing in hedge funds and private equity firms could increase their opaqueness as these investment vehicles are already opaque in their own investments. SWFs might indirectly cause price fluctuation through the activities of these funds. Speculations in financial markets caused by SWFs' non-transparency would be more likely to happen in countries, particularly the emerging markets or less developed markets, with inadequate regulations. Unlike developed financial markets which are in a better position to cope with price swings, the less developed financial markets do not have strong fundamentals to support large swings in prices. In addition, the USA and the EU have laws and regulations that provide considerable comprehensive mandatory disclosure regimes when major holdings in a listed company are acquired or disposed of. SWFs would have to comply with these. Therefore, the disclosure of SWFs' strategic asset allocations is more important for less developed markets or markets which do not require mandatory disclosure for major transactions.

In fact, SWFs can be used as a tool to prevent the potential financial destability that might arise due to global imbalances. The accumulation of US treasuries and US dollar assets by Asia and the Middle East can be partially adjusted using SWFs. Both the Asian economies, (who have accumulated) large foreign reserves) and the Middle Eastern countries (who hold a large number of petrodollars) have invested in US treasuries and other US assets. It is a matter of time before we see how these excessive holdings of US treasuries will adversely affect the financial markets. SWFs serve as an alternative for countries in these regions to invest their foreign currency in assets other than in bonds issued by developed countries, particularly US treasuries. For years the deficits in the USA and the UK have been funded by the surpluses from Asia and the Middle East, and the low interest rates have partly boosted asset prices in those countries. According to the estimates from the McKinsey Report (2007), the investments of Asian central banks in US treasuries has decreased the US long-term interest rates by 55 basis points, while the investments from petrodollars have reduced the rates by an additional 21 basis points.[23] These have distorted the real value of US treasuries and have fuelled a low

---

23 *"The new power brokers: How oil, Asia, hedge funds, and private equity are shaping global capital markets." McKinsey Global Institute. October 2007. http://www.mckinsey.com/mgi/publications/*

interest rate environment. The low interest rate was regarded as one of the factors that led to the subprime crisis, the argument being that cheap money had encouraged housing bubbles and free spending by US consumers. This shows the danger of pouring all the money into the same type of financial instrument. SWF investments are more diversified, with direct and indirect investments in different industries and different types of financial instruments. Having SWFs investing in diversified assets in different countries poses less of a threat than central banks investing in bonds issued by developed countries and US denominated dollars. Furthermore, a shift in central banks' reserves can be more disruptive to the market and has implications for monetary policy for many countries when they have to hedge against a fall in currency of developed countries such as the US dollar.

5.5 International Guidelines and SWFs

There are currently many debates on SWF guidelines and regulations to increase transparency in their operations. Basically a general consensus has been reached, but the adoption of the proposed guidelines is optional. The issue of regulations on SWF operations is controversial. Who should administer the guidelines and what can be done if these guidelines are not followed? How can a "penalty" be imposed on an SWF which does not follow the guidelines when the shareholder is a sovereign? These questions remain unanswered even though the Santiago Principles were initiated by the IMF in 2008 (see Chapter 2). The Santiago Principles are a good start but whether the initiative will work is questionable. Firstly, for countries where SWF operations are not separated from the state, the Santiago Principles have limited use. Secondly, different SWFs have different investment approaches and the Santiago Principles, which are "one-size-fits-all", are unlikely to work equally well for all. Thirdly, regulations and guidelines on SWFs which have been set and administered by western institutions or western-dominated institutions will not appeal to the SWFs from Asia and the Middle East. Though a good start, the Santiago Principles are non-binding, and this set of international guidelines and regulations may not work as well as intended.

The optimal solution to the problem is actually self-governance and voluntary disclosure. Any additional regulations will only increase the cost of implementation. Currently most countries have their own laws and regulations to deal with foreign investments, and the existing regulations and laws are sufficient to detect any non-economic motives of SWFs (see Chapter 3 for more on recipient countries' regulations on foreign investments). Furthermore, it is unlikely that SWFs will influence decisions that are against their interests or those of the recipient countries because SWFs typically take only a small stake. Despite this, SWFs that have taken bigger stakes and have the power to influence companies' actions need to consider carefully the cost of doing so since such an action could result in a complete loss of trust in SWFs. This will affect SWFs' open access to the global markets, and it would be too costly for SWFs to jeopardise their reputation. Polachek et al. (2007), in an empirical study on foreign direct investments and international relations, show that FDIs reduce conflicts and encourage cooperation. Similarly, it is in SWFs' own interests to cooperate with the recipient countries or companies as their welfare too is tied to the recipient countries and the companies they invest in. With developed countries running high deficits and Asian and Middle Eastern countries running high surpluses, promoting foreign direct investments can facilitate better capital flows. Both the SWF countries and the recipient countries need to negotiate a set of guidelines or regulations that are acceptable to all parties; failing to do so will result in resistance.

SWFs should disclose their primary asset allocation policies and their risk management policies to avoid high costs of entry into financial markets. This disclosure will avoid having protectionism imposed by recipient countries. SWFs should weigh the costs and benefits of transparency and make the optimal level of disclosure. The stakes are high for the the West could increase protectionist policies to restrict SWF investments in their countries thus reducing SWFs' opportunities to invest in the West. Chapter 3 shows that most SWFs have their cross-border investments in North America and Europe. If SWF investments were blocked in these countries, their investment strategies would be constrained as full geographical and industrial diversifications would no longer be possible. This would have serious implication on SWFs' operations because large SWFs are proactive in geographical diversification. Establishing trust between SWFs and the recipient countries is important both to avoid protectionism and to ensure the free flow of capital and investments across borders. While ADIA and the Australian Future Fund describe the Santiago Principles as a step to establish trust between SWFs and recipient countries,[24] China does not view

---

24 Press briefing on the International Working Group of sovereign wealth funds by co-Chairs, Mr. Hamad al Suwaidi of the Abu Dhabi Investment Authority, and Mr. Jaime Caruana of the

the Santiago Principles as a positive move. Gao Xiqing of CIC, commented that the adoption of the Santiago Principles would "hurt feelings".[25]

A lack of transparency in SWFs' operations would hinder the role they play in lowering the cost of capital in financial markets. Fears of political motives would result in protectionism and deter SWFs from entering into markets and industries that need the funds. It is natural for the West to feel sceptical about the motives of SWFs and to increase protectionism as most of the largest SWFs come from countries which lack full democratic rights. The shareholders of these funds are government-based and the threat of using them for political purposes is always apparently present. With suitable levels of disclosure, this fear would be eliminated and these funds would be encouraged to invest in those industries where huge investments are currently needed for long-term benefits.

Nevertheless, too many rules and regulations will only discourage the participation of SWFs in international investments and hinder the free flow of capital. With the high level of savings in Asia and petrodollars in the Middle East, capital should ideally flow to economies and industries where funds are most needed and can be effectively used. Hence, while policymakers and international institutions in the West are calling for operational transparency, they need to weigh the cost of increasing transparency. SWFs should be allowed a certain degree of non-disclosure similar to the level of non-disclosure allowed in private equity firms and hedge funds in their investment strategies. SWFs from China and the Middle East have warned that if OECD countries seek to impose stringent conditions on them regarding transparency and disclosure, they will locate their capital elsewhere. If this happens, we shall see the bulk of Asian savings and petrodollars moving to emerging markets only, and this will have adverse effects on those developed countries that have a high balance of payment deficit. Epstein and Rose (forthcoming) urge caution over regulating the SWFs. They argue that if US regulations keep SWFs away, the USA will lose the opportunity to strengthen ties with certain countries, which will adversely affect the dollar. These countries will switch their reserve currency away from the US dollar and, in extreme cases, possibly embark on a range of hostile actions towards the West.

International Monetary Fund, with David Murray of the Australia Future Fund and chair of the IWG's Drafting Group. 11 October 2008. http://www.iwg-swf.org/tr/swftr0802.htm

25 *"China investment an open book. 60 Minutes: Sovereign wealth fund's president promises transparency," 6 April 2008. http://www.cbsnews.com/stories/2008/04/04/60minutes/main3993933.shtml*

The corporate governance of SWFs should be improved as the funds develop. Even though the operations of most SWFs are separate from their ministries and government agencies, the boards of directors are mostly made up of government officials (see Table 2.2 on role of government in selected SWFs). With such a situation, it is not convincing to claim that SWFs operate independently from their governments. While some SWFs transfer their government officials from other government agencies to sit on the board of directors, the same question arises: how independent are these ex-government officials fresh from their government role? For some SWFs, external directors are appointed but it is unclear what voting rights they have, what role they play and how much influence they have. It is argued that having government officials sitting on SWF boards is an interim arrangement for new funds, but to this day government officials are still sitting in the board for some long-established SWFs.

Nevertheless, governments have a fiduciary duty to ensure that their SWFs are operated so as to contribute the best returns to their nation. They need to establish a proper arms-length relationship with the SWFs' boards of directors. While the board of directors is accountable to the government for the performance of SWFs, the government is in turn accountable to its citizens. These funds submit their audited annual accounts to the government in a similar way to privately-run companies submitting their accounts to shareholders. But most of the SWFs do not provide information on their performance, and even if there is disclosure of performance, only vague descriptions such as "return since the fund's inception" are produced which do not provide any useful information. A few exceptions are Norway's Government Pension Fund - Global and the Australian Future Fund which both provide detailed financial reports on their performance to the public.

In terms of accountability, SWFs are not publicly accountable. The public has no access to the audited accounts and is not informed of any fund's performance. As an SWF is created from a nation's wealth, so by rights the citizens of the country are the stakeholders, the state is the caretaker of the fund, the board of directors is the executor of the objectives and the executive director and managers are responsible for the management of the fund. All the arguments to support SWFs' transparency and disclosure have ignored the fact that the original and ultimate stakeholders of the funds are the citizens of those countries. Yet most of the public of these SWF countries do not have access to information on fund performance. Proper accountability of the SWFs' capital and resources is important and would act as a built-in mechanism to minimise the risk of misappropriation of funds. Increased accountability can ensure that funds are being used according to their objectives. An SWF's performance can have implications for the citizens of a country as the fund can be tapped into during an economic downturn. Norway's GPFG, for example, was tapped into in 2009, and there was a parliamentary debate in Singapore about the use of their SWFs to revive the economy. In the cases where SWFs are established to build wealth for future generations, the performance of the funds would have an impact on the provision of essential public services and the level of tax citizens have to pay. If an SWF cannot provide the fund for public services, the government should decide if it needs to reduce those public services or increase taxation; either choice will reduce the benefits to citizens.

5.6 The Conflicting Role of SWFs – State Capitalism and Free Market

Apart from the trend of capital flowing from the East to the West, another cause for concern for the West is that these SWFs are owned by the state. Fear of SWFs being used for political purpose has led Western governments to press Asian and Middle Eastern governments to adopt a "hands-off" approach in the running of their SWFs. While SWFs are owned by the state they can invest like other private investment vehicle. As cited in Truman (2008:3), "This redistribution from private to public hands implies a decision-making orientation that is at variance with the traditional private-sector, market-oriented framework with which most of us are comfortable even though our own system does not fully conform to that ideal." Is the emergence of SWFs a return to state capitalism or is it a new trend where governments are beginning to behave like corporations? "Do SWFs shake the logic of capitalism" (Lawrence Summer 2007)?[26] SWFs are owned by the state and this does not seem to fit comfortably into a definition of capitalism. Lyons (2007) views SWFs as "the rise of state capitalism" and the most problematic aspect of this is that these funds may take strategic stakes in sensitive industries in the developed countries. Despite the numerous criticisms of SWFs and the regulations established to monitor their activities, these funds are set to stay. They are changing the traditional role played by government and markets

26 Lawrence Summers, "Sovereign funds shake the logic of capitalism," Financial Times, 30 July 2007. http://www.ft.com/cms/s/0/8c9dea94-3e30-11dc-8f6a-0000779fd2ac.html

as "high finance can no longer be kept separate from high politics" (Cohen, 1986).

Western countries have been sceptical about the activities of Asian and Middle Eastern SWFs, which is why they have requested them to be transparent about their operations. They argue that some SWFs can be manipulated by governments to further their political ambitions. However, western countries have been good at mixing business with politics over the centuries, as witnessed in the practices of the East India Company in the British colonial days and the current US sanctions against Cuba. As noted by Sir John Gieve, Deputy Governor of Bank of England, as early as 1870s the UK had invested in emerging countries which had abundant land and natural resources but scarce capital and where the capital returns were high. They were able to build up a large stock of foreign assets 50 years before the First World War. As a result, they benefited from a surplus in their investment account for most of the period from 1870.[27] The existing SWFs differ from government investments in the past in that capital is flowing from emerging countries to developed countries. Theoretically, funds flow from developed countries which have abundant capital to developing or less developed countries which have abundant resources. However, the investments of Asian and Middle Eastern SWFs are not purely for investment returns but include objectives such as saving export revenues for future generations, hedging against the risk of a possible fall in the US dollar and knowledge transfer, etc. Therefore, the activities of the SWFs do not fit into the standard model where funds flow from developed to developing countries.

Government involvement in the private sector is not something new as nationalisation has always been an option after a financial crisis. In the case of the 1997/1998 Asian crisis, many Asian banks were nationalised and restructured. The recent subprime crisis has also brought about government involvement in the banking sector. An example is the nationalisation of Northern Rock by the UK government. There is a blurred boundary between the state and the private sector as the role of government can involve rescuing domestic companies. This shows that the level of government intervention is closely related to the business cycle. The recent investments in western financial institutions by Asian and Middle Eastern SWFs have the appearance of cross-border nationalisation but this is not exactly the case. If SWFs do not take up this role, there will be other state agencies playing such a role.

---

27 "Sovereign wealth funds and global imbalances," Speech by Sir John Gieve Deputy of England at Sovereign wealth management conference, London, 14 March 2008.

The key issue is that it is not possible to separate SWFs from the state completely. It is possible to have a set of good practices for the SWFs to follow, but it is questionable how independent they can be from the state which is their shareholder (or caretaker). There are always unavoidable grey areas due to the source or origin of the funds. The recent crisis made SWFs suffer great losses and the public has called on their governments to explain these losses, as in the case of the CIC and Temasek. Some even suggest that SWFs should invest in their domestic economies to help fight recession rather than investing overseas. Governments could avoid getting closely involved in SWF operations but they are unlikely to adopt a completely "hands-off" approach when it comes to the strategic direction of the funds.

Another issue that makes it nearly impossible for SWFs to operate as pure corporations is the attempt by politicians (mostly from non-SWF countries) to invite SWFs to invest or be actively involved in industries supporting clean energy in order to sustain the environment. How are SWFs supposed to operate purely for business interests when policymakers repeatedly suggest or dictate investment decision? There are a lot of controversial issues raised here.

To argue that the SWFs' investments are not motivated by strategic objectives or that they do not play a strategic role is incorrect. Decisions on some of the investments made are based on the government's strategic industrial policies. Diwan (2009) observed that SWFs from the Middle East are well-known for their strategic investments which take stakes in industries they are developing domestically to facilitate knowledge transfer. SWFs are also used to finance infrastructure development, recapitalising SOEs and strategic industries in domestic markets, so it is impossible to separate investment from politics. This is evident in Russia where the government has called upon the country's SWF to invest in its own domestic companies, and similarly, the objective of France's SWF is to protect its strategic industries. Recently SWFs have started investing in industries involved in clean energy and they are playing an important role in this industry. Such kinds of involvement are not a call for pure investment. The need for resources by these countries and the demand for expertise to facilitate their economic developments do result in SWFs investing strategically: China has been actively acquiring minerals in Africa and expanding its stake in oil industries in anticipation of increased demand for commodities as the country grows. Moreover, CIC has acquired stakes in some commodities related companies.

The existence and growth of Asian and Middle Eastern SWFs can be viewed as a strategic move by their governments to achieve certain objectives. The rapid growth of Asian SWFs reflects changes in Asia's economic structure. With the Asian economies becoming more developed and the growth of their domestic demand, they will be less reliant on exports to increase their foreign reserves. SWFs may be the Asian governments' answer to dwindling foreign reserves as a result of the fall in exports and rise in imports. They have learnt from the Asian crisis to keep sufficient foreign reserves as insurance for their countries. Moreover, Asian governments, excluding China and India, are looking for higher returns on their foreign reserves to cope with the ageing population in the region. This increasingly ageing population has urged its governments to look for alternatives to finance the future demand for pensions and social security. Outside Asia, Australia and Norway are also looking for higher returns from their SWFs to finance their future pension fund obligations.

The Asian and Middle Eastern governments are diversifying their US denominated assets into alternative assets to avoid the danger of tying all their national wealth to a single currency. The SWF provides them with the means to achieve this purpose. This is important so as to avoid shrinking the national wealth when the US dollar depreciates. When the Asian central banks adopt a more flexible exchange rate system, it is inevitable that the Asian currency will appreciate against the dollar and the US dollar will depreciate. Diversifying out of US assets gradually through SWF investments will lower the impact of US depreciation. There is already a trend for SWFs to invest in emerging markets: ADIA is investing in India and Khazanah Nasional is investing in China, while GIC and Temasek have actively invested in the Asia-Pacific region since their inceptions. The SWF allows these governments to invest in the private sector of emerging market (i.e. private companies) instead of investing in bonds issued by these countries.

Lastly, the SWF is labelled a "buyer of last resort" by the *Economist*.[28] Due to the subprime crisis and economic recession, SWFs are one of the few investment vehicles that have ample liquidity for investment even in times of uncertainty. SWFs were encouraged to invest in their domestic markets and provide liquidity to the financial markets during the credit crunch. The role of "buyers of last resort" is equivalent to the strategic role of "lenders of last resort" played by central banks. Acting as buyers of last resort, SWFs are assuming a strategic role taken to prevent asset prices from falling further

---

28 "Buyer of last resort, What China wants and can offer for its money," The Economist, 25 February 2009.

and to ensure that illiquidity in the financial markets will not paralyse the economy. During the Asian crisis in 1998, the Monetary Authority of Hong Kong (HKMA), Hong Kong's central bank, played such a role. To stabilise the Hong Kong stock market, the HKMA purchased shares and cushioned the effect of the Asian crisis. If the government had not played the role of buyer of last resort, the Hong Kong stock market and economy would have been badly hit by speculators. The shares were sold gradually in different stages after the market was stabilised. It would not be a surprise to see SWFs playing such a role in the future.

But are these SWFs turning the global financial markets into state capitalism? Are SWFs buying foreign businesses and trying to reverse the effect of privatisation into nationalisation? Or it is the other side of the coin where governments are behaving like corporations? Looking at Singapore and other Asian countries such as Japan, China and South Korea, we can see that the governments of these countries are active in their industrial policies. Most of these economies are run on a system based on planned industrial policy rather than the free market. Singapore is often called Singapore Inc. because of the government involvement in businesses within the country, and its SWF, Temasek, is one of the oldest SWFs in existence. The Singaporean government has created Government-Linked Corporations (GLCs) as part of its policy for economic development and for building various economic sectors in Singapore.[29] Unlike other Asian countries, the GLCs have been the major factor for Singapore's economic development and the presence of government involvement in business has been criticised, both overseas and domestically. The Chinese government, which set up its first SWF in 2007, is also involved in businesses through its state-owned enterprises, while Malaysia's SWF, Khazanah Nasional, is increasingly involved in domestic businesses via the GLCs. In the Middle East, the ruler of Dubai, the de facto CEO of Dubai Inc., also runs his country like a corporation.[30] Other part of the Middle East, such as Abu Dhabi, are run like a family-controlled business in which the government plays a dominant role in the economy and is also the largest investor in the private sector. In fact, the line between private and public business is unclear.[31] It would not be surprising to see that state-owned enterprises (SOEs), GLCs and SWFs invest in certain industries or countries to facilitate technology

---

29 Carlos D. Ramírez and Ling Hui Tan, "Singapore Inc versus the private sector: Are government-linked companies different?" IMF Working Paper, 2003, WP/03/156.
30 Pepe Escobar, "Dubai lives the post-oil Arab dream," Asia Times Online, 7 June 2006. http://www.atimes.com/atimes/Middle_East/HF07Ak01.html
31 Abu Dhabi invests to diversify its economy, 28 November 2005, Financial Times. http://www.ft.com/cms/s/0/7486689e-5fb3-11da-a628-0000779e2340.html

transfer, increase access to raw materials and expansion to overseas markets. Such strategies are also common in private corporations.

The recent episodes of Asian and Middle Eastern SWFs acquiring western financial institutions came about because, during the subprime crisis, it was a bargain for these funds to own an international brand at a reasonable price. Furthermore, the acquisition of investment banks allowed the SWFs to tap into their financial expertise to further their country's growth in the financial sector. This kind of shopping spree is likely to be a one-off event. Hence, looking at the future of SWFs, these funds are likely to hold a very diversified portfolio in terms of industry and geographical location. As these funds shift from the West to emerging markets or their own domestic markets, it is likely that we will see more developments in the emerging markets.

The western countries need to accept the fact that the rise of SWFs is a sign of the shift in the world economy to Asia and Middle East. More protectionism imposed by western countries would keep the SWFs away from these markets, which is not in the West's long-term best interests. The SWFs have currently started to invest in emerging markets and they are likely to increase these investments to get a higher return without facing criticisms from recipient countries. SWFs would be made welcome by many more politicians if the majority of funds were not amassed by undemocratic governments. It is not the SWFs that worry the politicians in the West, but the lack of democracy in these countries that underlies the controversy over SWFs.

This chapter has shown that controversies around SWFs are more political than financial and SWFs are positively valued by the market. There is no reason to worry about the emergence of SWFs if governments operate the funds with transparency, hold no dominant position in the companies in which they invest and have clear economic objectives. Concerns arise only when an SWF does not run the fund properly and when the operation threatens the public interest. The recent rapid expansion of SWFs is a reflection of the large and persistent global imbalance and the emergence of SWFs is a sign that the surplus countries want a higher return on these surpluses. If the growth of SWFs is to be contained, adjustments are needed from the deficit countries (developed countries) and surplus countries (developing countries).

CHAPTER 6 Conclusion

The rise of SWFs has provoked huge debates on their governance and investment motives. The thrust of this argument is the possibility of governments using SWFs to achieve their political agendas and threaten the security of recipient countries. This concern about these funds arises mainly from a lack of understanding of the funds. This book has aimed to provide an overview of the SWFs using several examples to illustrate their operations and investment strategies and, in part, reduce this fear.

The operational structure and degree of government involvement in SWF operations varies. The degree of government involvement in the SWFs is lower for western SWFs compared to their Asian and Middle Eastern counterpart. In addition, while the role of government in the SWF is clearly defined for the western SWFs, the role of government in SWF is ambiguous for most Asian and Middle Eastern SWFs. One notable observation is that the legal structure of SWFs does not determine the level of government involvement. SWFs established as a separate legal entity can have a high degree of government involvement yet SWFs established as pool of assets managed by central bank can have minimum government involvement. The Santiago Principles have specifically proposed guidelines to deal with the role of government in the SWFs' operations and the appropriate level of disclosure. However, it may take time for SWFs to adopt the guidelines proposed.

An examination of the operations and investment activities of SWFs does not show any evidence for SWFs acting for purely political motives. On the other hand, not all their activities are based purely on economic and financial considerations. Some investments are made to advance a country's industrial policy or to obtain expertise from foreign companies. In particular, SWFs from many Asian and Middle East countries have been used to enhance their governments' domestic industrial policy to invest in nascent industries and to bring in financial expertise to help their countries to develop as financial centers. However, even though the investments are made to enhance the countries' industrial policies, they pose no threat to the public or to other countries as a consequence of this.

Most SWFs invest in safe and liquid assets such as investment grade bonds and blue chip companies; only a few large SWFs from Asia and the Middle East invest in such risky assets as private equities and hedge funds. Some emerging trends suggest increasing investments in real estate, clean energy and infrastructure. A global report by CB Richard Ellis Group in August 2008 estimated that SWFs would invest $725 billion in real estate by 2015[1], most of which would be direct investments. The trend of investing in financial institutions in 2007-2008 is unlikely to continue as this kind of opportunistic investment only occurs when an industry is in distress. Furthermore, taking the lessons learnt from the investments in distressed banks during the subprime crisis, SWFs will be more cautious on such investments in the future and they are unlikely to take such an aggressive approach when the next round of opportunities occurs. SWFs are also increasing their investments in emerging markets after the subprime crisis. For example, there are recent reports on SWF investments in emerging markets like Brazil, India and Russia. In addition, there are increasing investments between respective SWF countries in the Middle East and China. There are reports on SWFs investing only in the stock markets in Hong Kong and Taiwan. However when financial markets in other SWFs countries become more liquid and open to foreign investors, SWFs are likely to increase their investments in these markets.

Despite growing concerns that SWF activities would destabilise the financial markets, many financial professionals are positive about their presence. Judging from SWF investments during the subprime crisis and the fact that the economies of the respective countries are highly dependent on the global economy, there is no reason to fear that SWFs are likely to destabilise the financial markets. The cost of market instability would be too high to compensate for any potential benefits derived. The SWFs' asset diversification approach is deemed to be better than the central bank's approach in holding government bonds and gold. Asset diversification is less likely to destabilise the market because first of all, investments are not concentrated in a few asset classes and secondly, until now the SWFs have not made any investments which affected the financial stability of the market. This implies that the funds have gradually re-balanced their portfolios instead of

---

1 Michael Haddock, "Sovereign wealth funds," *Global View Point*, CB Richard Ellis, Autumn 2008. http://www.cbre.com/NR/rdonlyres/2B0AFA46-D9BC-4DA0-84EF-F40DA64FD819/0/Global_ViewPoint__Sovereign_Wealth_Funds.pdf

making big shifts in asset classes. However, the low level of transparency of their investment activities could possibly lead to speculation, thus possibly destabilising the financial markets. Therefore, an optimal level of disclosure on these funds' strategic asset allocations is needed to ensure that speculation and the herding effect are kept to a minimum.

The emergence of SWFs is nothing new and cross-border state capitalism happened in the past when capital-rich countries invested in resource-abundant countries and companies. The only difference is that capital now also flows from developing countries to developed countries and recent acquisitions involve western financial institutions. This is the result of global imbalances and the shifting of economic power from the West to the East. The organisational structure of SWFs and the nature of these funds make it impossible to separate them completely from their governments. Since the funds manage the national wealth and hence are accountable to the government and the citizens of their countries, the governments will not adopt a hand-off approach. Yet it would be ideal if the Asian and Middle Eastern SWFs adopted the same approach as Norway's Government Pension Fund – Global which is accountable to the central bank but given a free rein in its operations. However, given that most big SWFs are owned by countries with minimally democratic governments, it is unlikely that the control of SWFs will be relinquished by the government.

In conclusion, the growth of SWFs is likely to continue and the funds will become significant players in the global financial markets, however the size and potential negative effects may have been over-rated by medias and policy-makers.

References

Aizenman, J and R, Glick (2008) *Sovereign wealth funds: stylized facts about their determinants and governance*. Working paper series 2008-33, Federal Reserve Bank of San Francisco.

Altbach E. G. and M.H. Cognato (2008) *Understanding China's new sovereign wealth fund*. NBR Analysis, July 2008.

Balding, C. (2008) *A portfolio analysis of sovereign wealth funds*. Available at SSRN: http://ssrn.com/abstract=1141531

Bernstein, S., J. Lerner and A. Schoar (2009) *The investment strategies of sovereign wealth funds*. Fondazione Eni Enrico Mattei.

Bortolotti, B., F.,Veljko, W., Megginson and W., Miracky (2009) *Sovereign wealth fund investment patterns and performance*. FEEM Working paper No. 2009. Available at SSRN: http://ssrn.com/abstract=1364862

Butt, S., Shivdasani, A., Stendevad, C. and Wyman, A., 2007. "Sovereign wealth funds: A growing global force in corporate finance." *Journal of Corporate Finance*, 19(1), 73-83.

Cassard, M. and D. Folkerts-Landau, (1997) "Risk management of sovereign assets and liabilities". *IMF Working Paper WP/97/166*, International Monetary Fund, Research Department,

Chen C. (2008) Sovereign wealth funds, macroeconomics policy alignment and financial stability. Available at SSRN: http://papers.ssrn.com/sol3/papers.cfm?abstract_id=1420614

Chhaochharia, V. and Laeven, L. (2008) *Sovereign Wealth Funds: Their investment Strategies and Performance*. CEPR Discussion Paper No. DP6959.

Clark, G. L. and Monk, A. H. B., "Government of Singapore Investment Corporation: Insurer of last resort and bulwark of nation-state legitimacy". *Pacific Review*, Forthcoming. Available at SSRN: http://ssrn.com/abstract=1397713

Clarke, G. L. and Monk, A. H.B. (2009) *The Oxford survey of sovereign wealth funds' asset managers*. Available at SSRN: http://ssrn.com/abstract=1432078

Cognato, M.H. (2008) "China Investment Corporation: Threat or opportunity?" *NBR Analysis*, The National Bureau of Asian Research.

Cohen, B. J. and Council on Foreign Relations (1986). *In whose interest? International Banking and American Foreign Policy*. New Haven: London, Yale University Press.

Das, S.U., Y. Lu, C., Mulder and A. Sy (2009) *Setting up sovereign wealth fund: Some policy and operational considerations*. IMF Working Paper WP/09/179. International Monetary Fund.

Drezner, D.W. (2008) "Sovereign wealth funds and the insecurity of global finance." *Journal of International Affairs*, Vol.62(1), 115-130.

Diwan, K.S. (2009) "Sovereign dilemmas: Saudi Arabia and sovereign wealth funds". *Geopolitics*, 14(2), 345-359.

Epstein, R.A. and A.M. Rose, "The regulation of sovereign wealth funds: The virtues of going slow." *University of Chicago Law Review*, Forthcoming, University of Chicago Law and Economics. Available at SSRN: http://ssrn.com/abstract=1394370

Gintschel, A. and Scherer, B. (2008) "Optimal asset allocation for sovereign wealth funds". *Journal of Asset Management*, 9(3), 215-238.

Government of Singapore Investment Corporation, *Report on the management of the Government's portfolio for year 2007/08*.

Government of Singapore Investment Corporation, *Report on the management of the Government's portfolio for year 2008/09*.

Hartwick, J.M. (1977) "Intergenerational Equity and the Investing of Rents from the Exhaustible Resources" *American Economics Review* 67(5), p972-974.

Hotelling H. (1931) "The Economics of Exhaustible Resources" *Journal of Political Economy*, 39(2), p137-175.

REFERENCES

IMF (2007) Global Financial Stability Report, *Financial Market Turbulence: Causes, Causes, Consequences and Policies.* International Monetary Fund, October 2007.

IMF(2008) Sovereign Wealth Funds – A work Agenda. Prepared by the Monetary and Capital Markets and Policy Development and Review Departments, 29 February 2008.

Kern, S. (2008) *SWFs and foreign investment policies – an update.* Deutsche Bank Research, October 2008.

Kern, S. (2009) *Sovereign wealth funds – state investments during the financial crisis.* Deutsche Bank Research, July 2009.

Lyons, G. (2007) *State capitalism: The rise of sovereign wealth funds, testimony before the committee on banking, housing and urban affairs,* United States Senate, 13 November 2007.

Maslakovic, M. (2009) *Sovereign wealth funds 2009.* International Financial Services London (IFSL) Report.

Mehrpouya, A., Huang, C., Barnett, T. (2009) *An analysis of proxy voting and engagement policies and practice of the SWFs.* IRRC Institute and RiskMetric Group.

Miracky, W., D. Dyer, D. Fisher, T. Goldner, L. Lagarde, and V. Piedrahita, (2008) *Assessing the risks: The behaviors of sovereign wealth funds in the global economy.* Monitor Group.

Monitor Group (2009) *Weathering the storm, Sovereign wealth funds in the global economic crisis of 2008.* SWF Annual Report 2008. Monitor Group and Fondazione Eni Enrico Mattei.

Norges Bank Investment Management, Government Pension Fund – Global Annual Report 2008.

Norges Bank Investment Management, Government Pension Fund – Global Quarterly Report, Third quarter 2009.

The Norwegian Government Pension Fund & NBIM, Presentation to Central Bank of Chile Santiago, 3 October 2007.

Pascuzzo, P. (2008) *Best practice asset allocation and risk management for sovereign wealth funds.* Mercer Investment Consulting, September 2008.

Polachek S, C. Seiglie and J. Xiang's (2007) "The impact of FDI on international conflict". *Defence and Peace Economics*, Vol.18(5), 415-429.

Rios-Morales, R. and Brennan, L. (2009) *The emergence of sovereign wealth funds as contributors of foreign direct investment*. 2009 Oxford Economics and Business Conference Program.

Rose, P. (2008) "Sovereign as shareholders". *North Carolina Law Review*, Fall 2008. Available at SSRN: http://ssrn.com/abstract=1102254

Setser, B. and R. Ziemba (2009) *GCC Sovereign funds, reversal of fortune*. Working Paper, Council on Foreign Relations (Center for Geo-economic Studies), January 2009.

Scherer, B. (2009) "A note on portfolio choice for sovereign wealth funds". *Financial Market Portfolio Management* 23(3), 315-327.

Shih, V. (2009) "Tools of survival: Sovereign wealth funds in Singapore and China" *Geopolitics*, 14, 328-344.

Sovereign Wealth Fund Institute, http://www.swfinstitute.org/

Sun, T. and Hesse (2009) *Sovereign wealth funds and financial stability - An event study analysis*. IMF Working paper, International Monetary Fund, Monetary and Capital Markets.

Temasek Holdings, Temasek Review 2007.

Temasel Holdings, Temasek Review 2008.

Temasek Holdings, Temasek Review 2009.

Wu, F. (2008) "Singapore's sovereign wealth funds: The political risk of overseas investments". Working paper no. 166, *S. Rajaratnam School of International Studies*, Singapore, 18 September 2008.

Useful Links

Information Sources and Reports

Deloitte LLP Reports – http://www.deloitte.com

Deutsche Bank Research – http://www.dbresearch.com

European Central Bank (ECB) – See 'The impact of sovereign wealth funds on global financial markets,' – Occasional Paper No. 91 July 2, 2008 – http://www.ecb.eu/home/html/index.en.html

Financial Times – In Depth – http://www.ft.com/indepth/sovereignfunds

International Monetary Fund (IMF) Global Financial Stability Report – A Report by the Monetary and Capital Markets Department on Market Developments and Issues – http://www.imf.org/external/pubs/ft/GFSR/index.htm

Harvard Business School – http://www.hbs.edu/

International Working Group of Sovereign Wealth Funds (IWG) – IWG is a voluntary forum of which SWFs will meet to discuss common issues. In particular, IWG bore the existence of the Generally Accepted Principles and Practices (GAPP)—Santiago Principles – http://www.iwg-swf.org/

Recently, IWG updated itself as the International Forum of Sovereign Wealth Funds (IFSWF) – http://www.ifswf.org/

IRRC Institute, Risk Metrics Group – See "An Analysis of Proxy Voting and Engagement Policies and Practices of the Sovereign Wealth Funds' – http://www.riskmetrics.com

Monitor Group – Economic Development and Security – http://www.monitor.com

Morgan Stanley – Research – http://www.morganstanley.com/institutional/research/index.html

Organisation for Economic Co-operation and Development – See 'OECD guidance on recipient country policies towards SWFs' – http://www.oecd.org

Oxford Economics – http://www.oef.com/

Oxford SWF Project – This is a project of Professor Gordon L. Clark and Dr. Ashby Monk at the University of Oxford which collates scholarly papers on SWFs. – http://oxfordswfproject.com/

Preqin – Research and Consulting Firm – http://www.preqin.com/

Social Science Resource Network – http://www.ssrn.com/

Sovereign Wealth Funds News – A news portal delivering the most up to date news on SWFs – http://www.sovereignwealthfundsnews.com/

SWF Institute – A portal providing essential information and research on SWFs. Recently launched *Sovereign Wealth Quarterly* and Sovereign Wealth Fund Transaction Database (SWFTD) – http://www.swfinstitute.org/

United States House Financial Services Committee – http://financialservices.house.gov/

United States-China Economic and Security Review Commission – http://www.uscc.gov/index.php

United States Federal Reserve Board – http://www.federalreserve.gov/

World Bank – http://econ.worldbank.org

World Economic Forum – http://www.weforum.org

Sovereign Wealth Funds

Algeria – Revenue Regulation Fund – http://www.bank-of-algeria.dz

Angola – Reserve Fund for Oil – http://www.minfin.gv.ao

Australia – Australian Government Future Fund (AGFF) – http://www.futurefund.gov.au

USEFUL LINKS

Azerbaijan – State Oil Fund – http://www.oilfund.az/en

Brunei – Brunei Investment Agency (BIA) – http://www.mof.gov.bn/English/BIA

Botswana – Pula Fund – http://www.finance.gov.bw

USA – Permanent Wyoming Mineral Trust Fund (PWMTF) – http://treasurer.state.wy.us

Canada – Alberta Heritage Fund (AHF) – http://www.aimco.alberta.ca/

Chile – Economic and Social Stabilization Fund (ESSF) – http://www.bcentral.cl/eng

China – China Investment Corporation – http://www.china-inv.cn

China – Central Hujin Investment Corp. – http://www.huijin-inv.cn

Hong Kong – Hong Kong Monetary Authority Investment Portfolio – http://www.info.gov.hk/hkma/eng/reserves/man_ex_fund.htm

East Timor – Timor-Leste Petroleum Fund – http://www.bancocentral.tl/PF/main.asp

Iran – Foreign Exchange Reserve Fund – http://www.cbi.ir

Ireland – National Pensions Reserve Fund (NPRF) – http://www.nprf.ie/

Kazakhstan – Kazakhstan National Fund (KNF) – http://www.nationalfund.kz

Kiribati – Revenue Equalisation Reserve Fund (RERF) – http://www.mfep.gov.ki

Kuwait – Kuwait Investment Authority – http://www.kia.gov.kw

Libya – Libyan Investment Authority – http://www.lia.ly

Malaysia – Khazanah Nasional BHD (KNB) – http://www.khazanah.com.my

Mauritania – National Fund for Hydrocarbon Reserves – http://www.bcm.mr

New Zealand – New Zealand Superannuation Fund – http://www.nzsuperfund.co.nz

Nigeria – Excess Crude Account – http://www.fmf.gov.ng

Norway – Government Pension Fund – Global – http://www.norges-bank.no/templates/article____69365.aspx

Oman – State General Stabilisation Fund (SGSF) – http://www.sgrf.gov.om

Papua New Guinea – Mineral Resources Stabilization Fund (MRSF) – http://www.bankpng.gov.pg

Russia – Stabilization Fund of Russian Federation – http://www.minfin.ru/en/stabfund

Saudi Arabia – SAMA Foreign Holdings – http://www.sama.gov.sa

Singapore – Government of Singapore Investment Corporation – http://www.gic.com.sg

Singapore – Temasek Holdings – http://www.temasekholdings.com.sg

South Korea – Korea Investment Corporation (KIC) – http://kic.go.kr/en

Taiwan – Taiwan National Stabilisation Fund (TNSF) – http://www.df.gov.tw

Uganda – Poverty Action Fund – http://www.udn.or.ug/PAF.htm

UAE, Abu Dhabi – Abu Dhabi Investment Authority – http://www.adia.ae

UAE, Dubai – Dubai Intern. Financial Centre Investments (DIFC) – http://www.difc.ae

USA – Alaska Permanent Reserve Fund Corperation (APRF) – http://www.apfc.org

USA – New Mexico State Investment Office Trust Funds – http://www.sic.state.nm.us

Venezuela – Investment Fund for Macroeconomic Stabilization (FIEM) – http://www.bcv.org.ve

Index

A
Abu Dhabi Commercial Bank 21
Abu Dhabi Investment Authority (ADIA) 2, 19, 83, 197–199
  case study 118–166, 118–167
  governance 19
  investments 40
  overview of investments 119–167
  recent investments 122
  summary of investment activities 124
Abu Dhabi Investment Council 119–167
  investments 15
ADIC 119–167
AEI 148–167
  Services 81
Agriculture Bank of China 130–167
Alaska Permanent Fund 100
Alberta Heritage Fund 2
  investment policies 71
al-Hajeri, Saeed Mubarak 121
al-Kindi, Khalifa 119
American International Group 137–167
  Asian Infrastructure 137–167
  Global Investment 85
Anglo-Persian Oil Company (APOC) 4
Apollo Management 98
Asian Crisis 82
Asset Liability Management (ALM) 92
Australian Future Fund 72, 87, 193–199

B
Bahrain Mumtalakat Holding 42
Bangkok Bank 137–167
Bank Danamon 138–167
Bank Holding Company Act 45
Bank International Indonesia 138–167
Bank of America 82
Barclays 67, 82, 139–167, 181–199
Beijing China Sciences General Energy and Environment Company 85
Benchmarking 164–167
Benetton 82
Blackstone Group 81, 84
British Land 150–167
British Petroleum (BP) 72, 98

C
Capital Land 138–167
Carlyle Group 74, 181–199
Case Studies 117-168
  summary of investment activities 163–167
Cathay Pacific 184–199
Central Huijin Investment (Central Huijin) 6, 126–167
Change in Bank Control Act 45
Chartered Semiconductor Manufacturing 135–167
Chile 6
China 2
China Development Bank 130–167
China Eastern Airlines 184–199

China Investment Corporation (CIC)
    6, 28, 81, 196–199
  actual areas of investment 128–167
  case study 125
  governance 25
  investments 82
  investments in domestic market
    130–167
  losses 24
  potential investment areas 127–167
  summary of investment strategy
    131–167
  will not invest in 126–167
China Jianyin Investment Ltd 128–167
China Railway 128–167
China Reinsurance 131–167
Chinese National Offshore Oil
    Corporation (CNOOC) 131–167
  bid for Unocal 100
Chrysler Building 45
Citigroup 99
Clean Energy 196–199
Commission of the European
    Community 85
Committee on Foreign Investment in
    the United States (CFIUS) 81

D
Deutsche Bank 81
Development Bank of Singapore
    (DBS) 137–167
Development Funds 10
Dhanabalan, S 25, 136
Distressed Companies 88
Dongfeng Motor 156–167
Dubai Inc 198–199
Dubai International Capital
  investments 84
Dubai International Financial Centre
  investments 81, 85
Dubai Ports 73, 85
Dubai Port World 99

E
East India Company 195–199
Emerging Market Partnership 137–167
Emerging Markets 87
Equities 86
Everbright Bank 130–167

F
Federal Law of the Russian Federation
    on Foreign Investments 97
Ferrari 74, 125–167
Fifth Schedule Company 13
Financial Institutions as SWF
    investments 82
Financial Markets, Implications of
    SWF Growth 179–199
Fisker Automotive 96
Foreign Direct Investment (FDI)
    Restrictiveness Index 97
Foreign Investment and National
    Security Act (2007) USA 96
France 74, 196–199
  investment policies 166

G
GAAP Principles 49
Gao Xiqing 29, 31, 127, 192–199
Generally Accepted Principles and
    Practices (GAAP) 47
Government Investment Corporation
    of Singapore (GIC) 2, 6, 150–166, 197–199
  case study 146
  governance 21
  investment portfolio by asset class
    148–167
  investments by geographical
    distribution 146–167
  Real Estate Pte Ltd 81, 149-167
  Special Investment Division 23
  summary of investments 150–167

INDEX

Global Integrated Monetary Fiscal
  Model 180–199
Gold 180–199
Goodyear, Charles 25
Government-Linked Corporations
  (GLCs) 23, 198–199
Government Pension Fund - Global
  (GPFG) 2, 31, 35, 82, 83, 87, 90,
  193–199, 194–199
  case study 152
  governance 42
  investment activities 156–167
  investment strategy 153–167
  investments 85
  summary of investment activities and
    strategies 162–167
GPFG, Alaska 139–166

H

Hartwick's Rule for Intergenerational
  Equity 11
Hedge Funds 74
Hedging 70
Herding Effects 188–199
Ho Ching 83, 136, 143
Ho Tian Yee 24
Hong Kong Monetary Authority 42
Hong Leong 151–167
Hotelling's Rule 10
Huijin Investment Ltd 29

I

India 12
  Central Bank 12
Indosat 99
Intercell AG 139–167
International Capital Corporation
  (CICC) 130–167
International Petroleum Investment
  Company (IPIC) 82, 118–167
International Standards 18
International Working Group of
  Sovereign Wealth Funds 6
Investment Fund for Macroeconomic
  Stabilisation, Venezuela 89

Investment Strategies 85
Israel, Simon 82
Istithmar 183–199

J

Japan 12, 171–199
JC Flowers & Company 82
JSC KazMunaiGas Exploration
  Production 129–167

K

Kazakhstan National Fund 70
Khalifa, Sheikh 118
Khazanah Nasional 10, 78, 197–199,
  196–197
  investment policies 72
  investments 6, 78, 87
Kiribati Revenue Equalisation Reserve
  Fund 1
Korea Investment Corporation 2, 71
Kuwait Investment Authority (KIA)
  2, 42
  BP investment 98
  investment policies 71
  investments 84
Kuwait Investment Board 1

L

Latin America 139–167
Lazard Asia Investment 137–167
Lee Kuan Yew 23
Lehman Global Aggregate Index 91
Leste-Timor 42
Li Yong 127, 131
Linaburg-Maduell Transparency
  Index 85
London Stock Exchange 23
Lou Jiwei 29, 126, 127, 129

M

Mapletree India-China Fund 138–167
Mapletree Investments 138–167
Maybank 138–167
Merkel, Angela 1

MerLion Pharmaceuticals 135–167
Merrill Lynch 6, 187-199
Microfinance 138–167
Mineral Resources Stabilisation Fund, Papua New Guinea 5, 69
Mitsubishi Corporation 137–167
Modern Portfolio Theory 28
Monetary Authority of Hong Kong (HKMA) 198–199
Monetary Authority of Singapore (MAS) 98, 146–167
Monopolies and Mergers Commission, UK 83
Moody 88
Morgan Stanley 85
Mount Charlotte Investments 151–167
MSCI World Index 101
Mubadala, investments 118–166

N
Ng Kok Song 151
Nobel Oil Group 129–167
Norges Bank 31, 154–167
  Investment Management (NBIM) 2
Northern Rock 195–199
Norway 5

O
Official Institutions Group 180–199
Optus 99
Organisation of Petroleum Exporting Countries (OPEC) 172–199

P
Pacific Asia Asset Management 24
Papua New Guinea 1
Pension Fund Act 32
Pension Funds, Different from SWFs 6
Pension Reserve Funds 6
People's Bank of China 178–199
Permanent Fund, Alaska 35
Permanent Mineral Trust, Wyoming 35, 131–166
PetroChina 131–167
Petrofac Ltd 150–166

PIK 150–167
Ping, Xie 74
Private Equity Funds 138–166

Q
Qatar Investment Authority 40, 74, 81, 82, 181–199, 187–199
  investments 85, 87
Qatar Investment Fund
  investment policies 73

R
Real Estate 87
  as SWF investment 83
Recipient Countries, investment Policies 95
Reco Bay NSW 166–167
Reco Landmark Tianjin Pte Ltd 149–167
Reco Pearl Pte Ltd 10
Reco Shahzan (M) Sdn Bhd 6
Russia 196–199
  New Growth Fund 139–167

S
SAFE Investment Company 13
Sainsbury's PLC 74
Santiago Principles 46, 190–199
Savings Funds 10
Seaprime Investments 149–167
Seet Ngee Huat 151
Shanmugaratnam, Tharman 98
Shin Corpporation 25, 138–167
Singapore 24
Singapore Airlines 25, 184–199
Singapore Companies Act (Chapter 50) 25
Singapore Technologies 12
Singapore Telecom 2
Song Bird Estates 129–167
South East Asia Property Company 149–167
South Korea 12
Sovereign Wealth Fund Institute (SWFI) 9
  Consensus Demand Meter 85

INDEX

Special Purpose Government Funds 6
Sri Lanka 9
  Central Bank 13
Stabilisation Fund of the Russian Federation 4, 13
Stabilisation Funds 25
Stable Investment Corporation 166–167
Standard and Poor's 166
Standard Chartered PLC 81
State Administration of Foreign Exchange (SAFE) 3
State Capitalism 194–199, 198–199
State-Owned Enterprises (SOEs, Different from SWFs 14
State Street Global Advisors 180–199
Sterilisation Bonds 9
Subprime Crisis 67
Summers, Lawrence 42
Superannuation Fund, New Zealand 1
Sovereign Wealth Funds (SWFs) 180–199
  accountability 193–199
  affect of history on investment decisions 90
  asset class correlation 90
  beliefs and approaches 90
  buyer of last resort 197–199
  commodity-based
    growth 172–199
  compared to foreign direct investments (FDIs) 184–199
  competitive advantages 94
  conflicting roles 194–199
  contingent liability 97
  controversial investments 34
  corporate structure 90
  currency composition 35
  current governance 34
  definition 42, 75
  effects on global financial stability 186–199
  estimated losses 91
  fear of 67
  future developments 169
  growth 171–199
  hedge portfolios 86
  implications of growth
    on financial markets 179–199
    on companies and recipient countries 182–199
  independence 193–199
  international guidelines 190
  investment activities 86
    in commodities 95
    in equities 77
  investment policies of recipient countries 77
  investments by
    sector 87
    region 91
  legal framework 5
  national strategic objectives 196–199
  non-commodity growth 177–199
  objectives 94
  origins 89

T
Tan, Dr, Keng Yam 23
Tan, Tony 93
Tasameem 166–167
Temasek Holdings 1, 35, 187–199
  case study 134
  governance 24
  international investments 138–167
  investment in Shin Corporation 98
  investments 78
    in domestic market 135
  losses 82
  regional investments 136–167
  summary of investments 140–167
Temasek Linked Companies) TLCs 78, 134–167
Teo Ming Kian 25
Texas Pacific Group 82
Thistle Hotels 136–167
Timor-Leste Petroleum Fund
  investment policies 72

Truman's (2008) Accountability and
    Transparency Indices 36
Truman's (2008) Scoreboard 18

U
Uganda 6
Union Bank of Switzerland (UBS) 15,
    81, 148–167
Unocal 100
US treasuries 12

V
Valeo SA 81
Venezuela 6

Vical Inc 139–167
Visa 128–167

W
Wang, Jesse 31, 125, 127
Wang Jianxi 129

GLOBAL professional publishing

Available online at
www.gppbooks.com

THE INTERNATIONAL HANDBOOK OF ISLAMIC BANKING AND FINANCE

ELISABETH JACKSON-MOORE

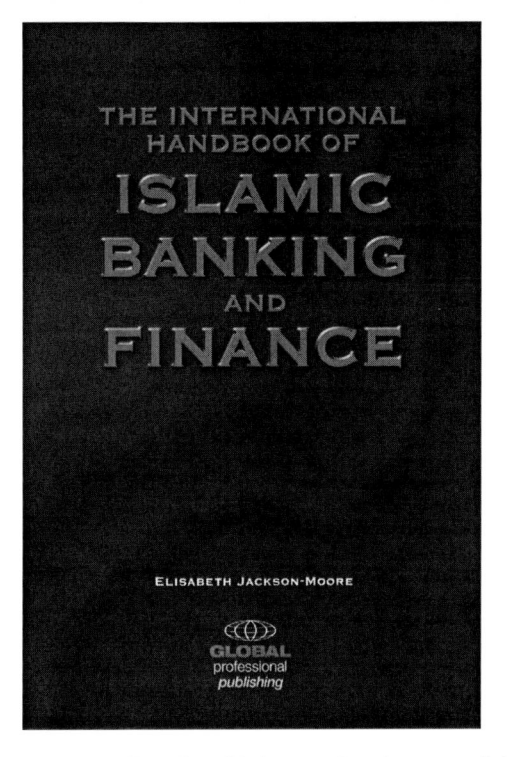

GLOBAL professional publishing

The International Handbook of Islamic Banking and Finance will give conventional bankers and financial advisers a detailed insight into Islamic banking. The book explains how it operates, what is the rationale behind it, the issues it raises, issues of compliance and how Islamic methods of banking relate to conventional banking and finance as well as the opportunities it presents.

While covering the ethical and religious basis of Islamic banking, Elizabeth Jackson-Moore concentrates on the details of how it provides all the services of any banking system: financing instruments, Islamic contracts, Islamic bonds, *Takaful* (basically Islamic insurance) as well as new developements in Islamic banking such as hedge funds.

All compliance and regulatory issues are covered from an international point of view and the author also surveys the world banking centres.

ISBN: 978-1-906403-31-7   272 pages

GLOBAL
professional
publishing

Available online at
www.gppbooks.com

the art of mathematics in business

analyzing facts and figures for smart business decisions

Dr Jae K Shim

A comprehensive, one-stop desk reference for managers who must use quantitative calculations to make daily operating and investing decisions. Its purpose is to provide the fundamentals of business math techniques that can be quickly applied to real-world problems. This unique resource will save countless hours of research time by making sound financial planning truly easy. It provides analyses as well as clear and understandable explanations of complex small business problems. Basic mathematical techniques are presented in a step-by-step fashion. The examples provide an invaluable and effective operating tool while this book also contains user-friendly personal computer techniques.

978-1-906403-32-4   406 pages

GLOBAL professional publishing

Available online at
www.gppbooks.com

WAVES OF CHANGE

MANAGING GLOBAL TRENDS
IN THE
FINANCIAL SERVICES INDUSTRY

PATRICK CALLIONI

We have had the sub-prime crisis. What comes next? How can the industry extract value from an apparent disaster? This book deals with the impact of technologies, both hard (eg information and communication technologies) and soft (new ways of working, eg teleworking) and the impact of the waves of change following the climate change juggernaut, including threats (eg reaction against globalization) and opportunities (eg cost reductions from the adoption of greener technologies, buildings and ways of working) and, finally, the impact of demographic change.

The author then returns to the scope defined in the early chapters and offers *practical* advice to the industry as a whole (and implicitly to governments) on how to deal with these global trends.

978-1-906403-38-6   376 pages

GLOBAL professional publishing

Available online at
www.gppbooks.com

GLOBAL professional publishing

Ratios: For Analysis, Control and Profit Planning

David E Vance

The book is designed to help ordinary people understand how to analyze and make sense of financial statements. It is also of great use to those in business so that they can understand how to measure, control and think about improving profit within their companies.

It starts by covering how to read financial statements while explaining how simple ratios can be used to evaluate profitability. It then explains cash flow, staffing and executive compensation. The author provides profit planning tools and explains the ratios banks use to value companies. The book concludes with a presentation and analysis of the key performance indicators used to derive peak performance in a variety of industries.

978-1-906403-53-9   179 pages

GLOBAL
professional
publishing

Available online at
www.gppbooks.com

Financial Management of Multinational Corporations

Jae K. Shim

Financial Management of Multinational Corporations provides a clear and concise introduction to international finance. The book is written and compiled for working professionals engaged in the fields of international finance, global trade, foreign investments, and banking. It may be used for both day-to-day practice and for technical research. It is a practical reference of proven techniques, strategies, and approaches that are successfully used by professionals to diagnose multinational finance and banking problems. The book covers virtually all important topics dealing with multinational business finance, investments, financial planning, financial economics, and banking.

978-1-906403-08-9   256 pages

GLOBAL professional *publishing*

Available online at
www.gppbooks.com

Strategic Business Forecasting provides a complete working knowledge of the fundamentals of business forecasting that can be applied in the real world regardless of firm size.

It takes the reader through basic forecasting methodology, and then practical applications. All aspects of business forecasting are discussed making this book a comprehensive and invaluable reference. It tries to avoid theoretical, rigorous, and mathematical discussions. Throughout the emphasis is on how to use it directly, when to use it, what it is used for, and what resources are required. It also integrates the use of computer and information technology. Finally, the book goes way beyond just sales forecasting. It encompasses a wide range of topics of major importance to practical business managers, including economic forecasting, cash flow forecasting, cost prediction, earnings forecasts, and much more.

978-1-908403-47-8   274 pages